STO

PSYCHIC MYSTERIES OF THE NORTH

Books by A. R. G. Owen

CAN WE EXPLAIN THE POLTERGEIST?

HYSTERIA, HYPNOSIS AND HEALING: THE WORK OF J. M. CHARCOT

SCIENCE AND THE SPOOK
(*with Victor Sims*)

POLYMORPHISMS WITH LINKED LOCI
(*with V. Arunachalam*)

Psychic Mysteries of the North

*Discoveries from the Maritime Provinces
and Beyond*

A. R. G. OWEN, Ph.D.

HARPER & ROW, PUBLISHERS
New York, Evanston, San Francisco, London

To
Donald C. Webster,
who made so much of it possible

This work was first published in Canada under the title *Psychic Mysteries of Canada.*

PSYCHIC MYSTERIES OF THE NORTH: DISCOVERIES FROM THE MARITIME PROVINCES AND BEYOND. Copyright © 1975 by A. R. G. Owen. All rights reserved. Printed in Canada. No part of this book may be used or reproduced in any manner whatsoever without written permission except in the case of brief quotations embodied in critical articles and reviews. For information address Harper & Row, Publishers, Inc., 10 East 53rd Street, New York, N.Y. 10022.

FIRST U.S. EDITION

Designed by C. Linda Dingler

Library of Congress Cataloging in Publication Data
Owen, Alan Robert George.
   Psychic mysteries of the north.
   Bibliography: p.
   1. Psychical research—Canada. 2. Occult sciences
—Canada. I. Title.
BF1028.5.C309   133'.0971   74–15845
ISBN 0–06–013266–3

75 76 77 78 79 10 9 8 7 6 5 4 3 2 1

CONTENTS

INTRODUCTION

This book is concerned with recent developments in the field known as psychical research, or parapsychology. It is particularly true of North America and to a lesser extent of the world in general that at the present time there is a vast interest in the "psychic" and related fields. As the reader is doubtless aware, "psychic" is used with two distinct meanings. "Psyche" is the word used by some psychologists for the totality of a person's thoughts, feelings, and urges, i.e., what the layman would call his "mind" or "soul." Indeed, "psyche" was the ancient Greek word for soul, and has been incorporated in such terms as psychology, the study of mind, and psychiatry, which means mental healing. However, psychical research is a special study mainly concerned with various strange happenings that seem to involve people's thoughts and feelings and which are therefore called psychic phenomena.

Of these occurrences telepathy, or thought transference, is the most familiar. Indeed, whether or not one believes that it actually does occur, almost everyone understands the idea of telepathy—it is almost a household word. The term "psychical research" came into use as relating particularly to telepathy and like problems in 1882, when the Society for Psychical Research was founded in England specially for the study of these questions. Besides telepathy, psychical research concerns itself with such strange happenings as precognition or presentiment (knowledge of the future), clairvoyance (direct knowledge of facts not known to any living person but subsequently verified as true), and psychokinesis or PK (movement of objects without physical contact or by means of known physical forces, such as electricity or magnetism). In addition, psychical research workers also interest themselves in the evidence that the human spirit survives death, the study of ghosts, visions, hallucinations, allegedly haunted houses, and poltergeist disturbances, as well as with the difficult problem of reincarnation. There is also the rather practical subject of "well witching" or "water divining" and the important problem of the mechanisms of healing by faith or "laying on of hands." The parapsychologist (as the psychic research worker is sometimes called) thus deals with a wide field penetrating human life at numerous points.

Insofar as the strange episodes with which psychical research concerns itself are not fully understood they may be said to belong to the sphere of the occult, in the primary sense of that word, which means "hidden." The term occult is, however, rather inoperative, as it is used in a popular sense nowadays to embrace a whole range of studies and activities past and present most of which are taught or engaged in with attitudes that are far from scientific. The subject matter contained in "the occult" is most diverse and in the popular mind embraces not only the phenomena studied in psychical research but various pseudo subjects such as fortune-telling, witchcraft, black magic, and the like. There is no objection to the study of the history of these movements or their psychology, but unfortunately besides being the province of harmless faddists, interest in them is, I regret to say, fostered both by uncritical enthusiasts and by people whose aim is an unscrupulous exploitation of the public.

These criticisms do not apply to a particular type of persons who are sincere seekers after what I would term "spiritual knowledge" or "spiritual philosophy." Their studies can also be said to be embraced by the all-inclusive term occult, but they are at the opposite end of the spectrum from the devotees of witchcraft and the like. These students of the unknown are usually activated by a tendency which is both intellectual and, in a general sense, religious. They study various bodies of teaching which have been built up both in modern and ancient times with reference to man's position in a spiritual world. Elements of this teaching are to be found in Freemasonry, Rosicrucianism, and Theosophy, to mention only a few. Judging by the people I know who engage in these studies, I rate this area as occupying the respectable end of the enormous spectrum embraced by the occult; I accept that the teachings are of real moral value and an influence for good in the world, and also that they inculcate spiritual and mental disciplines of value to their practitioners. For all I know to the contrary, the teaching, whether of ancient or modern origin, may contain genuine insights into the mastery of the psychic talents which, as a parapsychologist, I have found that some human beings possess.

However, though his subject—psychic phenomena—occupies a kind of center position in the occult, it would not be quite accurate to place the parapsychologist at the midpoint in the range of occultists. The psychical research worker stands slightly to the side of and apart from his fellow seekers after knowledge. This is because he strives for the knowledge he acquires to be "scientific" in the same sense as is that obtained by scientists working in universities, or in industrial laboratories, or in field surveys. For this reason the parapsychologist tends to limit his scope to such phenomena as he can find and assess in a scientific way. People trained in science will know immediately what I mean by a "scientific approach." Indeed, most readers will have a good appreciation of what this phrase implies, because we live in a very science-conscious age.

The fact that psychical research aims to be scientific in spirit does not, however, mean that the subject is dull; on the contrary, it is as varied as human life. Its subject matter, "psychic phenomena," is concerned essentially with attributes of human beings. My wife and I after many years of experience have formulated the maxim "Parapsychology is people," that is to say—people with all their human feelings, quirks, and nuances. Indeed, the psychic research worker forgets this only at his peril. If, as sometimes has happened, he treats a person with psychic talents as a prisoner in the dock, sternly required to prove his innocence to the court, he is likely to get no phenomena! Also, if he is not a good judge of human integrity and rejects testimony from reliable witnesses he is in danger of throwing out good-sized babies with the bathwater!

A word on nomenclature may be in order. In psychical research the term "psychic" is used a great deal. In fact, like "telepathy," it has overflowed into common parlance, as when people say, "You must be psychic to have guessed that"—whatever "that" might be. In psychic research a "psychic impression" is a thought or piece of information that comes as if "of itself" or out of the blue into the mind of the percipient instead of being communicated by speech or writing or by clues of various kinds. That is, a "psychic impression" comes via telepathy, clairvoyance, or precognition. To save us the trouble of listing these three words every time, we say that the information has been obtained by extrasensory perception, or ESP for short. If it validly seems that a person frequently acquires knowledge by ESP, he is often spoken of as being a "psychic sensitive," or simply as a "psychic" or a "sensitive," or he is said to be "psychic" or "sensitive." More loosely, a person who has the strange power of psychokinesis is sometimes called a "psychic," but this is not usually done unless the person also gives evidence of ESP, so that he would qualify as a "sensitive." Parapsychology is, of course, not restricted to the study only of people who have ESP so frequently that they can be ranked as psychics. Indeed, one of the most important branches of psychical research studies the sporadic experiences of ordinary people and many examples will be found in this book.

The purpose of this book is primarily to make known a number of discoveries in psychic research that have been made in Canada. I think they are sufficiently important for Canadians to be interested and take a pride in them. Also as news in this field tends to percolate somewhat slowly out of Canada, I think it is important to make these discoveries available to men of other nations. Being a true science, psychical research, like all science, is essentially international and proceeds fastest when new things are followed up in many parts of the world. For example, the Canadian discovery that the receipt of a telepathic message can be "seen" in the resulting electrical activity of the brain is clearly of the first importance, and possibly may revolutionize the entire subject of parapsychology. Further work has been done in Canada and will be published; however, we are pleased to learn that scientists in Scotland and New Zealand have decided to repeat this work. We hope that this kind of research will be engaged in in many countries. The work on the biological effects of healing hands initiated in Canada by Dr. Grad and carried out in the United States (an excellent example of international cooperation) is ripe for considerable extension in and out of Canada. Similarly our "Philip" research is of a kind that can easily be repeated wherever one or two (or perhaps I should say seven or eight) are gathered together.

While the main purpose of the book is to let these new fields of research be known, it is impossible to put them in perspective for the general reader without giving a general background of the subject matter of psychical research and the scientific approach to it. I felt that the simplest and most compact way to achieve this would be to take my examples from Canada, so as to give the reader an overview of the psychic as it has been experienced and written about by Canadians. While I hope this will interest Canadian readers, it need not deter the non-Canadian reader. As far as psychic talents are concerned, Canada is the same as any other nation. Indeed, ESP is indifferent to division of class, color, creed, or nation. It seems to be distributed most fairly and equitably among all parts of the world. Perhaps it is the one potentially universal form of communication that transcends all barriers of language!

Much of this book has been written out of my own personal experience, or in the light of it. I was first introduced to psychical research as a field worthy of serious study about twenty years ago by my senior colleague on the staff of Trinity College, Cambridge, England, the late Professor C. D. Broad, the eminent philosopher. Three of the founders of psychic research in the last century—Myers, Gurney, and Sidgwick—were Fellows of the college and since that time there have always been a few members of the college staff who maintain a lively interest in the subject. In 1970 I was invited to Canada to head up a small research institute founded through the generosity of a Canadian donor, Donald C. Webster, a businessman in venture capital. Parapsychology was among its terms of reference. As I have said, psychical research is a "people subject" and needs people not only as experimental "material" but as active participants in research. Many of the best ideas arise in group discussion and group experimental work. We therefore cooperated with others in founding the Toronto Society for Psychical Research (TSPR). Many of the results described in this book were obtained by members of the society, which is an entirely voluntary and self-governing one. Their work is unpaid and unrewarded except for the satisfaction of making new and real contributions to human knowledge. If this book required a further dedication it should perhaps be to them.

Though I have tried to describe, or at least mention, all genuine research work that has been done in Canada, I am all too aware that I may have omitted important and significant investigations for the simple reason that I do not know of them. Canada is a vast territory and communications between the provinces are still less than perfect. I apologize to any serious investigators whose work has been, in all innocence, disregarded. We try to improve communication by publishing results obtained by the New Horizons Research Foundation and the Toronto Society for Psychical Research in the journal *New Horizons* (obtainable from Box 427, "F" Station, Toronto, Ontario) which is often cited in the bibliographical references. As the emphasis is put on research I have not sought to list the societies and other organizations in Canada that undertake the task of teaching and lecturing on matters psychic.

While I have written about the psychic always from a scientist's point of view, and therefore have expressed myself somewhat conservatively as to what in my opinion can be taken to have been "proved," I have not aimed to rob the subject of its intense human interest. The results of psychical research, which in the opinion not only of myself, but of many eminent scientists are important, have a manifold bearing on our ideas of human destiny. Precognition challenges our accepted vision either of time itself or of the way in which human life is managed. With respect to clairvoyance, thoughtography, and psychokinesis, the results of research are truly awesome in what they suggest of the immense power of mind in the universe. I think that parapsychology is a true science which is obliged to pursue the patient task of investigation without fear or favor, and also that it is not the handmaiden of either philosophy or religion. However, it is perfectly fair for those interested in either of these spheres to make such intellectual use of its results as, with honesty, they can. Which is a somewhat dry way of putting the obvious fact that psychical research gives us some hint that possibly it would be premature to write the death certificate of religion at the present time, though equally it would be premature to say just which religious insights, Western or Eastern, may ultimately be validated by parapsychology. The implications of psychical research for other sciences, such as the widely separated disciplines of psychology and physics, are matters that I discuss at the end of this book.

From time to time, therefore, in my account of Canadian parapsychology I have made asides concerning the wider implications of our subject. Also, where merited by the "state of the art" as I have presented it, I have not hesitated to discuss possibilities and unresolved issues as honestly as I can. Most work in parapsychology, just as in any other science, proceeds less on the analogy of proving things in a courtroom and more on the lines of a detective story: we are looking for clues—for enlightenment as to where next we should go. As we know, it is fun finding out. One can enjoy parapsychology without necessarily forgetting its solemn overtones and the actual encounters with tragedy that color some individual psychic experiences. But the subject spans the whole range of human acts and feelings from the sublime to the humorous. I hope that I have succeeded in communicating some of the adventure, humanity, and even humor to be found in psychical research.

1

THE FIRST CANADIANS

The first Canadians—the Indians who preceded the white man here by many thousands of years—certainly had a most active belief in all aspects of the psychic. This is shown very clearly by the Indian paintings done in red-ochre upon rock faces of the Canadian Shield in a huge area north of the Great Lakes extending from Trois Rivières in Quebec to Lake Winnipeg in Manitoba. These paintings were almost unknown until recently when they were surveyed by Selwyn Dewdney, a research associate of the Royal Ontario Museum, who is also an artist, author, and art therapist at Westminster Hospital, London, Ontario. Dewdney's explorations disclosed a vast number of red-ochre paintings whose age is uncertain, except that they predate the arrival of the white man. Besides representations of animals such as bears, serpents, and deer, there are numerous pictures of mythological beings such as rabbit-men, men with heads like sunflowers, as well as beings of grotesque form that presumably are spirits. There are also little men with horns which the present-day Ojibway Indians of the area call *Maymaygwayshi.* These are a species of nature spirit who are supposed to live in the wild like the elves and gnomes of European mythology.

Some of the modern Ojibway say that the rock paintings were made by the *Maymaygwayshi,* but others say that they were made by the Indians to commemorate dreams they had had at these sites. The latter explanation is likely to be true, because all North American Indians were deeply affected by dreams, which they explained as communications from spirits. Dreams or visions were specially sought for in wild and desolate places both by ordinary hunters and by the shamans, or professional psychics. Many of the rock paintings, it may be supposed, record dreams which came spontaneously or in response to an active "vision quest." In modern Ojibway belief the rock paintings are at "places of *Manitou*," i.e. the haunts of mighty spirits.

The word *manito*, which means "spirit," survives in the names Manitoba and Manitoulin. Dewdney's rock paintings were probably made by the ancestors of the modern Ojibway, whose religious and spirit beliefs have been studied by Dr. Ruth Landes, professor of anthropology at McMaster University, Hamilton, Ontario. The Ojibway believed that the universe was activated by innumerable types and grades of manitos, ranging from the minor nature spirits up to the Great Spirit—the Creator of the World. The North Wind was a manito hostile to man. Ice and Snow were capricious manitos, sometimes friendly, but often treacherous. Each species of animal, such as bear, had its own manito "bear" conceived of as ancestral to the bear species, and perhaps ancestral to humans of the bear clan or totem. Because of this identification of man, animal species, and spirit, we have to accept that many of the rock paintings of animals were intended not as portraits of actual individual animals, but as representations of the spirit animal, the manito of the species, Superbear or Supermoose. Indeed, one of the objects of the vision quests, in which the young hunter voluntarily endured a lonely and lengthy vigil in the wilderness, was to obtain the patronage of one of the animal manitos who would continue throughout life to act as a "guardian spirit" of the visionary. Only if the hunter or apprentice shaman received an appropriate dream or vision would he feel confident that he had acquired a spirit guardian. In the absence of a vision he would be subject to extreme depression as one scorned by the spirit powers, and the object of derision by his fellow tribesmen. The idea of the animal helper spirit was held in common by most North American Indians, as well as by Canada's other indigenous people, the Eskimos. Dr. William Taylor, director of the National Museum of Canada, Ottawa, and Professor George Swinton, of the School of Art of the University of Manitoba, have given many examples of prehistoric Eskimo carved effigies of animals, such as bears, which have little actual resemblance to real animals. The distorted forms of these carvings are intended to represent spirit animals, the magical helpers of the hunter and the fisherman. Though some people today believe in spirit animals, at least to the extent of holding the view that if humans have souls then so do animals, the concept of Superbear and Supermoose as manitos of their species is quite alien to modern ideas even among those sympathetic to the existence of a spirit world. More akin to European thought is the Ojibway belief, shared with many other groups of North Americans, that the human soul survives death. The Ojibway word for the spiritual component that persists after the body fails means "shadow." According to Ojibway belief, after death the shadow first haunts the vicinity of its home and family. To reach the permanent abode of the dead it has to make a perilous journey beyond the western horizon—the place of the setting sun. The Ojibways believed that the shadow could make this journey safely and successfully only if aided by the special funeral rites performed by shamans specially qualified for this work by membership in an exclusive group called the Midewiwin, or Mystic Society (*mide* = mystic, *wiwin* = society). Shamans graduated into the Midewiwin only if they could claim to have had astonishing visions. Once accepted into the Mystic Society they were addressed as "Manito" and assured at death of a direct and easy passage into the world beyond where they would occupy a place of honor.

The term "shaman," which is used by anthropologists to indicate a person who claims to communicate with spirits, is derived from the Siberian word *saman*. The activity called shamanism is rare in Africa but common among most primitive peoples in the land areas that ring the Pacific Ocean. Anthropologists distinguish between the work of the shaman and the medicine man. The latter will carry out medical treatment often of a fairly orthodox nature even by modern standards, e.g. setting bones, use of plaster and herbal remedies, as well as doing sorcery of various kinds. The shaman's essential business, however, is to communicate with spirits or even, in some cases, to be possessed or "taken over" by spirits. His other powers, such as healing, knowing the future, forecasting the weather, finding lost objects, exposing thieves, and defending people against sorcery, are, so he believes, obtained from the spirits or are the actual work of his spirit patrons. In some North American communities the medicine man and the shaman were quite distinct persons. But often their functions were combined in the same person, usually referred to as medicine man rather than as shaman. Some of the Ojibway rock paintings certainly portray medicine men in shamanistic roles.

2

CANADA'S FIRST
PSYCHICAL INVESTIGATORS

Those explorers and missionaries of New France who encountered shamanism in action in what are now the provinces of Ontario, Quebec, and Nova Scotia may properly be claimed to be Canada's first psychical researchers. For a lucid and well-written account of their experiences among the Indians of eastern Canada we are indebted to R. S. Lambert, the distinguished Canadian author and broadcaster. In the early chapters of his historical work on psychic occurrences in Canada—*Exploring the Supernatural*—he draws on the memoirs of the early travelers, French and English, who were greatly intrigued and genuinely puzzled by the feats of the Indian medicine men.

In 1609 the great explorer and colonizer Samuel de Champlain went as an ally of the Huron, Algonquin, and Montagnais Indians in their fratricidal war against the Iroquois. He was surprised that when they encamped the Indians maintained no lookouts, but depended on their *pilotois,* or medicine men, who performed a ritual every night to foretell the future and ascertain whether there was any impending danger. The shaman set up a small tent of beaver skins over pinewood stakes. Lying down inside the tent, he pronounced certain words to invoke the spirits. Eventually he became worked up, leapt about with much writhing of his body, and cried out in a variety of different voices. (These voices were, presumably, heard alternately and not simultaneously.) At this stage the tent shook vigorously. De Champlain was unimpressed and regarded the medicine men as plain tricksters consciously altering their voices and shaking the tents themselves. But later students found the shamanistic phenomena more enigmatic. Such a one was Père Paul Le Jeune, head of the Jesuit mission to New France, who spent seven years in Quebec. From October 1634 to April 1635 he shared the rigors of winter life out in the wilds with the Montagnais Indians. He earned their respect but found it difficult to convert them to Christianity in the face of the opposition of their medicine men, whom he sought to discredit as mountebanks. He watched shamanistic demonstrations with observation as close and as critical as that which many investigators in the nineteenth and twentieth centuries have brought to the doings of spirit mediums. He remained constant in his belief that the spirit voices resulted from conscious trickery by the medium but was genuinely puzzled by the violence of the shaking of the tent, which was constructed of extremely heavy, stiff, and well-rooted poles. He conceded that it was difficult to see how any man of ordinary strength could have exerted such force. He remained skeptical, however, concerning the origin of the sparks that flew out of the opening at the apex of the tepee, and of the fact, alleged by the Indians, that the medicine man's body was levitated within the tent. The Indians ascribed both the asserted lifting up of the shaman and the shaking of the tent to a violent wind that the spirits generated within it. Le Jeune was unimpressed also with the medicine men's prognostications of the future, e.g. the amount of snow to come or the abundance of moose or elk.

The English trader Alexander Henry the Elder in his *Travels and Adventures* gave an eyewitness account of the shamanistic tent ritual performed by Ojibways at Sault Sainte Marie in 1764. The Ojibways were invited by the British to send a delegation to Fort Niagara to conclude a peace treaty. The Ojibway chief, concerned lest this be a trap, decided that Mikinak, the Great Turtle (their most revered manito), should advise them on their course of action. The ceremony began at nightfall with Henry and the leaders of the tribe gathered in a large wigwam specially erected for the purpose. Inside this wigwam stood a small tepee, four feet in diameter at its base, with poles set two feet deep in the ground, and its mooseskin cover fastened tightly except for one loose flap by which the medicine man entered. Henry said that the sounds of numerous voices were heard, apparently simultaneously, and mingled with yells, sobs, howling as of wolves and barking as of dogs, and human speech in an unknown tongue. Then came "a low and feeble voice, resembling the cry of a young puppy," which pleased the Ojibways, who recognized it as the voice of the Great Turtle. The medicine man, speaking in his own voice, announced Mikinak's presence and his willingness to answer questions. The chief asked as to the intentions of the British and if there were many redcoats at Fort Niagara, whereupon the tent shook so violently that Henry expected it to collapse. With a piercing cry Great Turtle departed for an aerial reconnaissance over Lake Huron, proceeding via Fort Niagara to Montreal—for thus was the ensuing silence of fifteen minutes' duration interpreted by the Indian bystanders. The medicine man then reported on behalf of the manito that redcoats were numerous in the whole area, but that the Ojibways would be well received at Niagara.

By 1846, when the artist Paul Kane made his journey through western Canada, Indian religious and magical practices had much declined in the east and survived in vigorous form only in the territories of the Hudson's Bay Company. However, on his way home Kane saw the shaking tent in operation at Dog's Head near Lake Winnipeg. Kane, who had been asleep, was awakened by the shaman's incantations and approached the tent silently in complete darkness. He was astonished when the shaman ceased his incantation and declared that a white man was present. This would seem to have been an instance of extrasensory or psychic perception. About the same time, the Anglican Bishop of Montreal, visiting the Red River area of what is now Manitoba, saw shaking tents which, though tall, were very narrow. He noticed that the medicine man was put into the tent with his hands and feet bound with knotted cords, but that, nonetheless, the tent became violently agitated.

Both the Jesuits of the seventeenth century and the Protestant clergy of the nineteenth dismissed most of the effects produced by the shamans as tricks, but admitted a residue of doubt as to whether there was not also a paranormal factor involved. Père Le Jeune's colleagues ascribed this inexplicable residue to the work of the Devil, as did some of the Bishop of Montreal's fellow clerics. However, the Bishop himself, though puzzled, did not suppose that Satan actually produced these strange effects, merely that the Adversary created delusion in the minds of the observers.

Looked at with the hindsight of nearly a century of modern psychical research and numerous anthropological studies on North American Indians, we can appreciate their difficulty. Studies of spirit mediums conducted both in Europe and in North America in the latter half of the nineteenth century and the earlier decades of the twentieth century showed that it was extremely difficult for even disinterested and unbiased investigators to separate out truly paranormal phenomena from results that were or might have been produced by trickery. If a general conclusion on spirit mediumship can be enunciated on the basis of this admittedly somewhat unsatisfactory experience, it would probably be to the following effect:

Some mediums were totally fraudulent.

Some mediums were mainly fraudulent but showed flashes of paranormal ability.

Some mediums (e.g. Eusapia Palladino) had great paranormal powers but would also resort to fraud.

A few mediums were completely honest and the powers they manifested were usually paranormal (Mrs. Leonard belonged to this class, it would seem, with high probability, and there is a good case for regarding D. D. Home similarly).

On the principle that there is an underlying genetic similarity between men of all races we would expect Canadian shamans to present a similar spectrum with respect to paranormal ability. This can also be plausibly argued from anthropological findings. In some North American tribes the office of medicine man or shaman was hereditary and those who entered the profession by this route may be expected to have employed the tricks of the trade learned at their fathers' knees. However, in other groups, such as the Ojibway, shamanism was not a profession but a vocation; the shamans were self-elected on the basis of their visionary experience. More properly speaking, looked at from his own point of view, the shaman was one who had "received his call"; the spirits through their visionary manifestations, or via presumptively psychic impressions they had engendered in the shaman's mind, had called him to their service and elected him as intermediary between themselves and mankind. While the visionary or psychic experience was, then as now, more likely than not to be illusory, nonetheless a proportion of these vocational shamans would in some degree or other have been psychic sensitives and possessed of some paranormal powers.

In the middle of the last century the German anthropologist J. G. Kohl took a statement from a white man settled in the Lake Superior area who reported himself extremely puzzled by the violent movements of a hut ten feet high, in which a shaman was singing and beating a drum. Thirty years later Kohl's informant chanced to be present at the deathbed of the same shaman, now converted to Christianity. When questioned, the shaman declared that he did not move the lodge, that it was shaken by the power of the spirits. "The top of the lodge was full of them, and before them the sky and woodlands lay expanded. I could see a great distance about me, and believed I could recognize the most distant objects." Kohl's witness described this statement as made "with such an expression of simple truth and firm conviction that it seemed to me at least, that he did not consider himself a deceiver, and believed in the efficacy of his magic arts and in the reality of his visions." Another deathbed confession—or nonconfession—was told to Henry Schoolcraft, the Indian agent on the United States side of Sault Sainte Marie who studied the birchbark pictographic texts of the Midewiwin shamans and was one of the first to notice the rock paintings on the shores of Lake Superior. The author of two important books, *The American Indians* and *The Intellectual Capacity, and Character of the Indian Race,* he inspired Longfellow to write *Hiawatha,* which was based on his collection of Ojibway legends. The dying man was Wan-Chas-Co, an ex-shaman and Christian convert who said he never attempted to move the tent, but that as soon as he commenced drumming an incantation he would feel the presence of his personal manitos who generated currents of air, which spun like a whirlwind. These spirits also revealed knowledge to him. Unfortunately we do not have enough comparative knowledge of deathbed statements of white spirit mediums to permit us to form a reliable judgment of the value of such declarations however solemnly made, but it would seem fair to allow some weight to them.

Tent shaking had been observed in 1879 among the Blackfoot on the Red Deer River by Sir Cecil Denny, an official of the North West Mounted Police. He was particularly impressed, as he was present himself with the medicine man inside the tent, which in this case was a large wigwam. The medicine man sat quietly throughout smoking a ceremonial pipe, but the tent rocked dramatically at points, heaving its base a foot off the ground. From time to time Denny slipped out of the tent to look for an accomplice, but saw none, although the tent was in an empty clearing well lit by the moon. As late as 1929 A. H. Black, an official of the Hudson's Bay Company at White Sands in the Mackenzie River basin, was impressed by a demonstration of tent shaking given by a celebrated medicine man named August. The wigwam was constructed in Black's presence and thoroughly tested for mobility and found to be immovable. However, it started to shake violently as soon as August entered it. What Black found even more uncanny was the fact that a conversation ensued between the medicine man's own voice, coming from low down in the wigwam, and what seemed to be an entirely different-sounding voice coming from the top of the tent. At the end of the performance, when August came out of the tent, Black stripped off its bark covering and was surprised to find the poles as firmly tied together and as solidly rooted in the ground as formerly.

Apropos of the 1967 Centenary of the Confederation of Canada, Dr. Winifred Barton published *Canada's Psi-Century,* an interesting collection of narratives of psychic experiences by Canadians. These narratives were obtained through the cooperation of weekly and daily newspapers who asked their readers to send in their accounts of any strange events they had encountered. As every psychic investigator knows, or should know, it is impossible to be sure that written narratives are not fabrications or, even if basically true, are free from embellishments or inaccuracies due to faulty memory. This is especially true when, as was the case with many in Dr. Barton's collection, the accounts were written many years after the event. When time and funds allow, corroboration of stories of this kind can sometimes be gathered by interviewing the narrators and by getting confirmation of some of the details by other witnesses. But this is counsel of perfection, especially in a country as large as Canada. Failing vigorous checking out, a person familiar with this field can, however, form some estimate of the reliability of a statement from the style in which it is written and from the subject matter itself. I have read hundreds of narratives of this kind. The majority of stories in Dr. Barton's collection do in fact "ring true." The events they describe are, for the most part, typical of "standard" types of psychic experience as reported in many other parts of the world and are written in an honest, straightforward style which, I think, is characteristic of the way in which these experiences are usually reported by people who are impressed by what has occurred and understand some of its significance, but are not immersed in occultism or extensive study of the psychic. I think, therefore, that credence can be given to an account of tent shaking first published in Dr. Barton's collection over the initials E. R. (a correspondent whose name and address were given to Dr. Barton) from Winnipeg, Manitoba.

In 1920 E. R. was a clerk in the Hudson's Bay Company in a post adjacent to an Indian reserve on the shore of one of the lakes in the north of Manitoba, where there was a quarrel in progress between a newly arrived self-styled medicine man and the established incumbent, an elderly, longtime resident. The local RCMP corporal decided to stage a competition in magic between the two wizards, hoping simultaneously to discredit both and to restore peace and tranquility to the neighborhood. In the event, this proved to be one of those plans that "gang aglay." At the break of day the young aspirant built a Migawap, i.e. a tepee almost twenty feet tall made of four poles of poplar covered with canvas, with no aperture except a small opening at the top. The rigidity of the structure was tested strenuously by E. R., the corporal, and many Indians. A tin can filled with pebbles was suspended in the tent about ten feet from the apex. The tepee was sufficiently narrow for E. R. and the corporal, standing on opposite sides, to keep all of it in view. During the contest no one came nearer than within three feet of it. The senior shaman was invited to rattle the pebbles by use of his occult powers. After half an hour of singing and dancing without any effect whatever he retired weary and dejected. His rival was more successful; he followed a similar, though more vigorous, routine and within ten minutes the tepee was vibrating and the pebbles loudly rattling. The corporal, suspecting that an accomplice had sneaked into the tent, slit the canvas with a knife but it was seen to be empty. Within a few weeks, says E. R., the new shaman had more influence in the village than even its chief and his council.

If E. R.'s account is to be relied on, it would seem that on occasion a real physical force of mysterious origin did come into play during shamanistic rituals. The shaman's own explanation was that this force was exerted not by himself but by the spirits. Though this explanation is one which would be accepted by modern spiritualists, it is not necessarily the correct one, though admittedly it cannot be proved wrong. As we shall see, the same problem of how to explain mysteriously produced movements of physical objects occurs elsewhere in psychical research, sometimes in situations where the spiritualist explanation seems inappropriate, even if (as is usually the case) it does not allow of actual disproof. In these situations it is customary to speak of the physical effects as happening by psychokinesis (or PK). Here the underlying assumption is that in some way the person concerned is doing it himself. How he does it we do not know, but the fact is interesting and of profound importance to our understanding both of man and the nature of the universe. Situations in which PK occurs apparently without the assistance of spirits may be listed as follows: cases where, in the laboratory, people by conscious willing seem able to slightly influence the fall of dice (these effects are usually small but a great deal of data of this sort has been accumulated, particularly in the United States during the last forty years); cases where the motion of a light object has been influenced or controlled by the deliberately conscious choice of an experimenter (the exploits of Madame Mikhailova in Russia are very well known; later in this book the reader will become acquainted with the work of Jan Merta in Canada); last, cases where objects move spontaneously of their own volition (this kind of happening sometimes occurs sporadically and sometimes in what is called a poltergeist case; examples of each situation will be discussed later).

The other type of phenomena, truly paranormal or fakes, claimed by the shamans fall into the type which psychical research workers call mental phenomena (as opposed to physical ones). These are the receipt of information which the shaman could not acquire by normal means, and "traveling clairvoyance," whereby the shaman "sees" things that are far away. It may well be that the information is imparted by the spirits, and that the shaman in some ethereal or spirit form is borne by the spirits to distant places. These phenomena can, however, equally be explained in terms of extrasensory perception (or ESP for short). That is, the information is obtained by telepathy, clairvoyance, or precognition. In so saying we do not claim to understand how these phenomena work— all we are saying is that according to this mode of explanation it is the shaman's own powers that are operating without the intervention of spirits. Just as with physical phenomena the choice of alternative explanations (via the spirits or via the medium's own

powers) presents itself in any consideration of the mental phenomena of modern spirit mediums.

In the shamanistic rituals the messages of the spirits are delivered
in two different modes. Sometimes, as in Alexander Henry's case,
the shaman merely passes on the intelligence conveyed to him by
Great Turtle or his spirit helper, whoever that may be. However,
it appeared that, just as with the modern trance medium (whom we
shall discuss later), the shaman, though doing the actual speaking,
simulates a voice different from his normal one. When this happens,
then, as with contemporary trance mediums, we have the problem
of deciding among three different possibilities:

The shaman was consciously faking.

He was not consciously faking but like many trance mediums
(perhaps the majority) was in an altered state of consciousness, i.e., some secondary personality had come to the fore. In
this state the secondary personality may have been talking pure
fantasy; on the other hand, it may have (part of the time at least)
been conveying genuine information acquired by ESP or by
the "spirits."

The shaman is "possessed" by a spirit who uses his vocal cords
to communicate.

Sometimes, as in Black's observations at White Sands in 1929
(an impressive case because it is, relatively speaking, fairly recent),
the "spirit voice" seemed to come from a point several feet away
from the shaman. Just possibly, this was an example of the "direct
voice" as it is known in spiritualist circles. The voice seems to
come not from the medium but from a point in midair.

As readers with a knowledge of Spiritualism will recognize, the
resemblance between the Canadian shaman and the spirit mediums
who appeared for the first time in North America in the second
half of the nineteenth century is a very close one. Modern Spiritualism among white people is supposed to have received its initial
impetus from the case of the Fox sisters at Hydesville, near Roch-
ester, New York, in 1848, whose home was disturbed by loud

knockings of mysterious origin. Little, if anything, is recorded of spirit mediumship prior to that among whites. However, within a few years the practice of mediumistic séances had spread through the United States and thence to Britain and Europe. The anthropologist Kohl was the first to claim the existence of similarities between the technique and apparatus of the medicine man and the nineteenth-century spirit medium. There is indeed a parallel between the shaman's tepee and the medium's cabinet—a curtained-off section of the room. There is also something of a parallel, though perhaps a less close one, between the use of hymns and chants, the tambourine and the drum, as well as the trembling and shaking that sometimes preceded the medium's entry into trance. If there is a historic connection, it may have occurred via the sect of the Shakers. Descendants of English Quakers, by the mid-nineteenth century Shakers were found in New York State, New England, Ohio, Kentucky, and Indiana. Some of these communities believed that the spirits of deceased Indians visited their religious meetings and "'possessed" their members, compelling them to shout, dance and sing, and shake in Indian fashion. It seems that the Shakers had a theory concerning these spirits rather similar to that sometimes encountered among present-day spiritualists: they believed the Indian spirits were "earthbound souls" to be rescued by religious conversion from the limbo in which they were stranded. According to R. S. Lambert it is likely that the Davenport brothers, who were the first recorded professional spirit mediums, were inspired by the Shakers. However, they introduced the medium's cabinet, and among their feats was that of escaping from bonds while in the cabinet. As this was a feature of Ojibway shamanism it is likely that they drew considerably on Ojibway examples. But the origins of Spiritualism are still rather obscure.

Each modern spirit medium almost invariably has a spirit guide permanently on call. When the medium goes into trance it is usually the voice of the spirit guide that first comes through. Sometimes he alone talks with the sitters, bringing them messages that purport to come from deceased persons. Sometimes, however, the spirit guide will offer to "bring" someone else or to yield his place to another spirit. The Davenports' spirit guide was said to be the spirit of an Indian who claimed to be the chief of a band of 150 deceased Indians, presumably present with him in the Happy Hunting Grounds. His name was John King. Perhaps, more precisely, one should say *is,* because he has been claimed as spirit guide by many later mediums. In 1930 he manifested as the control of a medium in Winnipeg. "Katy King," the spirit guide of the famous English medium Florence Cook, who worked with Sir William Crookes in England in the late nineteenth century, was accounted a daughter of John King. Since the Davenport brothers many mediums have had North American Indians as spirit guides. Some critics have found this puzzling. If it is not to be explained on historical grounds, then weight must be given to the spiritualist explanation that spiritually, even if not materially, the North American Indians are a highly developed people.

Ojibway and Cree were both celebrated for conjuring feats of various kinds. Though these were represented as magical or spirit phenomena, and though also we have admitted the possibility of some genuine paranormal happenings being mixed in with the shamanistic repertoire, it would be naïve to suppose that the feats of the medicine men were not as a general rule merely tricks of the trade. Demonstrations of "fire-eating" given by Ojibway magicians appear to have closely resembled stunts performed by white men today in which the "fire-eater" fills his mouth with a flammable liquid which he then ignites, while expelling it forcibly. The flame is then always an inch or so beyond his mouth. It was said that the Ojibway used to chew a certain root which made their breath flammable. However, in the seventeenth century the French missionaries to both the Montagnais and the Hurons were genuinely puzzled by demonstrations of insensitivity to heat with a corresponding failure of the skin to show signs of burning. Père Le Jeune saw a fire ceremony in 1637 which had been organized by the Montagnais for the purpose of curing one of their number of some ailment (not specified). Twenty-four Montagnais, while singing and chanting, heated a number of stones to red heat in a fire. To Le Jeune's astonishment the Montagnais with their bare hands parted the burning firebrands and lifted out the stones and held them between their teeth. Walking up to the patient, they stood with the stones still in their mouths, blowing the while. Le Jeune kept one of the stones, which was about the size of a goose's egg. When discarded by the sorcerer in whose mouth it had been, and dropped on the ground, glowing sparks fell off at impact. (Père Pijart also kept a stone which had been used similarly by Hurons. Being a calcareous rock it had softened in the heat and bore the sorcerer's tooth-marks.)

Fire-walking and related practices have always interested some psychical research workers, not because they necessarily assume that factors other than psychological and physiological ones are involved, but because, being very incompletely understood, the phenomenon of immunity to heat may, for all that we know to the contrary, depend on something very strange and interesting. Sometimes the immunity is purely apparent; the contact is so brief that there is no time for an appreciable transfer of heat; we all can pass our hands through a flame or dab ourselves with a lighted cigarette. This will also be true of the traditional ordeals of licking or stroking a piece of hot iron. An alternative explanation is sometimes offered for success or failure in licking the iron. Fear is supposed to dry the mouth and, presumably, the tongue, which is thereby deprived of its protective layer of moisture, is burned unless the person, being innocent, trusts in God and his clear conscience. It is said (though I do not know with what experimental justification) that a person of sufficiently strong nerve can, without injury, plunge his hand briefly into molten lead. It is alleged that the natural moisture of the skin forms a layer of vapor which during the short time that the contact is maintained effectively insulates against the heat. If this is the true explanation, then boiling lead would not be very appropriate as a lie detector. It is well known that when one is tense or excited the skin exudes more moisture than when one is relaxed. This is the principle upon which the modern lie detector works. It is presumed that the liar is under more stress than the honest man; his skin is moister so that the electrical resistance between two locations on it will be lowered. The lie detector operates by recording the drop in skin resistance. Only in recent years has it been recognized that there may be a fallacy in the psychological theory underlying the use of the lie detector. An honest man of nervous disposition may react with considerable tension when he is asked a question that he recognizes to be a key one. The lie detector would seem to be merely a modern form of trial by ordeal, and appears in criminal investigations to be following the older method into oblivion.

Some instances of simple fire-walking as practiced by various primitive peoples seem to be explicable in terms of the toughness and thickening of the soles of the feet acquired by a lifetime on bare feet, supplemented by special treatment—soaking the feet in alum or anointing the soles with infusions of various plants. The Zuñi Indians of the Southwestern United States are said to have used yarrow (*Achilles borealis*) and Navajo fire dancers to have rubbed their feet with white clay and crushed cedar. The Heyoka Society of the Omaha Indians had a ritual ordeal requiring them to pluck objects out of boiling water; in preparation they rubbed their hands and arms with chewed leaves of red false marrow (*Malvestrum coccineum*). Recently a young stage performer in Montreal, one of whose "acts" was fire-walking, came to the attention of Allen Spraggett and Dr. Bernard Grad. His performance was not unimpressive; however, he burned his feet to a degree that he found painful and inconvenient. It seems that he wore socks which (presumably like his feet) were impregnated with some chemical mixture; the contretemps resulted from some negligence or error in the preparations. Père Le Jeune's observations, however, if correct, do not appear to be explicable in terms of medication of the skin of the practitioners. One of Le Jeune's colleagues insisted on looking into the mouth of one of the Indians who had filled his mouth with live coals, but found no sign of burning or blistering. Le Jeune goes on, "And not only these persons, but even the sick people were not burnt. They let their bodies be rubbed with glowing cinders without showing any evidence of pain, and without their skin appearing in the least affected."

We would be inclined to dismiss Père Le Jeune's observations as inadequately made, or even, following the lead of the nineteenth-century Anglican clergy of Montreal, speculate as to some element of hallucination, hypnotism, or suggestibility, were it not a fact that immunity to heat crops up from time to time in quite different contexts. Before any missionaries went to Canada somewhat similar abilities had been recorded of various eminent Catholic mystics. It was said that the Venerable Domenica del Paradiso (1473-1553) could carry live charcoal in her hands. Numerous incidents of this sort were reported of Saint Francis of Paola (1416-1507), such as putting his hands into boiling oil or mending hot lime kilns. Saint Catherine of Siena (1347-1389) was said to have been miraculously preserved from scorching when she lay in a trance for an appreciable time in contact with the kitchen fire. It is unlikely that Père Le Jeune was familiar with these happenings and thus predisposed to see the same phenomena among the Indians in Canada (where, of course, they would have the status of diabolical miracles according to the theological maxim that what God can do, the Devil, subject to Divine permission and certain limitations, can do also). The Catholic Church tended to be suspicious of and reticent about the more extraordinary happenings in the cloister, and it is unlikely that Père Le Jeune, who was a pastoral priest and not a theologian, and who left France as a young man, was *au fait* with the miracles of Italian saints.

The interest attached to the data concerning the saints is that they were in fact saints and not mountebanks, and cannot be accused of sleight of hand or soaking themselves in alum. It may be objected, however, that we are not comparing like with like. It is legitimate to take the view that the mystic incombustibility of holy persons is a divine miracle, and so, being a law to itself, casts no light on the mechanisms operative in other contexts. But the same objection cannot easily be made with respect to D. D. Home;

though little, if anything, is known to his discredit, he is not usually classified as a saint. One of the feats ascribed to Home was the handling of red-hot coals and an ability to enable others to handle them without injury. With regard to D. D. Home it is worth remarking that while some modern critics have very properly and validly shown how *some* of his exploits *might* have been done by trickery, no investigator either in his own time or subsequently has *proved* fraud on Home's part. Neither were Home's effects obtained in circumstances such as to engender *a priori* suspicion of fraud; he used no cabinet and did not work in complete darkness like some of his contemporaries. Frank Podmore, a highly qualified critic and a very skeptical one, did his best to scrutinize rigorously Home's record, and certainly made no concessions where Home was concerned. It is therefore well worth quoting Podmore when he says that Home's resistance to heat was ". . . the least readily explicable and the best attested of all the phenomena presented by Home. The evidence for the fire-ordeal is abundant; it is in some cases of high quality; and from the nature of the experiment, the illumination of the room was generally more adequate than in the case of the levitations. . . ."

There is, therefore, a case for believing that what Père Le Jeune saw was not the result of imposture but represents a phenomenon which is strange and not easily understandable. I was present a few years back in Kansas when a Hindu swami, eminent in his own country, who works from time to time with the Menninger Foundation in Topeka, said that by appropriate meditation techniques performed for a few hours he could put his body into a state resistant to a variety of physical assaults, e.g. by strong acid. I cannot recollect whether heat was mentioned but would deem it to be implied on the principle that the greater includes the lesser. This ties in vaguely with a proposition enunciated by Jan Merta (of whom more will be heard in Chapter 14) to the effect that when a karate exponent shatters a plank of wood by an edgewise blow of his hand without sustaining injury, it is because the karate expert has in some way modified not his physical body but its "astral" counterpart.

The idea of the astral body is a very old one. Greek philosophers thought that the stars were made of a form of matter more refined than our mortal clay and called it *asteron,* or "star stuff." In the early years of the Christian era Stoic and Platonist philosophers thought that the soul of a righteous man, conceived of as made of *asteron,* rose up to dwell among the stars. Later the theory was elaborated that in addition to his physical body every human being has within him an astral body consisting of this rarefied material which is of the same size and shape as his physical body. Whether it is, like Oliver Cromwell's portrait, absolutely identical "warts and all," to the physical body is a delicate matter that has not yet been adjudicated; however, a marked degree of resemblance is usually implied by those who believe in the astral body's existence. The concept of the astral body, which is an ancient one, has something in common with the Ojibway idea of the "shadow." Indeed, most primitive peoples believe in the existence of the "shade" or "spirit double" of the living person. It is the shade which is supposed to visit people in dreams or to travel about during sleep, thus "explaining" why, in dreams, the dreamer seems to visit places, near or far. The idea of the astral body is deeply rooted in many systems of thought such as Spiritualism and Theosophy. As we have noted, it bears a strong resemblance to the ideas of primitive peoples. This does not imply that it is necessarily a mistaken notion. If every idea that had ancient antecedents were wrong, then such well-established happenings as telepathy would have to be rejected. However, the position with regard to the astral body is somewhat different from that with respect to telepathy. Happenings that can be explained in terms of the existence of the astral body can also be explained in other ways and as yet it cannot be said that its existence has been proved.

No one branch of mankind has a monopoly of psychic abilities, which seem to occur in all times and places irrespective of race or color. This is entirely what we would expect from the underlying biological unity of the human race. However, it would appear that religion and culture can have some effect on how these abilities are manifested. As we have seen, some of the more dramatic phases of Canadian Indian shamanism survived into the thirties of the present century. In the same period, Professor Landes found the Midewiwin religion and shamanism still alive among the Ojibway. How the matter stands today is unknown. Some decline may be surmised. However, in the last hundred years the Indians of North America have defied all the confident predictions of their imminent decease, and have stubbornly and resolutely refused to fade away like the Patagonians or Tierra del Fuegans. With characteristic unconformity, they have also retained much of their old beliefs and philosophy. This cannot be blamed on the "childlike simplicity" which the white man once ascribed to the "savages" with whom he came in contact, possibly on account of their lack of "business sense" in dealing with the intruders in their land and an unsophisticated tendency to accept the white man's word. As the experiences of educationalists with Indian children show, theirs is a race of quick intelligence, even if they cannot all accept the necessity of working in nine-to-five jobs. The visionary life still seems to answer a deep-rooted desire in the Indian mind. In the present century the vision quest has been reanimated in some areas by the spread of peyotism—the use of peyote, the Mexican cactus, whose active principle is mescaline. In the course of about a hundred years the use of peyote has spread from Mexico via Indian tribes of the desert states and the Great Plains into Saskatchewan. Peyote users in Canada and the United States are organized in the Native American Church of North America. An even more recent and apparently independent development is the founding of the Church of the Great Spirit. Whether these movements will create a milieu especially favorable to psychic phenomena remains to be seen.

3

CANADIAN POLTERGEISTERY

In his historical review of psychic and related matters in Canada
R. S. Lambert found that the most extensive literature referred to a
particular type of haunting that psychical researchers call poltergeist cases. Though these cases are very complex from one point
of view, looked at in another way, they are simpler and in some
ways more easy to understand than other problems in the psychic
field. Also, they involve psychokinesis and so the study of them
follows on in a rather natural way from that of the Indian shamanistic phenomena.

The word "poltergeist" was originally a German folklore term
made up from *polter* (a noise) and *geist* (a spirit or sprite), and
meant a nature spirit akin to elf or goblin or "things that go
bump in the night." Phenomena that were ascribed to the activity
of poltergeists included a remarkable variety of alleged happenings: movements of domestic objects, flinging of mud or stones,
teleportation (the mysterious conveyance of articles into closed
rooms), as well as the production of noises such as raps, bangs, or
scratchings, and sounds imitating the human voice whistling, singing, or talking. Despite the apparently fantastic nature of the alleged
phenomena, serious investigators in psychical research in England
and Europe in the nineteenth century, such as Frederic Myers,
Frank Podmore, and the criminologist Cesare Lombroso, thought
them very worthy of unbiased study. But in order not to prejudge
the issue—i.e. not to assume at the outset that the happenings were
really due to the action of a "spirit"—they tended to use the word

"poltergeist" as an adjective and not a noun, speaking of "poltergeist outbreaks" or "poltergeist disturbances" in order to indicate the kind of occurrence that took place. I find it convenient to use the word "poltergeistery" to refer to "goings on" of this kind.

It is necessary to say at the outset that not all alleged poltergeistery is genuine. In many instances the happenings are due to natural causes which are poorly observed. For example, noises caused by shrinking of timbers or by underground water may be quite dramatic yet completely normal phenomena. Also, the happenings may be fraudulent, as when objects are moved by trickery. However, as I showed some years ago (Owen, 1964) there have been a vast number of cases in which the evidence of eyewitnesses was so abundant and well corroborated that it is not possible to doubt that the phenomena did occur and cannot be explained in normal terms. For well-evidenced cases of this kind, the problem is not their genuineness but how they are to be interpreted.

In the Middle Ages if a scholar or priest encountered poltergeistery and did not regard it as due to trickery or natural causes he would have blamed it on elves or goblins rather than on witches or demons. During the Reformation period, however, belief in the power of witches spread throughout Europe, and was still rampant in the seventeenth century. Consequently, witchcraft was invoked to explain a poltergeist outbreak among the colonists of New France in 1661. The phenomena occurred in the vicinity of a young woman; they included noises and, so it was said by the Venerable Mother Mary of the Incarnation (well known as a religious person of that time), "stones were detached from the walls, flying hither and thither." These exploits were blamed on *esprits follets* (mischievous spirits) who, it was supposed, were activated through the exercise of witchcraft by a young miller whose advances had been rejected by the girl. Though the laws against witchcraft in Quebec were basically the same as those in Old France, any penalties actually imposed on persons convicted of witchcraft seem to have been relatively light; there were no executions such as occurred in Massachusetts in 1692, and even later in Scotland. This is to the credit of the Quebequois; as R. S. Lambert points out, as late as 1830 the Scottish Canadians of Baldoon in Ontario were inclined to believe in witchcraft as the source of a poltergeist outbreak there.

At this stage, I ought to take time out to explain that I do not believe in witchcraft, magic, and sorcery. Doubtless the majority of readers share this complete disbelief and will wonder why I trouble to mention something so obvious. Twenty years ago no literate person believed in the efficacy of magic and the like. But this is no longer true. It seems that a proportion of educated persons, especially among the young, have developed a literal belief in the actual efficacy of witchcraft, meaning magic and spells and the employment of discarnate entities (spirits, demons, and the like) to do one's bidding. This is due in part to the books of unscrupulous writers and the operations of even more unscrupulous and venal groups who exploit the public. The matter is not helped by people who are not necessarily unscrupulous or excessively venal but who claim to be both "psychic sensitives" *and* "witches." Charitably, I (provisionally) exonerate them from willful deceit but not from the charge of muddle-headedness, which if kept to themselves would be harmless. As it is, they greatly confuse otherwise intelligent people who are attracted to the occult.

Witchcraft beliefs are either old superstitions or modern errors. In this they differ from the findings of psychical research, which is a true science employing the methods of science, and from the theories held by spiritualists, which are based on observation of the phenomena of spirit mediums and also have a very strong ethical content. Persons who have a strong inclination to dabble in witchcraft or who genuinely fear the activities of "witches" should examine their motives, which undoubtedly stem from unconscious psychological forces. To our surprise, one day a woman of mature age came to our home. As representatives of the Toronto Society for Psychical Research, would we put her in touch with a competent witch? When we replied that we wouldn't and couldn't, she turned somewhat nasty and departed, accusing us of dereliction of duty. It was lucky that we did not believe in witches or we might have felt uneasy at having offended her. With high-school witchcraft, things have their lighter side (see Vicki Branden's article); all the same, children should not be encouraged in foolishness.

In recent decades the subject of witchcraft has been further confused, not only by the emergence of "Satanist" sects, but by groups who claim to perpetuate the pre-Christian religion of Europe, which consists of simple nature rites, dancing in the open air (clothed or nude), and the worship of deities such as the Celtic Bran or a mother goddess. They call themselves "witches" and claim that *their* witchcraft is merely the old religion of nature. However, things are rarely kept as simple as this, and the modern practitioners of the "Old Religion" usually claim also to have psychic powers and to exercise them in beneficent witchcraft for healing and the like. In unguarded moments they sometimes confess to "hexing" people of whom they disapprove.

If, following my line of reasoning, the reader is prepared to admit that some poltergeist cases involve genuinely paranormal phenomena but cannot be explained by witchcraft, then he has to ask what other modes of explanation are available. A psychical research worker when presented with the record of any particular poltergeist case examines it carefully to see whether all the phenomena happened within the same house. When this is so, the case might still be one of poltergeistery, but equally it could be of a kind that is more complicated and much less well understood—a "haunted house" case. Very few cases of this kind have ever been reported in Canada. But there have been quite a number of cases in which the strange events have not been confined to any particular location but appear to happen only in the vicinity of certain people. A very clear-cut instance of this occurred in Forest Hill, Toronto, in 1947. In January, noises such as rappings, moans, and whistlings occurred in the home of Mr. and Mrs. Sherman in Silverwood Avenue. More dramatically, from time to time, large pieces of plaster would be "blown off" the interior walls of the house. Each event of this kind was accompanied by a loud report, as if there had been an explosion in the wall. Consultants called in to examine the plaster could find no abnormality or rational cause for the "explosions." Outbreaks of knockings then occurred in the homes of the Donnerfields in Ardmore Road and of Mrs. Young in Hillholme Road. The police were unable to discover how they were caused. However, there was one fact common to all the disturbed houses—the events happened only when a certain young woman, employed as a domestic, was present. Clearly, therefore, the poltergeistery was not attached to the house but was in some way connected with the presence of this girl.

In a case at Chilliwack, British Columbia, knockings broke out late in 1951 in the home of Miss Duryba. Lambert quotes the firsthand evidence of a witness who described the knockings as "rapid, violent rappings on the outer wall." The house was floodlit outside but no prankster was seen in the vicinity of the knockings either inside or outside the house. It would seem that these sounds were genuinely paranormal phenomena. No cause could be ascertained for the rappings. However, when Miss Duryba's fourteen-year-old niece, Kathleen, was sent to Vancouver for ten days the manifestations completely ceased, only to resume on her return to Chilliwack. Here again, the phenomena would seem to be attached to a person—Kathleen—rather than to the building itself. Over the Christmas period in 1937 the Hilchie family's home at Eastern Passage near Halifax, Nova Scotia, suffered a variety of poltergeist disturbances. From time to time deep, hollow knocks were heard in the walls. Also, sporadically, objects would move. For example, at breakfast on Christmas Day a table suddenly "moved itself" across the floor. Light switches were seen to move between the on and off positions without human contact. Objects would take off by themselves and move through the air. These included diverse objects such as dishes, items of food, tools, and pillows. It was noticed that these strange phenomena always occurred in the presence of Catherine, the Hilchies' fifteen-year-old daughter. Mrs. Hilchie tried the experiment of taking Catherine with her to her mother's home at Sheffield Mills. Raps followed them on the train journey and into a restaurant at Kentville as well as into the grand-mother's house, and returned with them to their home at Eastern Passage. This experiment was conclusive in demonstrating that the phenomena were not caused by the house itself but by one of its three inmates—Mrs. Hilchie, Catherine, or her elder sister, Rita, who accompanied them to Sheffield Mills.

Lambert has assembled about a dozen Canadian poltergeist cases, all falling into this pattern—strange and definitely para-normal production of sounds and movements of objects, occurring in various locations but always in the vicinity of one particular person—a "poltergeist focus." The pattern is one which has been repeated in hundreds of cases throughout the world (see Owen, 1964). There is no doubt that the phenomena really occur and are not due to trickery or to ordinary natural causes. It is not easy to convince oneself of the correctness of this conclusion without considerable study of the evidence, but it is one which all serious scholars who have considered these cases have arrived at. We are obliged to deduce that, on occasion, a physical force of unknown nature is exerted in a sporadic but fairly directed way. This force can move objects and produce sounds. (As sound is generated by vibration of solids and is transmitted by vibration of the air, we can, in this context, regard it as a form of mechanical movement.)

What is the origin of the poltergeist force? We can say nothing, as yet, as to its nature, but we can form some opinion (though not a conclusion) as to its *origin*. Having cast witches, demons, and elves out of our intellectual scheme of things, there are only two admissible theories—the "psychological" and the "mediumistic." On the mediumistic theory the poltergeist person or focus—i.e. Kathleen at Chilliwack, or Catherine at Eastern Passage—is really a "medium." In Spiritualism a medium is a person who functions as a link or intermediary for a disembodied spirit to manifest its presence. In this view, two elements are required for poltergeistery: a spirit and a living medium. In the simplest form of the medium-istic theory it is the visiting spirit that actually moves the objects or vibrates the air or the walls to produce the sounds. A more complex form of the mediumistic theory might argue that the spirit merely endows the medium with the power to exert the mysterious poltergeist force by psychokinesis. On the psychological theory it is the poltergeist person herself who produces the phenomena by psychokinesis.

In favor of the psychological theory we may note that poltergeist phenomena are chaotic and rarely hint at any attempt to communicate a message. Apparitions are rarely reported in poltergeist cases. Poltergeist phenomena differ somewhat from the physical phenomena of the spiritualist séance: they occur in full lighting conditions; ectoplasm is absent; the poltergeist person rarely goes into trance; but even in cases where trances are reported the physical phenomena seem not to happen during the trances but rather when the medium is awake. Another difference between spirit mediumship and poltergeistery is exhibited in the age distribution of the persons concerned. The famous spirit mediums seem to have developed their powers in their late teens or soon after the age of twenty and to have retained them for long periods, sometimes for thirty or forty years. The majority of poltergeist persons are young, between ten and twenty years of age (though a small proportion can be older), and the poltergeistery surrounding them is of short duration, lasting at most for a year or two, and more usually for only a few weeks.

From a study of poltergeist literature there emerges a fact especially favorable to the psychological theory. In a large proportion of cases there is evidence to suggest that the poltergeist person is in a situation which prior to the poltergeist outbreak has put her into a state of emotional tension involving masked anger, fear, or resentment. On the psychological theory we suppose:

> The poltergeist person is of a rare biological type in that she possesses as a hereditary endowment the latent psychic talent of PK, or psychokinesis.
>
> She has a tendency to suppress, repress, or "hold in" her emotions.

She unconsciously "works off" her emotions via the poltergeist phenomena, which usually seem to have "meaning" only in a very vague and broad sense, i.e., they seem to signify a general desire to annoy her family, employers, or workmates—a kind of protest.

Here I have given only the merest sketch of the psychological theory of poltergeistery which can be argued with much more refinement of detail, as I have done elsewhere (see my article in *Man, Myth and Magic*).

In the foregoing I have used the feminine gender in referring to poltergeist persons. This is not a concession to feminism, nor on the contrary is it intended as derogatory to the female sex. It just happens that in the Canadian cases as marshaled by Lambert, poltergeist people appear to have been girls. This, however, is doubtless merely a sampling effect. When poltergeistery is considered on a worldwide scale it appears that there is only a small preponderance of girls, many boys having been at the center of famous poltergeist cases. Something also needs to be said about the age factor. It is rare for a poltergeist person to be over twenty years of age but not impossible; cases of poltergeist persons in their thirties and even forties are known. Nonetheless, the phenomenon appears to be age-limited, and older people usually seem to be capable of precipitating only an isolated event. For interest, I extract from the journal *New Horizons* (1972) a report of such an isolated event. It is interesting as being quite typical of the flight of a common domestic object as observed in numerous poltergeist cases.

The event took place on Saturday, November 21st, 1971. A buffet supper had been arranged in the dining room at Dr. and Mrs. Owen's home, the guests at that time having a pre-dinner drink in the living room. Frank McInnis and Iris Owen were having a conversation in the kitchen which adjoins the dining room. Frank was standing at the sink (having collected some glasses up), and Iris was standing in the doorway, half turned towards him, and halfway towards the table. Frank was completely facing the dining table, as he had turned to answer a remark by Iris. His eyes went past, and he said "Look at that spoon!" Iris turned completely and saw the spoon referred to just landing on the floor underneath the rung of one of the dining chairs, and some three feet away from the table. Frank saw the spoon rise from the bowl on which it was laid, float horizontally for a couple of feet, and then go down under the rung of the chair. It made just a tinkling sound as it landed.

The spoon had been placed some minutes before on the top of the bowl of rice in the centre part of the table. The rice was only warm, not hot, as there had not been room for it to be heated in the oven. If the spoon had fallen in the normal way it would have landed on the table, and the bowl was fully 18 inches from any edge of the table. Nothing else moved at all.

(Signed) Frank McInnis, M.D., Iris M. Owen
23 November 1971

As is usual with isolated events there was not enough to go on to decide who the medium or psychokinetic person was. A number of other guests were in an adjoining room, and these included one or two with psychic talents.

If one has read several hundred accounts of poltergeist cases, then levitation of spoons, perambulations of tables or chairs, and knocks, raps, and bangs come to seem the most natural things in the world. However, it would be unfair to the reader to suggest that all instances of poltergeistery are as simple as this. In some we encounter the "direct voice," which puts us in mind of the old Indian shamans. This fact, which is certainly a stumbling block in the way of belief, cannot be brushed under the carpet because it was evidenced (by very abundant testimony) in a Canadian poltergeist case which raged at the village of Clarendon, near Shawville, north of the Ottawa River in the province of Quebec, in 1889. The central character was Dinah Burdon McLean, a Scottish child recently arrived in the country who had spent some time in the Home for Orphaned Children at Belleville, Ontario. At the age of eleven she was adopted by George and Susan Dagg, who maintained a farm at Clarendon and had two small children of their own, Susan and Johnny. Shortly after Dinah's arrival the Dagg farmhouse was plagued by poltergeist activities of the usual kind. The case aroused the interest of Percy Woodcock, a distinguished artist and member of the Royal Canadian Academy, who agreed to prepare a report on it for the *Brockville Recorder and Times*. He spent two days at the house and on the basis of a great deal of evidence from the family and neighbors became convinced that the reported phenomena were genuine. But he tried to verify one phenomenon for himself. This was a gruff voice which, people alleged, they had heard speaking to Dinah. Woodcock took Dinah to a shed at the back of the house where she said she had seen an apparition. Dinah said, "Are you there, Mister?" To Woodcock's extreme astonishment, "A deep gruff voice, as of an old man, seemingly within four or five feet distance, instantly replied in language which cannot be repeated here." When Woodcock asked who it was, it said, "I am the devil. I'll have you in my clutches. Get out of this or I'll break your neck." The voice also used a great deal of bad language.

Woodcock examined the shed carefully and his account insists that there was no place of concealment for a third person. He told Dinah to fill her mouth with water, which she did, but the voice continued unaltered. In any case it was deep and rough, while Dinah's own voice was exceptionally high-pitched. When they returned to the house the voice followed them and maintained conversation for several hours in the presence finally of almost twenty neighbors, who had dropped in during the course of the day. Woodcock made repeated inspections, inside and out, of the Daggs' log-built house and found no place where a prankster could be concealed. During the conversation the voice modified its aggressive tone and became amiable and conciliatory. It apologized for the poltergeist phenomena and said it had done them for "fun" and meant no real harm. It also claimed that a neighbor, Mrs. Wallace, using the "Black Art" had sent it to plague the Daggs. At this, Woodcock fetched Mrs. Wallace and challenged the voice to accuse her to her face. At length Mrs. Wallace entangled the voice in several self-contradictory statements, whereupon it lost its temper and burst out plaintively, "Oh, don't bother me so much—you make me lie." It became conciliatory again and said it was sorry for its bad behavior. It promised that on the next night (a Sunday) it would say goodbye and leave the house for good. When Sunday came the voice was on its best behavior, but answered questions and made comments on people as they entered the house. Some remarks were humorous and displayed intimate knowledge of the private lives of the questioners. (In a small village this is, of course, not necessarily paranormal.) The voice claimed, "I am not the person who used the filthy language. I am an angel from Heaven sent . . . to drive away that fellow." However, as time went on the voice relaxed and, getting entangled in some of its answers, lost its temper and said many things out of harmony with its supposed heavenly origin. However, it continued until 3 A.M., changing character once more, and singing hymns in a beautiful flutelike voice. It said it had adopted the gruff tone previously to protect Dinah from being accused of impersonating a spirit.

Though Woodcock seems not to have been a careless investigator, all this happened a long time ago and is difficult to accept. However, there have been a few other cases reported from various parts of the world where voices spoke apparently from thin air, the most recent being in Saragossa, Spain, in 1934. It seems, therefore, that all one can do is to keep the "direct voice" in mind as a possibly true but rare phenomenon. In direct-voice poltergeist cases the voice is usually facetious and abusive, which does not accord very well with the mediumistic theory of poltergeistery but is rather what we would expect on the psychological theory. One of the difficulties with psychical research is that if the subject is to be truthfully presented one is required to mention a number of alleged happenings which are too fantastic to be accepted as definitely proved, but which have to be kept in view as possibly true. For those who do not already have a thorough knowledge of the subject matter of psychical research this can have the effect of diminishing belief in those parts of the subject matter of psychical research which are in fact solidly established, such as extrasensory perception. However, awkward as this may be, it means only that psychical research is a developing science and not a dogma.

The Clarendon poltergeist case also illustrates another type of fantastic phenomenon that is difficult to accept. Indeed, to adapt a well-known phrase, "it sticks like a bone in the throat." This is the alleged teleportation of objects. Interestingly enough, it is also alleged to occur sometimes at spiritualist séances. In very many poltergeist cases objects are said to vanish in midair, sometimes to reappear elsewhere or within closed rooms. Equally, objects are said sometimes to appear suddenly in midair as from nowhere. These are always ordinary mundane objects—stones, pennies, domestic tools and utensils, and the like. Because the Daggs at Clarendon had been mystified by apparent instances of teleportation a local resident, Mr. Smart, maintained a watch on a cupboard. He sat facing it and saw Mrs. Dagg put two pans of fresh bread into it. Ten minutes later Mrs. Dagg found one of the pans, still full of bread, in the back kitchen. She told Mr. Smart. He opened the cupboard and found only one there. Mr. Smart said that this event was so staggering that it forced him to change the view that he had previously held that the poltergeist phenomena were fraudulent.

Even if true, teleportation phenomena are very hard to understand, and if they are ever proved beyond all scientific doubt will require us profoundly to revise our ideas of what matter is, and perhaps of what space is. This, of course, is what makes psychical research so interesting, as it suggests that there are still revolutionary and fundamental discoveries to be made about the universe we live in. Curiously, teleportation is alleged in quite a large proportion of poltergeist cases, often where the testimony of witnesses seems to be quite reliable. Teleportation is sometimes reported as an isolated occurrence which causes great mystification.

Shortly after we came to Toronto a woman telephoned us, asking if we could explain a completely baffling incident which had happened to her. She described the events as follows: some five years previously, when her child was approximately one year old, she had laid him on a table to change his diaper. The child was playing with a small phonograph record, one that had been delivered in the mail, and which the child had been given and had chewed and played with. As she was attending to the child an astonishing thing happened. She saw the child throw the record up in the air and it vanish in front of her eyes. She immediately searched for it; as she says, she really could not believe her eyes. She could not find the record even after moving all the furniture, searching behind the radiator, and lifting the rugs. She remained completely puzzled. The loss of the record became a talking point and a puzzle for some time, as during the next five years the decor and furniture of the room were changed. No trace was ever found of this record until just a short time before her telephone call to us; she related that she was having guests for dinner and had gone to the record player just after their arrival to put on some music. When she lifted the lid of the record player, there on the turntable, ready to be played, was the record that had been missing for five years. She recognized it by the baby's toothmarks, which were still visible! The baby was now six years old, and he denied having found the record. As the mother said, "If he had, where had it been these last five years?" There was another small child in the house, two years old, but she was unable to reach and open the record player, so if she had found the record she would not have placed it where it was. The woman's mother usually acted as babysitter, and she denied having found the record—she was in any case very familiar with the story of its disappearance and would have certainly told them if she had found it. The woman concerned was very disappointed that no explanation could be offered her and remarked that she would continue to feel very puzzled until she could arrive at an explanation.

4

EXTRASENSORY PERCEPTION

Extrasensory perception, known for short as ESP, is the term used to cover all cases where a person acquires accurate items of information without using any of his five senses. ESP is the best attested of all paranormal phenomena and its genuineness has been amply verified in scientifically designed laboratory experiments. ESP experiences also occur quite often in everyday life. Consequently, a surprisingly large proportion of people accept the possibility of ESP and that it actually happens. Thus, "telepathy" has become a household word and ESP is on the way to being so; it is even becoming a verb, as when one says, "I have *espped* it!"

The most common experiences, such as the simultaneous exchange of letters by friends who have not corresponded for some time, or being called just at the moment one is thinking about the other, are hard to distinguish from ordinary coincidences on the principle that like-minded people are apt to think alike. The same principle doubtless accounts for a large proportion of parallel thoughts and behavior in identical twins. But there are some instances which are not easy to explain convincingly as coincidences. Dr. Helen Creighton, the well-known authority on Canadian folklore, first published in 1957 her book *Bluenose Ghosts,* which deals with the "supernatural" in the folklore of Nova Scotia. In the prologue to the book she explains that her interest in the spooky Nova Scotian stories was aroused not only by the tales themselves, but by psychic experiences she herself had had at sundry times. They are interesting, not only on account of Dr. Creighton's excellent standing as a witness, but because they include examples of actions performed under strong inner compulsion instead of being in accordance with a rationally thought out plan. One day, while walking to Halifax, Dr. Creighton suddenly "knew" she should cross to the other side of the street. This was irrational in the circumstances, because that side of the street was both less pleasant and more crowded than the one she was on. "Nevertheless," says Dr. Creighton, "the urge was strong, and for curiosity's sake more than anything else, I obeyed. The reason was given immediately when a friend got off the tram and upon seeing me looked greatly relieved and said, 'I've been trying all day to get you on the telephone.' The message was important." The chance that this experience was coincidental seems very small. As Dr. Creighton was consciously in the forefront of her friend's mind that day the most likely explanation is that of telepathy, the transfer of thought from one mind to another. Dr. Creighton's case is interesting because the information as such, that her friend wished to contact her, did not rise into her own consciousness but affected her at a subconscious level, emerging only as a hunch, an urging to do something not indicated rationally by the facts as consciously known to her.

Sometimes the information goes explicitly into the ESP percipient's conscious mind. For example, a Toronto woman who some years ago had a twelve-year-old foster daughter says that one day as she was in the kitchen ironing she distinctly "saw" the child sitting on the wall of the games field beyond the local school, surrounded by the roughest kids of the area. The mother walked up the hill beyond the school and, she says, ". . . there she was, sitting exactly as I had seen her in my mind." At a later date the mother was standing at the intersection of Bay and Queen streets in Toronto, preparing to cross the road. She told a companion that the child was near her. She hurriedly began looking all about but failed to see the girl. The sense of the child's nearness faded quickly. The child telephoned her later in the evening and asked why she had not glanced up at the passing streetcar, because she was on it. The second example is doubtless one of telepathy, but the first may have involved clairvoyance. For want of a better name, "clairvoyance" is the word used to indicate the process of getting knowledge directly, rather than from the mind of another person. It is an excessively implausible phenomenon, but we are obliged to accept that it happens occasionally. It has often been demonstrated in simple laboratory experiments. For example, a pack of cards can be shuffled mechanically in such a way that no living person knows their order. Some ESP experimental subjects, however, are capable of guessing the order to a degree of accuracy that far exceeds the chance probability of so doing. Similarly, a few people can get results of the same degree of unlikelihood with random numbers typed out by a machine before anyone has looked at them. It is theoretically possible to explain all cases of apparent telepathy as really being ones of clairvoyance. However, few students of the subject go to that extreme. Correspondingly, some cases which are claimed to be clairvoyance could well be telepathy; a very careful study of all the circumstances is required before a psychic experience can be claimed as pure clairvoyance.

Dreams occur during a particular phase of sleep in which consciousness is muted but not extinguished and its boundaries with the subconscious mind become indistinct. It is not surprising, then, that psychic impressions are relatively frequent in dreams. In Dr. Barton's collection of Canadian narratives a woman, F. F. of Calgary, speaks of dreams she had while her husband was overseas during World War II. On his return he started to tell her of a narrow escape he had had. F. F. stopped him and said,

"Let me tell *you*. You and another fellow were in a small boat on the River Thames. Your boat just about capsized from the wash of a larger boat that passed too close."

This episode, which she had seen represented in a dream, was correct in all details.

Sometimes in the waking state the psychic impression does not take the form of a mental impression or even a hunch, but that of a hallucinatory sensation. Dr. Barton's correspondent F. F. narrates that on the day her husband received his inoculations at Camp Borden her arm was sore. This would seem to be an example of "sympathetic pain." Quite often, when a person knows that a close relative has pain he or she will get a "sympathetic" ache. This is easily explainable in ordinary psychological terms as the result of autosuggestion. However, sympathetic pains induced, it would seem, by ESP are also encountered when the person experiencing them is quite ignorant of the fact that his relative is ailing. This phenomenon is extremely interesting because it suggests that the ESP message is accepted only on subconscious levels but in some way activates that mechanism or region of the brain whose excitation corresponds to a mental perception of pain.

In this example, the perception of pain is called hallucinatory because the wife's arm had no real pain in it, and the sensation of pain was, in a sense, illusory. The mental experience was, in fact, a hallucination of pain. There is an amusing old jingle that deals with hallucinations.

> At the turning of the stair,
> I saw a man who wasn't there.
> He wasn't there again today;
> O, how I wish he'd go away!

Here the hallucinatory perception is of a human figure or an apparition—something which appears to be there with no corresponding concrete reality actually present.

ESP appears sometimes to be responsible for hallucinatory smells. Normally we have the sensation of smelling something only if molecules derived from the odiferous substance stimulate the olfactory cells in the nasal cavity; the resulting excitation is then carried by nerve fibers to the higher centers of the brain. However, as with telepathic pains, sometimes people have telepathic olfactory sensations. F. F. (mentioned above) once smelled gas in her home and searched diligently but unsuccessfully for a gas leak. It proved later that this happened just at the time that at Camp

Borden her husband was being indoctrinated with the necessity for carrying a gas mask. The instruction was reinforced by passing the recruits through a gas chamber. Recently a Toronto housewife had set a ham to boil in her kitchen and then had gone marketing for groceries, having forgotten to turn down the stove to the simmering point. At the market she was suddenly assailed by the smell of hot and burning fat, at which she hurried home just in time to forestall a fire. As the reader will note, this case is not quite watertight as an example of ESP, because it might only signify that her unconscious mind remembered her omission and issued an alarm signal. Even so, this is interesting as exemplifying the peculiar forms in which unconscious knowledge can be drawn to the attention of the conscious mind. In Dr. Barton's collection, however, there is a case of olfactory hallucination which (provided the correspondent, W. B. of St. James, Manitoba, has given the facts correctly) is hard to explain other than by ESP. One morning, leaving her house and garden unoccupied, she took the bus to Winnipeg. Almost immediately she noticed a smell of burning. No cause was visible and the other passengers seemed quite unaware of it. W. B. formed the conviction that she must return home immediately so she left the bus at the next stop and caught one in the other direction. Back at the house, she searched thoroughly but found nothing amiss, so she sat down at the kitchen table to take a cup of coffee and assess the situation. Glancing idly out the window, she noticed a tiny puff of smoke rising from a wall of the wooden garage. Rushing to the site, she found the wall smoldering at the base. Unless this was a pure coincidence this experience must be attributed to ESP because the event was not one that W. B. could have foreseen and fretted about either consciously or unconsciously. It was also, very possibly, an example of clairvoyance, as no one was present at the site to have knowledge of the fact. However, it ought to be said that this conclusion is not absolutely certain. W. B. thought that the fire had been caused by someone burning garbage in the back lane, near her garage, at a place where its brick siding was missing. It is conceivable that she had been telepathizing from the mind of the (unknown) inadvertent incendiary. This argument may seem farfetched, but it exemplifies the problems one runs into when analyzing ESP cases. For this reason psychical research workers often speak of GESP—general extrasensory perception—in circumstances where they think ESP has occurred but do not know for certain whether it is telepathy, clairvoyance, or precognition.

Clairvoyant experiences are hard to explain; even more difficult to understand are those of precognition or premonition, known in Scotland (and therefore to many Canadians) as instances of the "second sight." Premonitions involve knowledge of future events. Usually we would not use the word premonition to describe an expectation based on logical deductions from the facts as known to us. But the word is often used to describe cases where we feel we have a good idea that something is going to happen without being able to give a logical reason why we have that opinion. In such cases, the premonition may be a completely normal phenomenon based on unconscious processes of observation and reasoning that are more subtle than we think. However, other premonitions may involve paranormal happenings. Sometimes they are applicable purely in terms of telepathy. For instance, R. S. Lambert gives a story of the eighteenth century which the Governor of New France got from his mother-in-law, Madame de Marson. This lady was anxious because her husband, who commanded a military post in Acadia, had not yet returned to Quebec, though the appointed day had passed. An Indian woman, noting her concern, told her that her husband would return at a certain day and hour with a gray hat on his head. Seeing that Madame de Marson doubted this, as well she might, the Indian woman came to her at the predicted time and led her to a point on the riverbank. Almost immediately Monsieur de Marson appeared in a canoe with a gray hat on his head, quite astonished that his time and place of arrival could have been anticipated. A stern critic could argue that this story, even if it happened as stated, is explicable in terms of telepathy from de Marson to the Indian woman.

The same could not be said of a story, if true, narrated by Mère Marie de l'Incarnation, of an Indian girl in 1663. The girl had intelligence and character and was a convert to Christianity. In her cabin, two nights running, she heard a voice warning of an earthquake which was to occur on the third day between 5 and 6 P.M. In the event, the Great Quebec Earthquake occurred at exactly that time. This is quite typical of disaster warnings. The hallucinatory voice (or auditory apparition as it is sometimes called) is a very common form in which paranormal information is supplied. If it was a true prediction before the event we would have to ascribe it to the phenomenon of precognition—that is, knowledge of the future obtained neither by telepathy nor by unconscious reasoning—because we can hardly suppose the Indian girl, however intelligent, to be able to make a prediction that would be difficult or impossible for a modern seismologist.

Warnings of disaster often come as compulsive hunches. Thus, Dr. Helen Creighton in 1917, when very young, received an impulse to move down under the bedclothes at the very moment of a large explosion in Halifax, when part of the window casing with the nails facing downward imbedded itself in her pillow. Occasionally the warning comes very explicitly. Among Dr. Barton's correspondents were D. H. and G. F. of Vancouver, British Columbia. In February 1959 they drove to work with two other men in a new Chevrolet which they owned collectively. On arrival, one of the men jumped out precipitately instead of sitting in the car to keep warm until the rest of the work team had arrived. He explained his action in what D. H. and G. F. described as a "strange manner," saying that they could stay in the car if they liked, but he was getting out because in a few minutes the car would be wrecked and everyone in it would be killed. He was very positive and insistent, so they got out and sheltered from the cold in a small shack on the site. In about three minutes they heard a speeding car which collided with the Chevrolet amidships denting it in at exactly where the first man out had been sitting.

Sometimes premonitions take the form of an auditory apparition which is not a warning voice but a kind of preview (or rather pre-audition) of the sounds associated with a future event. I do not know of a contemporary Canadian example; however, Mary Fraser, in her *Folk Lore of Nova Scotia*, reports a story she received first-hand, which may therefore be reliable. In the 1890s on a frosty February morning a truck laden with lumber came to a farmhouse where an old man had died during the night. The driver and his partner noisily unloaded the timber, which they had brought to make a coffin. The mistress of the house declared that all winter she had heard a truck drive up every night with all the sounds of unloading, followed by sawing, planing, and hammering. She took this as a prediction of a death in the family. In this story, if interpreted in Nova Scotian terms, the premonitory truck would be regarded as a phantom—a "forerunner" of its actual self. It is simpler to think of it as a premonition in which the sounds of a future event presented themselves as an auditory apparition.

Sometimes the premonition takes the form of an actual vision of the future event. Cases of this sort occur throughout the world, but I cannot bring to mind many Canadian examples that are entirely typical. Curiously enough, Lambert quotes two narratives which, if true, represent a very odd kind of premonition. It is claimed that in 1888 at Mule River, Nova Scotia, a young man, walking in the dark, was terrified to see a large black object traveling away from him, down the road. It had a large red eye in the center of its back, while from its front came two streams of light. It passed around the house to which the young man was going, and then returned down the road so swiftly that he had to jump out of its way. Only twenty-five years later did the percipient identify his vision as an automobile. The experience of two women on the highway at Port Hawkesbury, Cape Breton Island, was similar. A huge "thing" pursued them and then passed them with a noisy clatter and loud rushing sound, and then apparently passed through a fish house nearby. Many years later the Inverness Railway was built and its track ran through the site of the fish house. It is unusual, though not altogether unknown, for two percipients to share the same vision. Also, it is faintly suspicious that two stories of rather similar character should come from much the same part of the world, but it is just possible that one or both of the stories are true.

A story of more orthodox type was told to Dr. Creighton by a young Nova Scotian. Walking to his home at Broad Cover near Petite Rivière on a foggy night, he saw a woman on the roadside who, as he said, was a "mass of fire." A few nights later he heard his mother scream. The lamp she was carrying had overturned and set fire to her nightgown. He was badly burned while trying to extinguish the mass of flame, but she died.

Another story concerns a visual warning which took the form not of a picture of the future event, but the apparition of a deceased relative. Mr. Donovan was a steam engineer in the electric power station at Halifax. He told Dr. Creighton that once at 4 A.M. he was sitting on a bench in the boiler room while his assistant was clearing out the ashes. Something prompted him to turn his head and he then saw an apparition of his father to the left of him. Interestingly enough, this was what he called an incomplete apparition, possessing only a head and shoulders. This oddity, so far from detracting from the credibility of the story, in fact, makes it very believable. Psychical research workers are aware that an appreciable proportion of the apparitional or hallucinatory appearances that people see are incomplete. This fact is unknown to the general public however; the story is therefore unlikely to be a fabrication. The apparition of Mr. Donovan's father had an angry expression on its face and seemed to move somewhat in the direction of the boiler. Mr. Donovan took this as a warning and examined the boiler, but found nothing amiss. He had sat down again (the apparition having disappeared) when the boiler exploded, without injuring either of the engineers but covering them with soot and ashes. The experience, of course, may not have been a true precognition, and could, for all we know to the contrary, have resulted from unconscious anxiety about the boiler, but the form of the premonition is interesting.

True precognition in the sense of premonition not explicable as telepathy or clairvoyance is exceedingly difficult to understand. But there is a great deal of evidence for it and most psychical research workers accept it as a true phenomenon. Baffling as clairvoyance is, true precognition is even more enigmatic. Naturally, many thousands of words have been written as to its significance and doubtless many thousands more are to come. Questions that arise in other areas of psychical research, such as whether certain phenomena are to be ascribed to the action of "spirits" rather than to the embodied psyche of the living human being, have no special relevance here. For how do the "spirits" know the future? If one believes in a personal deity, how do the spirits know what He has foreordained? Are they privy to His counsels? Or do they have a privileged mobility allowing them to catch glimpses of memos from the Head of the Firm? If precognition is the human soul's own doing, then again we ask, "How?" Is it the case, as Hindu philosophers think, that the "atman," which is the core of the individual human psyche, is one with Brahman the Cosmic Consciousness, which is the soul, motive force, and very Being of the Universe? It is easier to multiply questions than to answer any single one of them.

5

CRISIS COMMUNICATIONS

Accounts of ghosts and of hauntings, other than those which are recognized as clear-cut examples of poltergeistery, are among the most troublesome material that the psychical research worker has to do with. But there is one type of phantom which occurs so commonly that we can regard it almost as a normal kind of happening. We may describe it as a "crisis apparition" because it is associated with a crisis, sometimes death, sometimes illness or accident. The apparition of the person who dies or who is involved in a catastrophe or stressful situation sometimes appears to a relative or friend at about the same time as the crisis, or shortly afterward. Sometimes the apparition is recognizably an apparition— e.g. it is seen in transparent form, or it vanishes suddenly. Often however, strangely enough, the percipient sees what appears to all intents and purposes to be the person himself, fitting naturally into the surroundings. Sometimes the apparition is recognized as being an apparition only because the person whose likeness it is is known to be far away. Canada's most famous "ghost" was, as can be seen from Lambert's account of it, of precisely this character.

The apparition in question was that of John Otto Wynyard, a lieutenant in a British regiment in India. It was seen simultaneously by his brother Lieutenant George Wynyard and Captain John Cope Sherbrooke, who were then serving in King George III's 33rd Foot Regiment at Sydney, Nova Scotia, half the world away from India. Both officers subsequently had distinguished careers, Wynyard becoming a colonel, and Sherbrooke, after serving as Wellington's second-in-command in Spain, becoming a viscount and governor-general of Canada. They were sitting together studying, in Wynyard's apartment in the Sydney barracks at 4 P.M. in the afternoon of 15 October 1785. They had dined, but had taken no wine or liquor. Sherbrooke, happening to look up, saw a tall young man, apparently about twenty years old, standing at the door. He looked sickly and was dressed in a light indoor costume, which contrasted with their own heavy clothes and furs. Sherbrooke exclaimed in surprise and Wynyard looked up. Seeing the figure, he blanched and seemed dumbfounded, having, as Sherbrooke later described it, "the appearance of a corpse." The figure walked past them slowly, gazing at Wynyard with a sad expression. It then went through an open doorway leading into Wynyard's bedroom, which had no other exit, the window having been sealed up for the winter. Wynyard seized Sherbrooke's arm and exclaimed, "Great Heavens! My brother!" Sherbrooke thought there was some mistake. They both rushed into the bedroom, but found no one there. Wynyard was very affected by this episode and convinced that his brother in India was either dead or ill. Sherbrooke was skeptical and thinking their brother officers might have played a trick, he interrogated one of them, Lieutenant Gore, who succeeded in convincing him that there had been no practical joking. Gore also recommended that they make a precise note of the time of the occurrence. It was not until 6 June 1786 that news arrived concerning John Wynyard; this came in a letter to Sherbrooke asking him to tell George Wynyard of the death of his favorite brother, John. It is said that in due course it was confirmed that John died in India about the same time as his apparition appeared in Sydney.

The incident had a curious sequel. Sherbrooke had never met John Wynyard in the flesh. A few years later while walking in Piccadilly, London, England, he was surprised to see, on the other side of the street, a man with a striking resemblance to the apparition. Sherbrooke went over and told the gentleman that he had seen him before, and told him of John Wynyard's apparition. The gentleman replied that, though he had never been out of England, he had known John Wynyard, and that people who had seen them together had been apt to take them for twin brothers, such was the degree of resemblance between them.

This case is interesting in several respects. The evidence seems good. The apparition was remarkably lifelike and fitted in coherently with the surroundings as if it were a real person. There is no doubt that it closely resembled John Wynyard. Though we are not told in any detail exactly how the time of John Wynyard's death was ascertained, it is likely that the assertion that it coincided more or less with that of the apparition is true. An unusual feature of the Wynyard apparition is that it was seen simultaneously by two people. Though this is unusual, it is, however, recorded of a number of crisis apparitions occurring at sundry times and places. Curiously enough, it was reported also of another Canadian crisis apparition seen in 1844 at Eldon House, London, Ontario, the seat of the well-known Harris family, who were giving a party to which they had invited a beau for their daughter, Sarah. He did not arrive, but later in the evening Sarah, while dancing, saw him standing in the doorway of the room watching her. Sarah's father and sister spoke to him and were puzzled and offended when he turned away and walked into the hall. Next morning their hurt was converted into astonishment when the young man's servant came to Eldon House in search of his master, who, the day previous, had asked for his evening clothes to be laid out, saying that he was going to Eldon House and expected to be late back. His riderless horse found its way home, and the servant had come to look for him. Eventually his body was found in a ford of the nearby river. His watch had stopped at 6 P.M., when, it would seem, he had been thrown from his horse and hit his head on a stone. The main outlines of this story are undoubtedly true. One is at liberty to be skeptical of the apparition being seen by two other members of the family besides Sarah, and it would be permissible to regard this as an elaboration. However, the apparition's failure to reply to them rings true, as the silence of this type of specter is a characteristic feature of crisis apparitions.

The two instances of crisis phantoms that we have cited are especially good and clear-cut ones because in each case the phantom appeared when the fact of the person's death was unknown and unexpected. Otherwise we might interpret the phantom as a pure hallucination, resulting from the percipient's mind alone, perhaps because the percipient is either expectant of death or disaster befalling a person he esteems or is generally concerned for his well-being. An experience of Dr. Helen Creighton's illustrates the difficulties of interpretation that can be encountered in analyzing even what are apparently simple cases. It relates to a dream and not to an apparition seen while the percipient is awake, but nevertheless serves perfectly to illustrate the point. Archdeacon Wilcox of Dartmouth, Nova Scotia, was greatly loved and esteemed by all who knew him. He had a long illness, and, as Dr. Creighton says, "the time came when death was imminent. One morning I awoke very early and then went to sleep again. I dreamed that I was walking along a street and that I saw the archdeacon walking towards me, but on the opposite side." She goes on to say that normally he would have seen and greeted her but, in her dream, he seemed unaware of his surroundings, and walked steadily on, gazing as if at a point "about the level of the housetops." Dr. Creighton in her dream said to herself, "Archdeacon Wilcox is much too ill to be walking," and then, while still dreaming, explained it to herself by saying, "That's not the Archdeacon; that's his Spirit." Now, in reality, as Dr. Creighton was able to ascertain, the archdeacon had died during her second period of sleep, probably at the time that she had dreamed of him, and the dream might have come about by her extrasensorial perception of the fact. On the other hand, it might have arisen merely from her concern for the archdeacon without any paranormal causation. On this interpretation the accuracy of the timing would be purely a coincidence.

Care, therefore, needs to be applied before either a dream experience or the sighting of an apparition can be assumed to have a cause outside the mind of the percipient. If there is no external cause traceable, even a psychical research worker will describe an apparition as a pure hallucination. A crisis apparition differs from a pure hallucination in that there is an external cause, namely the fact of the death or crisis in the life of the apparitional person. The fact is communicated to the percipient by his seeing the form of the apparitional person. We should note that a surprising number of people, including extremely sane ones, do, on occasion, have visual hallucinations. Sometimes there is no doubt that the apparition is a pure hallucination, because sometimes it is a fictional person. Thus, Sir Francis Galton recorded the case of a novelist who assured him that she once saw the principal character in one of her novels enter the room by coming through the door and glide toward her. This experience must have originated within some level of the novelist's own mind. Even "pure" hallucinations are not all of the same kind. Some of them seem to be expressions of a "visionary" tendency, i.e. thoughts sometimes rise up in a very vivid form. Others appear to be freak events, a flicker in the brain—often a perfectly healthy brain. Yet others seem to be due to internal emotional stress, manifesting itself in hallucinatory form. One other group should be mentioned, the "hypnagogic hallucinations." These are the phantasms that can occur when one is on the borderline of sleep and wakefulness. These waking dreams, which are sometimes experienced as if they were apparitions, are difficult to regard as much different from ordinary dreams. Often, of course, like dreams, they have ESP content.

An apparition, irrespective of whether it is a pure hallucination or a genuine apparition (i.e. has a cause external to the mind of the percipient), may show itself not to be an actual real person by disappearing abruptly. Thus, in 1931, Mrs. Mainwaring of Brockville, Ontario, visited Allan's Point, a forested property nearby. According to the account in Sheila Hervey's book *Some Canadian Ghosts*, at dusk Mrs. Mainwaring, who had been sitting outdoors all afternoon, chanced to look to her right at a rock some twenty yards away that sloped down to the water's edge. She was surprised to see a man sitting there quietly gazing upriver. The story, as received by Sheila Hervey, says that Mrs. Mainwaring, being startled to see an unexpected intruder, stared silently at him. Her little dog, however, leapt to its feet, growling, with hackles rising. At that, to Mrs. Mainwaring's astonishment, the figure for the first time manifested its unsubstantial nature by "melting into the rock" so that it vanished without trace.

Apparitions do not always act so eccentrically as to disclose their apparitional nature. As with John Wynyard's, an apparition often takes itself out of view in a perfectly natural way, just as a real person might, by going round the corner or through an open doorway. According to careful surveys of apparitional experiences which have been made, an apparition is not as a rule a vague, misty figure like the ghosts of tradition. The background can only rarely be seen through it. Also, the apparition may speak. If so, this will seem quite natural to the beholder, as if the real person were present in the flesh. The apparition may also appear to pick up and move some object or to open a door and go out. However, it will subsequently be found that the apparition, no matter what it may have seemed to do, actually leaves no physical traces of its passage. There will be no footprints. Objects that seemingly were moved will, in fact, be still in their original places, and the door will, in reality, not have been opened. All this suggests that there is not, at any time, anything physical present, even though the apparition is not a pure hallucination but derives from an external cause.

But how does the "genuine" apparition arise? Primitive peoples throughout the world were impressed by two facts, that in dreams they saw the forms of both living and dead friends, and also that the dreamer found himself visiting, as it were, numerous scenes and places. Anthropologists believe that these experiences are the origin of the belief in the shade, or spirit double, of the living person. If one is not a skeptical thinker it seems very natural to explain dreams, apparitions, and hallucinations by supposing that everyone, besides possessing an ordinary physical body, has also a shade, shadow, or spirit body which resembles the physical body but is altogether of a more subtle construction. The shade is supposed to travel and to visit friends in dreams. One can also assume, like the Ojibway, that the shade survives death. Nowadays the shade is usually referred to as the astral body, or etheric double. (Both terms are in use and some people dispute whether they are the same, but it seems premature at this stage of knowledge to make additional refinements and distinctions.)

The astral body is commonly invoked to explain crisis apparitions. On this theory George Wynyard saw his brother John because John's astral body was there to see. One line of thought that could be applied to this problem is to argue that if the astral body can be seen, then, presumably, it can be photographed. However, evidence is lacking on the point for the simple reason that the percipient of a crisis apparition is not expecting it, and is not set up for photography. Another approach takes its point of departure from the fact that crisis apparitions usually wear clothes! This really does raise a problem. One can imagine a person being born with an astral body in addition to his mortal one, of flesh and blood, but it passes belief that every garment he puts on should have an astral counterpart. The question of the sartorial completeness of ghosts has been discussed, on and off, over the last three centuries. The usual answer which various sages have put forward at various times is that ghosts wear clothes for the same reason as they wear bodies. The soul has an astral body of somewhat indeterminate form on which it can impose any outward shape it pleases, clothes and all!

At this stage in the discussion it becomes clear that the explanation of crisis apparitions in terms of the astral body, instead of being simple, is rather complicated. Perhaps therefore we should seek to explain a crisis apparition in terms of telepathy. On the telepathy theory no astral body travels to the vicinity of the percipient. Instead, we suppose that the person in crisis, either consciously or unconsciously, transmits what, for the sake of a better word, we may call a thought or idea of himself. When this reaches the percipient it is probably registered on some subconscious level of the mind, and then is translated by some means or other into a picture of the person concerned. Alternatively, we may suppose that it is not the mind of the crisis person but that of the percipient which unconsciously perceives clairvoyantly the state of the crisis person. The sequel is, however, the same; whether the message is received telepathically or clairvoyantly, it enters via the subconscious prior to rising as a visual image into the consciousness of the percipient.

As we saw earlier, ESP impressions can enter subconsciousness in a variety of disguised forms. Does a "message" which is predisposed to entering consciousness as a visual image of a crisis person ever fail to be adequately translated, so that it emerges only as a distorted or incomplete manifestation? I know of two English cases in which apparitions, occurring at the time of death of distant persons, took misty or indeterminate forms. In one case the percipient saw a shapeless gray mass resembling, as much as anything, cement, for a brief period before it "sank" through the floor. In the other case the apparition of a deceased airman appeared in incomplete form—the head and flying helmet were formed, but not the rest of the body, which was wavering, gray, and fluid. Of course, this can be interpreted as the astral body incompletely subjected to the formative mental powers of the decedent. On the other hand, the interpretation as an imperfectly transmitted message is interesting and plausible enough to be set up as an alternative. On 3 September 1970 an apparition of indeterminate form was seen by a young woman, Helen, at her home near Toronto. Her aunt was ill in the hospital and was expected to live only a few days more. One evening Helen was alone at home and sitting on her bed. She heard a noise in the hall. When she looked out into the hall "there was a huge blob." It had an indefinite shape and was slightly transparent. "It hovered over the clothes hamper and disappeared." Helen's aunt was still alive at the time of the apparition but died the next day. Helen says she realized it was "something" but did not know what. Several weeks later she read an article which said that when a person is dying his soul can leave his body and go to a loved one. "I knew then that what I saw was my aunt coming to say good-bye to me." If this was a crisis apparition it preceded the actual death by several hours, thus falling into the group of events often called forerunners (particularly in Scottish and Nova Scotian folklore). This in itself is not enough to prevent the incident being classified as a crisis apparition, but here it could reasonably be objected that it was a pure hallucination induced by Helen's anxiety for her aunt, to whom she was obviously devoted. Be that as it may, it is irrelevant to the point under discussion, which is the "mistranslation" or imperfect translation of a thought in the unconscious mind into an image in the consciousness.

If crisis apparitions were never seen by more than one person the telepathic theory would be the simplest and best explanation for them. However, in psychical research nothing is ever simple. Quite a number of crisis apparitions are experienced collectively by two or more witnesses in the way that the phantom of John Wynyard was seen by Sherbrooke and George Wynyard. Also, the phantom is seen as essentially the same figure by the different percipients, but from different optical perspectives, just as if it were a real person being observed from the different locations of the percipients. At this stage, telepathic explanations become very complicated. This does not mean that the astral body theory can be immediately reinstated; it shows, however, how deep and difficult are the problems encountered in interpreting even those phenomena which, like crisis apparitions, are well attested and relatively clear-cut.

Deaths and other crises are often accompanied by auditory apparitions. Thus, Dr. Creighton once heard her own name called when the mother of a friend died. Mrs. Margaret Page of Toronto told us that in 1929 her sister in England was awakened by the voice of their mother on the night that she died in Chicago. One of Dr. Barton's correspondents, V. G. from Regina, described how one day in 1917, while as a young girl working as a waitress in a restaurant, she encountered the cook, Elizabeth, looking ghastly and clutching the edge of a table. She explained that in the middle of serving up the mashed potatoes she had heard her husband's voice calling to her with the words "I've had it, Liz, I'm a goner."

A month later Elizabeth received official notification of her husband's death in the trenches in France. Another correspondent, Mrs. Mott, wrote concerning an auditory apparition she experienced in 1914 which related not to a death but to an accident which befell her father. He was in England, but she had come to Canada to be housekeeper on a large farm in Saskatchewan. One morning, while clearing up the breakfast dishes, she heard him calling, "Minnie! I have fallen over the stile and broken my arm!" She said that the voice was very clear, ". . . as though we were walking together." Sometime later she received a letter from England with news of her father's broken arm, and giving the time of the accident, from which it appeared that his cry of pain reached her at the instant he fell.

Auditory apparitions at times of crisis seem to be as frequent as visual ones. Usually they are heard only by one person at a time, but like visual apparitions, it seems that on occasion they are heard simultaneously by two or more witnesses. It is not easy to decide, even in cases of that type, whether the "voice" is merely a vivid psychic impression or an actual physical happening—a "direct voice"—though possibly opinion among psychical research workers would have to favor the former theory.

The famous "death raps" of which instances are known the world over, however, seem very often to be heard collectively by all the persons present. Dr. Creighton describes an event of this nature that occurred not long prior to 1928, a few days before the death of her sister-in-law, who had suffered a long illness—very hard on both the patient and her family. To help distract the children, Kathleen and Barbara, Dr. Creighton was sitting with them in the drawing room one evening playing cards. They were startled by a loud knocking. There was no door on that side of the house. Barbara went to the nearest door and satisfied herself that there was no one at all in the neighborhood of the building. Later, after she had started collecting Nova Scotian folklore, Dr. Creighton identified the knocking with the raps traditionally equated with forerunners of death. One of Dr. Barton's cases occurred many years ago at Transcona, Manitoba, when her correspondent, C. E. P., was twelve years old. He was present with four other members of the family at the lunch table. There came a knocking on the door leading from the dining room into another part of the house. "The blows were very powerful, they came three or four times, as though someone were rapping with the ball of the hand. My father got up and opened the door but no one was visible there. My grandfather, who was quite hard of hearing in those days, looked up and said, 'That was Margaret.' He was referring to his last living sister, my aunt Margaret, who lived about thirty miles away. She . . . had been perfectly well the last time we had seen her. Later we heard that she had died that morning unexpectedly, after having been sick for only two or three days."

The sounds that, it would seem, advise of deaths or difficulties are not always rappings. Thus, M. K. G. of Whitehorse in the Yukon, a Canadian minister of religion, wrote to Dr. Barton to say that in April 1965 his sister-in-law was killed instantly in a motor accident. On the day of her death he was working in his office when he heard footsteps on the stairway and the sound of a door banging. Thinking that a parishioner had come to see him, he opened the door but found no one there. Next morning he received news that his relative had died about half an hour previous to this occurrence. A correspondent, Y. A. S. of Calgary, relates that in the 1920s she was being courted by a young man, Walter, who in due course became her husband. He was in the merchant navy and whenever he came to the house during his shore leave he would buzz the morse code signal for "W" on the doorbell. One evening while Walter was at sea, a "Di-Dah-Dah" came on the doorbell. The young woman ran to the door but found no one there. The evidence for this event being paranormal is better than most because the house was so designed that there was a clear view of the exterior of the front door from the living room window, where the girl's father was sitting, as was his wont, watching any activity in the street. Happily, Walter surmounted his crisis. He wrote to say that he had had pneumonia and was told by the nurse that while delirious he had been calling his fiancée's name.

In all these cases, even those with multiple witnesses, it is difficult to decide whether the sounds are hallucinatory (i.e. shared psychic impressions) or result from actual physical vibrations of the air or of the doors and walls. Traditionally, there is another group of happenings which are supposed to be associated with distant deaths or disasters: the broken picture cord or the smashed ornament. I cannot recall a Canadian example. However, in Dr. Barton's collection there occurs an instance of an actual physical phenomenon related to a death. C. D. wrote from New Burnaby in British Columbia to say that one morning as he and his wife went to get the car out of the garage, a can of antifreeze "hurtled from the shelf striking the far side of the garage for no apparent reason. Later that day we learned that my wife's father, who had originally brought us the antifreeze, had died in an industrial accident at just that time." This account is most interesting. I would say that all elements of hallucination are absent. We have a definite physical phenomenon. Naturally, a variety of explanations can be attempted. For instance, it could have been that Mrs. C. D.'s father, doubtless unbeknownst to himself, moved the antifreeze can by very remote psychokinesis. Alternatively, we could speculate that Mr. C. D. (or more plausibly Mrs. C. D. as more closely related to the decedent) received an ESP message, which emerged not into consciousness, but as a psychokinetic action of mildly symbolic type, since it chose as its *point d'appui* an object associated with the dying person. Instead, we could suppose that the astral body of Mrs. C. D.'s father sped invisibly to the garage and exerted a physical force on what was to him a familiar object.

6

GHOSTS AND HAUNTED HOUSES

Except for poltergeistery, which seems to have been relatively abundant, Canada does not seem to be especially well provided with haunted houses. This is probably not a real deficiency and represents only a lack of folklore such as in England is engendered by the numerous mansions, abbeys, and castles surviving from Tudor and even medieval times. Even in Canada there is a noticeable tendency for the older buildings to accumulate their legends. It also appears from a study of Lambert's book that "ghost stories" of traditional types are scarce except in the Maritime Provinces, where, as Dr. Creighton has shown, particularly for Nova Scotia, every conceivable type of "spooky" narrative is still told, even today. Consequently, while *Bluenose Ghosts* contains many accounts of experiences of a kind frequently encountered by psychical research workers, and which, therefore, can be considered either to be true as they stand or to derive from actual happenings, many of the stories (as freely admitted by Dr. Creighton) are the product of "imagination and superstition" and so have only the status of "tales," more strange than true. In the category of tales we can with fair confidence put the visions of phantom ships, pirates, with or without longboats and treasure chests, and including the legends attached to Captain Kidd, the Bay of Fundy, and, of course, Oak Island. Similarly, we can take with a grain of salt all those monitory tales which detail the not fully intended consequences of rash oaths, such as "Devil take me!" Also we need not take too seriously those stories whose motif is the ghostly consequences of disturbing the bones of the dead or failing to comply with their last wishes. Though here it must be admitted that some of those narratives may contain a kernel of truth, because guilt (especially in a superstitious environment) can stimulate hallucinations or even paranormal phenomena. According to Sheila Hervey, in the remoter territories of Canada a legend still current is that of the phantom trapper, complete with sled and fourteen white huskies. In this legend he seeks out lost travelers and guides them to safety through the blizzard before he disappears again into the raging storm. These stories would seem to be a native counterpart of local legends of helpful saints such as Saint Christopher or Saint Hubert of the Ardennes forest told in European countries.

There is one tale that is worth looking at, not because it is true, but because it illustrates how tales go the rounds, being retold each time as if they had actually happened to the narrator or to someone he knew well. This is the tale of the phantom girl hitchhiker. I first encountered this story in 1967 when it was told to my friend Victor Sims, a veteran reporter and feature writer for the *Sunday Mirror* in England. A man in Bedfordshire, England, told it to Victor with all solemnity as an experience he had actually had. We included it in our book *Science and the Spook* as an illustration of an uncorroborated tale that could be judged as certainly false. In our rejection we employed no criteria from psychical research; it was sufficient for Victor to apply to the story itself, irrespective of its spooky content, the criteria used by good reporters, lawyers, and detectives, to test a story for plausibility. The teller of the story claimed that, somewhat reluctantly, on a wet and windy night, he gave a young girl a lift on the pillion of his motorcycle. "I asked her where she would like a lift to and she gave me an address some twenty miles distant, a place that I would pass through on my way home." She seemed so light that he kept glancing over his shoulder to see if she was still there. The third time he turned his head he discovered, to his horror, that he no longer had a passenger. He turned about and searched the road for three miles back. He finally returned home without mentioning the episode to his wife or anyone else. Next morning, still frantic with worry, he called at the address the girl had mentioned. He asked the old lady who answered the door if her daughter had got home all right the preceding night. She replied, "Young man, my daughter was killed on a motorcycle just a year ago last night."

Quite recently I was interested to find that essentially the same tale was commented on by Dr. Creighton ten years ago. She says that for many years it has been quoted as occurring in places all over the United States. She inquired to see if the tale was known in Nova Scotia and eventually got a version of it from Earl Morash of East Chester, who was told it by a Toronto man, who claimed to have had the experience in Winnipeg, while driving a car. He picked up his passenger at a railroad crossing. She sat in the car and conversed with him normally. On arrival at her home he reached across to open the car door for her and suddenly realized that she wasn't there. After fruitlessly searching he inquired at the house, where he saw the girl's picture hanging. He was told that she had been killed two years previously at the railroad crossing. The story is still going strong. A few weeks ago we saw it in the English weekly *Psychic News*, which had reprinted it from the *Sunday People*. The hero, Luigi Torres, in Sicily, is again a motorcyclist. He was impressed by her "strange coldness" so he put his overcoat on her. This time she did not disappear en route. He left her at home (in Sassore, it is said) saying he would call for the coat the next day. When he returned and asked for the coat, an old woman told him her daughter had died three years before. In its Sicilian form the story has some artful embellishments. The "stunned" Luigi goes to the cemetery and recognizes the portrait of his passenger on a tombstone. Next to the grave lies his overcoat. Luigi, we are to understand, is now under care for mental shock!

The kind of ghost story that is likely to be truth and not fiction is invariably simpler and plainer altogether than these flights of the imagination. "True" ghost stories are, of course, subject to interpretation, and though we may accept that the percipient actually had the experience which he claimed, it is not always clear just what the experience signifies. Thus Sheila Hervey tells of two Nova Scotian women, Rita and Agnes, who had been schoolmates and business colleagues until they got married, when Rita remained in Halifax and Agnes moved to Sydney, N.S. They had made a pact that whichever one died first should "return" and manifest herself to her friend. As it happened, Agnes died in 1947, at the tragically young age of thirty-two. One night, climbing the stairs of her house in Halifax, Rita saw a shape in an alcove beside the staircase. The shape took form and was that of Agnes, young and smiling. Rita tried to speak to the apparition but before she could find words it vanished. Maybe it was the spirit of Agnes returning to fulfill her promise. On the other hand, a critic could dismiss it as a pure hallucination engendered by Rita's state of psychological expectancy.

A similar interpretation can be put on the experience of Johanne Allison of Lower Town, Quebec, an eight-year-old child, in 1967. Visiting the grotto behind the main church buildings of Notre-Dame-de-Grâce, she made three wishes: to be given a bicycle, for her father to become wealthy, and to see her deceased mother once more. Johanne said that she then saw her mother's face, which appeared beside the statue of the Virgin Mary. We may, if we wish, interpret this happening in purely religious terms as a special dispensation of Divine power. But if we choose to discuss it as an ordinary problem of psychical research we are left with the same alternatives as in Rita's case—a pure hallucination or the return of a spirit.

A more complex case is given in *Canada's Psi-Century*, over the initials of J. C., a woman in New Brunswick. She and her husband had lost their son Gary, aged nineteen, in a car accident on 27 December 1963. At 1:45 A.M. on 15 November 1964 she awoke suddenly and saw Gary standing at her bedside. After a brief moment of surprise and shock, J. C.'s first thought was to reach over and awaken her husband in his twin bed about three feet away.

"Seeming to anticipate my thoughts, our son Gary floated over to my husband's bed. Though my husband was sound asleep he sat bolt upright saying that he couldn't understand what it was that woke him. Then I told him what I had seen. I also got the feeling that Gary had come to warn me about something so I asked my husband to be extra careful as he is a miner and does dangerous work." In any event, disaster struck J. C.'s younger son, whose legs were crushed when he was hit by a truck three days later. J. C. adds, "Twice since the first visitation I've heard knocking on the door and found no one there, and each time it was immediately before an illness in the family. So you see, I know that my dead son has been warning me. And I know now that there is a life after death." The alternative interpretation is that J. C. has a precognitive faculty which does not present the future events explicitly to her consciousness but operates by producing visual and auditory apparitions. J. C.'s experience is really parallel to that of Mr. Donovan, the engineer at Halifax. We could have discussed it under precognition and equally have dealt with Mr. Donovan's case in this chapter.

Apparitions of deceased friends or relatives admit of various quite plausible interpretations, even if usually no one of these interpretations can be accepted as demonstrably the true one. More puzzling are the apparitions of total strangers that intelligent people in their right minds occasionally see. Thus, a clergyman told Dr. Creighton of an experience he had once had which perplexed him for years after. One dark night on Citadel Hill in Halifax he was walking parallel to a high timber fence when he heard footsteps behind him. As the man seemed to be walking faster than he was, he thought he might as well let him pass. So he stepped to the side and saw the man as he went by. (Dr. Creighton does not give a description of the man; we may presume that his appearance was quite normal and ordinary.) The man was now walking between the clergyman and the high fence on a better-lighted part of the hill. The clergyman expected that the man would proceed parallel to the fence, heading for the same path he was making for. However, the figure suddenly turned to the right, approached the fence, and vanished, much to the bewilderment of the observer, who could not figure out how he could have gone through the fence or over it.

Somewhat similar is the instance of a nameless apparition quoted by Sheila Hervey from *Summerland Spirit* by F. E. Atkinson, of Summerland, British Columbia. It is a little difficult to guess the status of this report as Hervey gives no clue as to whether *Summerland Spirit* is a book, pamphlet, or a magazine. Some very fictional stories can become included in local histories and magazines. The story, however, is typical of many more authenticated cases from other parts of the world. Two boys, Sam, fourteen, and Edward, twenty, on a moonlit summer night were walking to pastureland to move their horses. While Edward was retethering his horse about a hundred feet from the road, Sam saw a man who was fairly heavy-set and dressed entirely in white, his coat being in the style of a Norfolk jacket. Sam called out, "Where are you going?" The stranger stopped and faced him, but then walked away. Sam was disturbed because he made no sound whatever while treading the road. He then followed the road to the far side of the house, where the front door was, and thus went out of view. The boys hurried to the house but, according to the family, there had been no visitor nor any knock at the door. The man in white was presumed to have evanesced. It is very difficult to learn much about isolated unidentified apparitions. We do not know whether they are pure hallucinations or if, instead, they are genuine glimpses of the past. It is characteristic of isolated apparitions to maintain complete silence; it is as if they were moving pictures, mere representations, not "living" spirits.

There are on record few Canadian cases where an apparition not recognized at the time has subsequently been identified. The reader will recall the apparition of a man seen sitting on a rock by Mrs. Mainwaring at Allan's Point. It was not recognized at the time. According to Sheila Hervey, Mrs. Mainwaring described it to Judge Edmund Reynolds and his wife, who had resided for a long time at Brockville. They identified it from its appearance as the likeness of Travers Allan. Unfortunately, descriptions of neither Travers Allan nor the apparition seem to be available in print, so that the reader has no means of assessing the reliability of this identification. Hervey gives as reference for a story of an apparition in Vancouver, "Harold Weir, Nov. 2, 1961." It is not clear whether this is a newspaper item, a statement by an eyewitness, or merely a narrative at second or third hand. Possibly Weir was an eyewitness, because Hervey says that the people who saw the "vision" (in the early 1930s) are now free to talk, the "fear and shock" having worn off. The story goes that a young couple bought a house built only six months before by a middle-aged couple. The wife had died of a sudden illness so the husband sold it to them. The young people, it is said, felt uneasy in the house. However, they made extensive internal modifications and held a housewarming party. The guests were animated until "an icy chill" descended on the drawing room. Suddenly, at one end of the room there appeared the apparition of a complete tableau. "On a massive bed lay a woman who was obviously very near death. She stared in terror at the man sitting beside the bed. The man wore a small self-satisfied smile." One of the guests declared that the man was the man who built the house and the woman his wife. The lady of the house commented to the effect that the place of the vision was where the master bedroom had been prior to the alterations. The vision is said to have faded as silently as it had appeared. Now there are cases on record elsewhere in the world, which seem well attested, in which apparitions appear as whole scenes or tableaux. So this story may be true. It must be admitted that any self-respecting psychical research worker would prefer a more circumstantial narrative giving particulars as to just who of the assembled company saw what. The writer, however, has an additional uneasiness concerning an appendix to the story, which goes as follows. The owners of the house sold it immediately and sent all their new furnishings to auction. One of the guests went to the auction rooms and looked at the drawing room carpet. To her astonishment she saw there were four deep, clear indentations in it, at about the places expected if the spectral bedstead had been there in reality! Like Luigi Torres's overcoat, this additional turn of the screw, so far from adding to conviction, merely weakens belief, because it has the air of an embellishment tacked onto an original story which might have stood better on its own. In so saying, the writer may be doing an injustice, but it is difficult in conscience to say otherwise when a detailed firsthand narrative is lacking.

Tom Thomson, the Canadian landscape painter and one of the famous Group of Seven, was found dead in Canoe Lake, Algonquin Park, on 16 July 1917. He had been missing since 8 July, when he had gone out in his gray canoe. It is said that his specter has been seen paddling the canoe on some evenings at dusk. Gray, of course, is the color of many of those apparitions, like gray monks and nuns, which throughout the British Isles are often seen in half-light. The majority of such appearances must, it would seem, be classified as optical or visual illusions, the tricks of light and sight. This is likely to be true also of an alleged sighting of Tom Thomson's gray canoe landing at the beach near Hayhurst Point. The observers (according to Sheila Hervey) followed it in to the beach but found nothing there. The vagaries of fog, mist, and lighting seem adequate also to explain sightings of an apparition on the rocky shoreline at Oak Bay, near Victoria, B.C. The figure seen is usually identified as the ghost of a woman who was strangled in 1936 on the Victoria golf course by her husband, who then drowned himself in the sea nearby.

It is a remarkable fact that throughout the world there are very few cases in which essentially the same apparition is allegedly seen repeatedly in the same building that will stand up to scrutiny. Consequently, we need not be surprised that Canadian cases of this kind are few in number and, so far as published reports go, evidentially weak. Sheila Hervey tells of a large house in Streetsville, Ontario, situated at the junction of Steeles Avenue and Mississauga Road. A woman who lived there from 1970 to 1972 saw no apparition, but was mystified by electric lights switching themselves on or off. The truth of this may be accepted because it is a common ingredient in poltergeistery and occurs quite often in houses reputed to be haunted. Some time prior to this woman's occupancy the house had been inhabited by a family with small children. Once the husband went to the staircase to investigate a strange rattling noise. It is said that he saw the apparition of a small girl with fair hair standing on the stairs with a toy in her hands. According to Hervey, previous occupants had seen this specter. These appear to include a doctor and his wife, who discussed it with newspaper reporters (though Hervey does not give a reference to any press account).

The information presented is really not adequate for us to be certain that essentially the same apparition has been seen repeatedly in the Streetsville house. But, for the sake of argument, let us suppose that this had been reliably established as a fact. Suppose also that, as does not seem to have been shown in this case, the apparition had been identified as closely resembling some previous inhabitant of the house. Can we take it that the apparition betokened the presence of a "real" ghost—the living spirit of the deceased child? Unfortunately not; the sightings of the apparition may merely have been vivid forms of psychic impressions received occasionally by subsequent occupants when in suitably receptive conditions. On this interpretation even ghosts that seem to walk around (exemplified by a few British cases) would be more in the nature of "moving pictures" that, in some sense, have remained latent in the place, but can, under rare conditions, be perceived by a person temporarily attuned or sensitive. In posing this question we have, in effect, outlined the restricted theory of ghosts which is believed by some students of the subject. We are asking whether living persons can impose on their surroundings some "trace" of themselves that can be reanimated now and again in a transitory fashion. This is an extremely interesting question, even if it does fall short of the traditional idea of a ghost, which envisages the presence of an active, self-moving, and motivated "spirit."

The remarkable subject of psychometry can perhaps throw some light on this possibility. In psychometry the psychic sensitive does not gather remote facts by just quietly thinking, but seems to utilize a material link between himself and the facts. The psychometrist likes to touch some object which has been in physical contact with a person. It is when this has been done that information concerning the person drifts into the sensitive's mind. The information received is often remarkable in both amount and accuracy. Psychometry, if it is a veritable ESP ability (and it seems to be so), is a remarkable accomplishment, and we cannot guess at all as to the mechanism by which it operates. It is certainly a curious amalgam of physical and mental aspects. However, it supplies a strong argument that ghost experiences are, in fact, possible, at least to the degree that such experiences may represent pictures from the past. Psychic impressions of the past do not necessarily need to take visual form; on this theory, auditory apparitions are just as likely. In *Canada's Psi-Century,* a Canadian woman recounts an experience of her mother (of Scottish descent) in the early 1920s in a hotel at Ramsgate, England. On the first night there she awoke to the sound of groans, as of people in pain. On making inquiries the next day, she was told that during the 1914-1918 war the hotel had been a hospital for wounded soldiers.

On the whole it must be said that visual apparitions are not usual or even very frequent in houses that acquire reputations for being haunted. There are, indeed, such houses both in Canada and elsewhere, but the phenomena tend in many ways to resemble those in poltergeist cases, though in more subdued form. Clocks will stop and start mysteriously; there will be little noises—tappings, clankings, or scratchings; small objects will be displaced from their usual positions, or disappear, to be found days or weeks later in unexpected locations. Quite frequently smells will come and go without any indication of their cause. Also, more obviously "ghostly" phenomena will be reported—phantom footfalls or noises as of dragging of furniture over the floor of closed uninhabited rooms. As the happenings are less spectacular than those in poltergeist cases it is often difficult to decide whether or not they are paranormal. Similarly, even if the investigator becomes convinced that they are indeed paranormal, it is still very difficult to assign a cause. The subject could be discussed at great length, but it is appropriate here only to list the possible theories that could be applied. The simplest one to envisage, though very hard to prove, is that the spirit of some deceased earlier inhabitant remains attached to the building and produces physical phenomena. Spiritualists describe these as "earthbound spirits." The other theory is that former inhabitants have left traces on the building and that somehow these traces interact with the present inhabitants (particularly if the latter have some latent psychic talents) so that these latter (living) people produce the physical phenomena by unconscious psychokinesis. This seems an exceptionally complicated theory, so much so that I would hesitate to advance it as definitely preferable to the earthbound spirit hypothesis.

A question that is always asked about hauntings, whether haunted houses or poltergeists, is whether exorcism is desirable or efficacious. The natural instincts of a psychical investigator are always against taking any measure that may do away with the phenomena he is investigating. However, he often prefers to yield to his humanitarian instincts. People who are subject to hauntings, real or imaginary, are often very genuinely troubled by the phenomena. In such cases, if they ask whether the phenomena can be terminated, it is best to let them try a service of prayer or exorcism. Provided it is done in a quiet, responsible, and unsensational way it will do no harm and may indeed have the desired effect or seem to do so. From November 1970 to February 1971 a team from the Toronto Society for Psychical Research, at the request of the occupants, investigated some relatively "mild" alleged haunting phenomena in a house in Scarborough, Toronto. The case was by no means sensational, as these things go, and perhaps its chief value was exemplification of the difficulties attendant on study of mild hauntings. The building is a town house at the end of a row. However, it adjoins a neighboring house which was occupied during the whole period. As the dividing wall between the dwellings is thin, it was difficult to exclude all extraneous noises. The team also discovered that winter in Canada is a bad time for investigating paranormal sounds, because the boiler and associated heating system generate a variety of noises. The house itself was of perfectly sound construction, and in good condition, and showed no signs of cracking, slipping, or foundering, which might have caused unusual sounds. (See Ingus, 1972.)

About two years previously, a housewife, B, resident there with her husband and children, committed suicide by hanging herself from a pipe near the ceiling of the laundry room of the basement. About a year later a woman, M, moved in with her husband, teenage son, and a daughter aged six. After she had been there about three months M was told of the tragedy. She was distressed to learn of it, and the effects of suggestion cannot be discounted in assessing her subsequent experiences, which commenced soon after. She told our team that she had felt uneasy in the house generally and was especially uncomfortable in the laundry. Also, over a long period, she had repeatedly heard noises which she could not account for as occurring by normal causes. These were raps on interior doors, sounds as of small objects falling on the floor, and sounds as if someone were walking around upstairs. M also had two dreams, separated by an interval of about a month, in which the figure of a woman had come toward her in a menacing manner. In the second dream the woman had attempted to strangle M. Two neighbors who were present at our first interview with M said that the physical description of the dream woman could apply to the appearance of B during life. However, the description given by M was a somewhat general one, and the investigators attached no significance to the resemblance. In the event, our team, in the course of various nightly vigils did audio-tape a few noises that seemed difficult to account for. M took some comfort from these proceedings, as people in these situations often do; it is reassuring to have one's problem taken seriously instead of having it discussed as "fancy" or "nerves." However, by March, she wondered if something could not be done to "settle" the house. The landlords of these properties, who were quite sympathetic to M, also told us that, if necessary, they would make another house available, but that if the nuisance, real or apparent, could be otherwise removed, they would be happy. We therefore arranged a simple service of scriptural readings and prayers for the peace of everyone who lived or had lived in the house. In this we followed the usual practice of most ministers of Protestant denominations. The service, which was conducted by an ordained minister of one of the Canadian churches, in no sense imitated a traditional ritual of exorcism. It was very quietly conducted in an atmosphere of sincerity. However, unsensational as it was, it worked! A few weeks afterward M said that all her feelings of unease when in the house had disappeared immediately following the service and she was now unaware of any uncanny phenomena.

Exorcism or services of prayer are not always so successful. Back in 1191 Gerald of Wales, commenting on a poltergeist case in Pembrokeshire, was puzzled that the "spirits" were apparently immune to all rituals of exorcism as well as to the presence of sacred relics, crucifixes, and sprinklings of holy water. Indeed, as happened in many attempted "layings" of poltergeists during the Middle Ages and the Reformation period, the priests themselves were liable to be pelted with a variety of domestic objects. This was a great puzzle to theologians, some of whom suggested that poltergeist phenomena were not the work of demons or truly evil spirits, but due to basically innocent but mischievous beings. A modern wag suggested to me that the trouble was that these spirits were too ignorant to appreciate the service—perhaps they did not understand Latin! The problem appears to be still with us in some degree. Sheila Hervey says that in 1969 violent poltergeistery attended a six-year-old child, Guylaine Saint-Onges, at Acton Vale in Quebec. The priests who were consulted studied the phenomena with a due degree of skepticism, and it was only after they had eliminated the possibility of trickery or natural causes for the events that they performed a service in the hope of terminating the happenings. Whether they used a traditional rite of exorcism or only a service of prayer is not quite clear, but the ritual was interrupted by a good deal of violence, in which a table and two religious statues were broken. However, after a few hours the phenomena ceased. According to Sheila Hervey, during another exorcism in a Quebec town in the 1960s an orange was thrown at the priest. In poltergeist cases in Europe it has often been noted that an exorcism produces a temporary cessation of activity lasting some days, or even weeks, to be followed by renewal of the phenomena. On the psychological theory this might be explicable in terms of the ritual affecting the poltergeist person psychologically, the influence being temporary and apt to wear off.

Sheila Hervey has pieced together the psychic episodes in the long history of the Mackenzie House, a favorite talking point for occult-minded Torontonians. Built in 1850 and occupied from 1859 to 1861 by William Lyon Mackenzie, the famous rebel, the Mackenzie House at 82 Bond Street, Toronto, is maintained as a historic site by the William Lyon Mackenzie Homestead Foundation. It was in 1861 that Mackenzie died there but no ghostly phenomena are claimed to have occurred prior to the mid-1950s. First to report phenomena were Mr. and Mrs. Dobban, who were caretakers from April to June 1960. But Andrew MacFarlane of the *Toronto Telegram* interviewed Mr. and Mrs. Edmunds, who had been caretakers from August 1956 to April 1960. They said that nearly every day there were the sounds of phantom footfalls on the stairs. One night Mrs. Edmunds woke up at midnight to see a woman with dark brown hair and long narrow face leaning over her. A critic might say this was a waking dream. However, a year later she saw the specter again; it struck her in the eye, which, on her waking, was purple and bloodshot. Sometimes Mrs. Edmunds saw a small bald man in a frockcoat in the bedrooms on the second floor. She does not seem to have identified this apparition with Mackenzie, who, says Sheila Hervey, was actually bald, though he wore a red wig. The Edmundses' son, Robert, while staying in the house overnight with his wife and two small children, heard (so he said) the piano playing in the parlor. The children, aged three and four, were once heard screaming in the bathroom. They said

there had been a lady in the bathroom who had disappeared. One
night when, so the Edmundses believed, the outer doors of the
house were all securely locked, all the plants in the house were
mysteriously watered and the curtains bespattered with mud.

The Dobbans testified that they heard footsteps, the piano playing by itself somewhat amateurishly, "as if someone were hitting the
keys with closed fists," and also a rumbling in the basement. When
they checked the oil burner they found it wasn't on. They likened
the noise to that which would be made by a printing press. As it
happens there was a printing press in the cellar—William Lyon
Mackenzie, who published *The Colonial Advocate,* installed it.
Though claimed to be still in working condition, it is kept locked.
These allegations concerning the house, when published in 1966,
led to a press controversy in the *Telegram* and the *Star*. The *Star*
organized a spiritualist séance at the house. No communication was
received. Archdeacon John Frank of Holy Trinity Anglican Church
responded to an appeal for exorcising the presence or presences by
saying prayers in each room, asking for God to send peace. He
added a prayer for William Lyon Mackenzie. Since then the house
appears to have been untroubled except for alleged outbreaks of
activity in 1962 and 1966. In 1962 workmen were renovating
the building, which was left uninhabited at night but supposed
to be securely locked up. They complained that sometimes when
they arrived in the morning they found that objects had been
moved in the night; these included a sawhorse, a rope, and the
dropsheet over the printing press. One of the team, Murdo Mac-
Donald, said that on coming in one morning he found a hang-
man's noose over the stairway. In 1966, the then caretaker, Mrs.
McCleary, said that the toilet flushed by itself and the hot water
tap turned itself on. She said also that sometimes she felt as if the
ghost was putting its arms around her. Bizarre as it all may seem,
nonetheless the reported activity at the Mackenzie House is no
more incredible than that reported of many houses around the
world. Indeed, with respect to muddle, incoherence, incon-
sequentiality, and general irrationality, the tale of 82 Bond Street

is completely typical of alleged hauntings the world over. It cannot be rejected out of hand as untrue, neither can it be neatly explained. We are stuck with it, as with many narratives of the same ilk, whether we like it or not.

The phenomena of haunting are extremely variable and enigmatic, as may be seen from the interesting narratives collected by Eileen Sonin.

7

COSMIC CONSCIOUSNESS

It is possible to be interested in psychical research without having any religious beliefs or even any curiosity about religion. This is because psychical research is a science in which we try to learn from observation, so that its methods and results are, or ought to be, independent of our private beliefs about religious matters. Of course, in some areas of psychical research, such as evidence for survival after death or for reincarnation, we come into direct contact with subjects concerning which most religions provide teaching. However, as investigators, we should seek only to ascertain the facts, rather than try to fit the facts to any preconceived dogma or religious teaching. When the facts have been reliably ascertained, it is, of course, perfectly legitimate for anyone to draw religious inferences from them, if he should wish, and is able to do in a logical way. Equally though, anyone who feels that the data of psychical research can be satisfactorily thought of in terms of the operation of certain natural forces without religious implications is perfectly at liberty to think in this way. Extrasensory perception is often thought of as a manifestation of a natural power with which the individual percipient is endowed. Some people, however (and this includes many of those who have psychic experiences), feel that some forms of ESP, especially clairvoyance and precognition, are too remarkable to be the work of a single human mind and have to be explained in terms of information reaching the percipient from some superhuman source.

Quite often people who have avoided disaster as a result of a precognitive warning interpret it somewhat vaguely in terms of the traditional Western religious backgrounds, and say that the message proceeded via the Divine Providence, that is from God or His messengers. Sometimes, particularly when the message appears in association with an apparition or impression of a deceased relative, the warning is attributed to the dead person's spirit. However, if the matter were analyzed further it would doubtless be felt that the departed spirit probably does not have knowledge of the future directly, but only through such access to a Higher Authority as it enjoys in its post-mortem condition. People brought up in other religious traditions would no doubt describe the source of precognitions in other terms, as coming from Allah, or from the Buddha, or from the Tao, or, if Hindu believers, would suppose it came from Atman-Brahman. The Tao and the Atman-Brahman represent concepts somewhat different from the Judeo-Christian-Islamic idea of the personal God distinct from the created world. Tao and Brahman are, in a sense, the totality of the world, embracing matter, God, man, mind, and spirit. The Atman is the individual spark of Brahman in the human soul. Presumably, in Brahmanic religion it is the fundamental identity of one's Atman with the cosmic Brahman that makes prophecy possible.

In outlining these theories of a superhuman or nonhuman source for some of the more remarkable instances of ESP, the writer wishes to make it clear that he is not necessarily advocating that any or all of them are true. But it has to be admitted that we do not know how precognition works, and it is certainly an extremely baffling problem. At our present stage of knowledge all possibilities have to be kept open, and explanations in terms of religious and philosophical ideas have to be kept in view. What in practice it comes down to is this: some, and possibly all forms of ESP *may* depend not only on the individual human participants, but on something that could claim to be at the least a kind of cosmic memory or repository of knowledge, but perhaps could rank even higher—a kind of universal mind.

Almost all religions teach that a universal mind does exist. However, even though a psychical research worker may, as a private person, have a religious belief, when he is doing his psychical research he should not let his prejudices color his work. He can therefore take an interest in religious *explanations* of ESP, but religious *implications* of ESP observations should be accepted only if they are logically necessary deductions from ascertained facts. This is what is called the "empirical" approach to knowledge, after an ancient Roman philosopher, Sextus Empiricus, who taught, in effect, that the only reliable sources of knowledge are observation and experiment. However, even this austere counsel allows some leeway to the scientist who is interested in religion. For example, he can legitimately ask whether religious experiences supply cogent evidence as to the validity of religious concepts such as God, personal immortality, and so on. This is primarily work for psychologists, but it is a field where psychical research workers can also make a contribution. Indeed, some areas of religious history are particularly amenable to the methods of psychical research though psychical research workers have not, as yet, ventured far in this direction. The type of religious experience that is most relevant to the existence of a universal mind is the kind that is called mystical.

Mystical experiences have been reported by men and by women in different times and lands. They are the prerogative of no one particular religion and come to Christians and Moslems, Hindus and Buddhists, as well as to people of other religions or without religion. A mystical experience is sometimes very brief, but occasionally can be of several hours' duration. Some mystical experiences appear to follow on a long preparation by way of meditation, prayer, and contemplation of religious themes. In this kind of experience the mystic will feel the presence of the deities or venerated personages of his own religion—for example, Catholic mystics feel they are communing with God, or Christ, or the Blessed Virgin. Thus, on occasion, Saint Ignatius Loyola "saw in a distinct manner the plan of divine wisdom in the creation of the world." It might be thought that mystic experiences consist in merely having visions of divine beings, but this seems to be less than the truth.

The experience seems to be more powerful than a purely visionary one. People with any religious background at all tend to speak of their mystical experiences in terms not of seeing God, however magnificently arrayed, from a distance, but of having an intense feeling of His near presence, a sense of unity with Him, and of being incorporated in Him.

Persons who would not be regarded as at all religious in the ordinary sense also have mystical experiences, just as intense as those of the orthodoxly devout. In their case the form of the experience is somewhat different, but it usually involves a feeling of oneness with the whole of nature and of union with a force behind, within, and above nature, which they tend as a rule to identify with mind or spirit. Mystical experience is a very peculiar fact and we cannot wonder that very astute thinkers with no religious ax to grind have considered it a very interesting and important fact. The phenomenon draws its importance from several peculiar features. No explanation for it has yet been given in psychological terms. Mystics are sane people, often more balanced than many of the colleagues they encounter in everyday life. The mystical episode has some of the characteristics of a trance in that the mystic during his experience will be "rapt"—i.e. like someone in deep thought or extended reverie—but unlike the subject of the hysterical, psychotic, or even the mediumistic trance, the mystic seems to have a good recollection of what went on. However, though he may recall his thoughts and feelings, he has great difficulty in expressing in words just what it was like. He will often say, in effect, what Bottom the Weaver said after his Midsummer Night's Dream, "I have had a dream, past the wit of man to say what dream it was. . . . Methought I was—there is no man can tell what. Methought I was, and methought I had. . . . The eye of man hath not heard, the ear of man hath not seen, man's hand is not able to taste, his tongue to conceive, nor his heart to report, what my dream was. . . . it shall be called Bottom's dream because it hath no bottom. . . ." As we all know, Bottom was fooled by the fairies, but as a description of the inexpressibility of a mystical experience, the incoherent words put by Shakespeare into Bottom's clumsy mouth can hardly be bettered. Like Bottom, the mystic is aware of a great profundity —a great depth of meaning—overwhelming significance, so that the experience is bottomless, and reaches to unsoundable depths. The mystic feels that he has been granted a great insight into the meaning and purpose of the universe. Even though he cannot fully or exactly put this meaning into words, he retains an unshakable conviction that he did have a revelation as to the why and wherefore of existence. Indeed, the experience in this respect always seems to him afterward to have been completely certain and authoritative. He feels that what he learned was in fact derived from or through intimate contact with the ultimate reality of the universe.

Some critics of mysticism, like Professor Zaehner, distinguish between mystic experiences in which religious beings such as God figure and those in which the mystic experiences only a sense of union and identity with nature. Whether any such distinction is a valid one is, however, very disputable. The fact that different language is used to describe or interpret the experiences does not mean that the nature of the experiences actually differs, only that the mystic in attempting to describe the episode uses the concepts he is most at home with. Hence his description is related to his usual philosophy and religion, if any. Quite irrespective of whether their experience is interpreted in terms of union with God or with nature, all mystics agree that it communicated to them an unalterable conviction that the universe is essentially good and its purpose sublime. The mystical experience, however, is not the same as religious conversion. The latter experience is more common than the mystical one, but differs from it in many respects. In particular, the emphasis is on the personal salvation of the recipient. The certitude he gains from his conversion experience relates to his redemption and immortality as an individual man and is less concerned with the totality of sentient beings.

The earliest Canadian mystic was a nun whom we have mentioned previously, the Venerable Mère Marie de l'Incarnation, whose contemplation attained to mystical heights. Like Saint Teresa of Avila, she combined this aspect of the religious life with an intensely practical and dynamic spirit, which took her to New France, where she pioneered in the field of education (Renardin, 1938). Of other Canadians who may have had mystical experience we know nothing, except of Dr. R. M. Bucke, whose book *Cosmic Consciousness* is widely read today, at least in the English-speaking world, and which in the present century has played a great role in drawing attention to mysticism and its possible implications. Published in 1901 it has gone through more than twenty-two editions and has never been out of print.

Richard Maurice Bucke was born in Norfolk, England, on 18 March 1837. His father was an Anglican curate and a descendant of Sir Robert Walpole. Bucke became a Canadian when about one year old. His parents settled on a pioneer homestead very close to the site of the present Ontario Hospital at London, Ontario. His father had been educated at Trinity College, Cambridge, where, later in the century, the three founders of psychical research, Henry Sidgwick, Edmund Gurney, and Frederic Myers, became scholars and teachers. Richard Bucke had no formal education but his father had brought seven thousand books in seven languages with him, and the children learned not only to read, but to do so in several languages. Professor Greenland (1966) tells us that Richard, besides participating in the life of the farmstead and reading learned treatises, enjoyed novels and books about wildlife and human behavior. Unable to accept Christian doctrine, he believed that "Jesus was a man—great and good, no doubt—but a man." He said later that he sometimes felt "a sort of ecstasy of curiosity and hope." At the age of ten years he longed to die in order to learn the secrets of the beyond, if such there was. At the age of sixteen he left home and worked as a laborer in various parts of the United States, eventually joining up with the miners Alan and Hosea Ghosh, the discoverers of the Comstock Lode. In 1857, Bucke and Alan Ghosh were caught for five days in a snowstorm on the mountains while on their way to California to register the Comstock claim. Alan died. Bucke had to have one foot completely amputated and the other partly cut off, leaving a wound that took forty years to heal. He returned to Canada and used a small legacy to put himself through medical school at McGill University, from which he graduated in 1862.

After two years of postgraduate study in England and France, he returned to Canada and married. After twelve years of general practice in Sarnia and a year as the superintendent of the mental hospital in Hamilton, he went to the Ontario Hospital at London, where he served for a quarter of a century, until his sudden death in 1902. His career was highly distinguished. Professor of nervous and mental diseases of the Medical School in London and a Fellow of the Royal Society of Canada, he became also president of the psychological section of the British Medical Association and president of the American Medico-Psychological Association. Always forward-looking, Bucke, who was a friend of Alexander Graham Bell, was the first telephone subscriber in London, Ontario, and the first public demonstration of the telephone took place between the asylum and Richmond Street.

Forward-looking in medical psychology also, Dr. Bucke took up the new Moral Treatment of the insane, which others were then introducing into Canada, but carried it further than anyone else had done hitherto. The idea of Moral Treatment was to treat mental patients so far as possible like normal human beings. His patients had restraints on their movements relaxed to the limit of feasibility and were given useful occupations. He declared that the object of treatment was the "rehumanization of the patient."

Dr. Bucke's theories on the treatment of the insane (which are now fully accepted) were only a part of his general philosophy. An avid reader and correspondent with numerous friends in professions of all kinds, his whole life was a "passionate note of interrogation, and unappeasable hunger for enlightenment," and was devoted, as Professor Greenland says, to understanding the nature of man's psychophysical interrelationships with the cosmos. Mental illness therefore was not simply an accidental aberration, but resulted from a failure of the total biological process by which mankind adapts to change. Besides his medical compassion there were two great influences on his development. The first occurred when he was thirty and read *Leaves of Grass* by Walt Whitman. When an old man, Dr. Bucke told the great physician Sir William Osler that *Leaves of Grass* had meant for him "spiritual enlightenment, a new power in life, new joys in a new existence on a plane higher than he had ever hoped to reach." Six years later, in the spring of 1872 while in London, England, Dr. Bucke had his own mystical experience. It happened at midnight while he was riding home in a hansom cab after an evening spent reading poetry with friends. His mind, he said, was calm and peaceful. He was in a state of almost passive enjoyment, letting ideas, images, and emotions flow of themselves through his mind. Then:

All at once, without warning of any kind, I found myself wrapped in a flame-coloured cloud. For an instant I thought of fire, an immense conflagration, somewhere close by the great city; the next, I knew that the fire was within myself. Directly afterward there came upon me a sense of exultation and immense joyousness accompanied, or immediately followed, by an intellectual illumination impossible to describe. Among other things, I did not merely come to believe, I saw that the Universe is not composed of dead matter, but is, on the contrary, a living Presence; I became conscious in myself of eternal life. It was not a conviction that I could have eternal life, but a consciousness that I possessed eternal life then; I saw that all men are immortal; that the cosmic order is such that without any peradventure all things work together for the good of each and all; that the foundation principle of the world, of all the world, is what we call love, and that the happiness of each and all is in the long run absolutely certain. The vision lasted a few seconds, and was gone, but the memory of it and the sense of the reality of what it taught have remained during the quarter of a century which has since elapsed. I knew that what the vision showed was true. I had attained to a point of view from which I saw that it must be true. That view, that conviction, I may say that consciousness, has never, even during periods of deepest depression, been lost.

It will be seen that Dr. Bucke's experience has all of the characteristics of a mystical experience as outlined above. Indeed it is one of the best statements in existence of the mystical episode as received by a man not orthodoxly religious.

Nowadays we are quite accustomed to speaking of "altered states of consciousness," where "altered" merely means a state different from the normal everyday kind of consciousness. We also know a great deal more about states of consciousness than did the psychologists of a century ago. We shall therefore be quite responsive to the phrase used by Dr. Bucke to describe his condition during his mystical experience. He regarded himself as having temporarily attained to a state of "cosmic consciousness," meaning cosmic awareness, i.e. awareness of the cosmos as a unitary and "living" entity. The phrase "cosmic consciousness" as used by Dr. Bucke is intended to mean a higher perception or consciousness of the cosmos or universe, rather than a consciousness possessed by the universe. However, his experience, if a truthful one (as he believed it was), implied that the universe had a consciousness, for otherwise his remarks about the universe as a "living Presence" with love as the foundation of the world would be nonsensical.

Except to his friends Dr. Bucke kept silent for twenty-two years. In 1894 he delivered a paper on "Cosmic Consciousness" to the American Medico-Psychological Association. By 1899 he had completed his now famous book *Cosmic Consciousness: A Study in the Evolution of the Human Mind,* which was published in 1901. In the book he examined fourteen cases of men who he believed had received sudden illumination of mind similar to his own, and gave thirty-six case histories of persons who had received it in lesser degrees. He formulated an evolutionary theory of the development of consciousness in animals and humans. He thought that there were three grades of consciousness. The lowest is *simple consciousness,* possessed by the higher animal. Above this is *self-consciousness,* enjoyed only by humans, who alone in the animal kingdom can step aside from themselves and be aware that they are aware. Finally, there is *cosmic consciousness,* whose possessor has a direct awareness of the universe and its life and order. Dr. Bucke believed that in the present age only a few people attain momentarily to cosmic consciousness but that in the future course of human evolution more and more humans would possess this faculty until it was shared by the whole species. In that era, life would be dominated by a new religion which would be a fusion of all true elements of the old faiths; there would be no rituals because man would commune directly with God.

Dr. Bucke's book was a remarkable achievement for a man who was not a professional scholar or religious historian. In 1899 though there were many lives of Catholic and Protestant mystics, and some literature on "other religions" available in the West, there were practically no general studies of mysticism in print (William James's *Varieties of Religious Experience,* based on the Gifford Lectures he gave at Oxford in 1901, was not published until 1902, the year that Richard Maurice Bucke died). Whatever its author's fate may have been in the great beyond, his book shows every promise of immortality.

Among the examples of major illumination cited by Dr. Bucke there was, besides obvious candidates such as Buddha, Jesus, Mohammed, and Dante, also Walt Whitman, who visited Bucke in Canada in 1880. Dr. Bucke's biography of Whitman was published 1883, some years prior to the poet's death at Camden, New Jersey, in 1892. Whitman, who described himself as "the mate and companion of people, all just as immortal and fathomless as myself," had an unshakable belief in eternal life, and it is this theme that the Whitman Fellowship incorporated in the Whitman Memorial at what is now Bon Echo Provincial Park, a tract of land donated to the province of Ontario by Merrill Dennison. Besides being one of the most beautiful, Bon Echo is one of the most interesting sites in Canada. It occupies one side of Mazinaw Lake, which it almost divides in two by a projecting strip of land which almost meets the opposite shore. "Shore" is a misnomer, for on this side is a huge granite cliff, about a hundred feet high, and a mile long, which is often referred to as Canada's Gibraltar. On the face of the cliff is one of the world's largest displays of Indian rock paintings, and on the top of the escarpment are assemblages of huge boulders which may possibly have been arranged by prehistoric Indians. Bon Echo owes its name to the echoing of sounds from the cliff face.

In what must be now an extremely rare pamphlet (shown to me by Professor Greenland), the issue for April 1920 of a little journal published by the Whitman Club of Bon Echo, Flora MacDonald describes how, as the culmination of the Whitman Centennial Convention in 1919, Horace Traubel dedicated the Whitman Memorial. In the rock of the cliff face a sentence from Walt Whitman's *Leaves of Grass* is engraved.

> My foothold is tenon'd and mortis'd in granite,
> I laugh at what you call dissolution,
> And I know the amplitude of time.

Horace Traubel of Camden, New Jersey, was a devoted friend and biographer of Whitman, and was highly respected by Dr. Bucke. Three days after the dedication, while looking across to "Gibraltar" from Flora MacDonald's house, Traubel said to Flora, "Look, look, Flora, quick, quick, he is going." Flora replied, "What, where, Horace? I do not see anyone." Horace answered, "Why, just over the Rock Walt appeared, head and shoulders and hat on, in a golden glory—brilliant and splendid. He reassured me, beckoned to me, and spoke to me. I heard his voice but did not understand all he said, only 'Come on.' " Horace Traubel was uplifted by his vision, but became ill a week later, and on 8 September he died. Colonel Cosgrave, who was sitting with him on the afternoon of 6 September, "saw" Walt Whitman on the opposite side of the bed and felt his presence. Then Walt "passed through the bed" and touched the Colonel's hand, which was in his pocket. The contact was like an electric shock. Horace was also aware of Walt's visible presence and said so. Whether these apparitions of Whitman are to be attributed to pure hallucination or not we have no way of knowing.

Dr. Bucke had some interest in paranormal phenomena, particularly psychokinesis. He attached some weight to the séance-room happenings that attended William Stainton Moses, a well-known

English nonprofessional medium. But in the course of a busy life he was able to give little time to these problems. He believed that some psychic phenomena did occur. He regarded psychic ability as a product of human evolution like the faculty of cosmic awareness. However, he regarded it as a different though almost equally worthy capability.

In 1964 the R. M. Bucke Memorial Society for the Study of Religious Experience was formed, its president being Professor Raymond Prince, M.D., of McGill University, and its honorary president George H. Stevenson, M.D. Its object is to study areas common to religion and psychiatry. Thus its membership is interdisciplinary, including psychiatrists, psychologists, members of several religious traditions, as well as anthropologists and other scientists. Its annual conferences have resulted in three important books dealing with various aspects of religious experience. Equally valuable articles are published in the society's newsletters.

8

REINCARNATION

Walt Whitman declared his belief in reincarnation in the words "And as to you, life, I reckon you are the leavings of many deaths. No doubt I have died myself a thousand times." Reincarnation is a belief widely disseminated among primitive peoples and for millennia has been firmly established in the thought of the Hindu and Buddhist inheritors of the ancient civilization of India. Curiously enough, the idea of reincarnation seems to have been totally absent from the religions of ancient Egypt and Babylonia. However, it was an article of faith in the creeds of the Pythagoreans and Orphics of ancient Greece; it occurs in the writings of Plato, and became known to the Romans. In Virgil's *Aeneid* the hero Aeneas, when visiting the world of the dead, receives instruction in the evolution of human souls. While alive on earth the soul, whose perception is obstructed by matter, acquires stains of guilt incurred by those deeds to which it is impelled by its emotions. After death it is cleansed, and then reborn. After many cycles of rebirth the soul attains to complete purity of consciousness—a spark of elemental fire; its abode is eternal bliss. Aeneas sees the candidates for rebirth drinking the waters of forgetfulness from the river Lethe, because in each incarnation the soul is required to forget its past.

Reincarnation had no place in Christian doctrine. After the foundation of the Theosophical Society in 1875 ideas strikingly similar to those expounded in the *Aeneid* have, of course, been disseminated throughout the Western world, but prior to that date they could hardly be said to be widely known. Literary men had, however, been familiar with the concept of reincarnation ever since the European Renaissance had revived interest in ancient writings.

For example, in *Twelfth Night* Shakespeare inserts a reference to the Pythagorean belief that the soul of one's grandmother might inhabit a wild fowl. This, of course, refers to the more extended theory of *metempsychosis,* or "transmigration of souls," which supposes that base or backward spirits may have animal incarnations—a theme susceptible of comic treatment, as in Shakespeare. When Walt Whitman in the first edition of *Leaves of Grass,* which he produced in 1855, spoke of the "perpetual transfers and promotions" of the soul in its long journey, the idea was by no means original with him.

According to Oriental mythology it is only the soul that has achieved complete detachment from desire for the things of this world that remembers its past lives. Only when, sitting under the famous bo tree, he had attained to Supreme Enlightenment, did the Buddha recall his millions of previous incarnations. The water of Lethe is indeed a powerful amnesiac. Now, from time to time, either spontaneously or under hypnotism, people do apparently have "recollections" which are inapplicable to actual events in their present lives. In such cases there is naturally a strong temptation to regard these recollections as memories of a former life. Though it may be different in Asia, it is extremely rare in the Western world for the alleged facts of the former life to be verified in any degree from records. Consequently, the great majority of Western instances of "reincarnation memories" fail entirely to prove the fact of rebirth. The essential point is that the supposed previous incarnation has to be an obscure person whose life is unknown by normal means to the person who "remembers" it. Only if a person answering closely to the description supplied by the "memories" is subsequently shown to have actually existed can we begin to consider the case as possible evidence of reincarnation. (Obviously, memories relating to the life of a well-known person, e.g. William Lyon Mackenzie, would be evidentially useless as the facts of his life are readily available in books.) Quite an interesting case occurred in Canada only a few years back. It illustrates not only the curious phenomenon of reincarnation memories but the difficulties encountered in verifying the existence of the presumed previous incarnation when this person is not a well-known historical character.

According to the account published by Jess Stearn, Joanne MacIver of Orillia, Ontario, was hypnotized "inadvertently" by her father, Ken MacIver, on 5 October 1962, when she was almost fourteen years old. Orillia is on Lake Couchiching, an appendage of Lake Simcoe and is the "Mariposa" which the Canadian humorist Stephen Leacock made world-famous. Joanne was born on 22 October 1948 (presumably at Orillia). Ken MacIver was born and educated in Toronto and served in the Royal Canadian Air Force during the Second World War, after which he married and settled in Orillia. Joanne was the eldest of five children. During the war MacIver learned to do hypnosis. It should be said that he was also an enthusiastic believer in reincarnation. On the evening of 5 October 1962 Joanne was at home playing cards with two school friends, Barbara White and Paul Torrance. The conversation having turned to hypnotism, Joanne vainly attempted to hypnotize Paul. When she failed she applied to her father for assistance. Ken MacIver also failed with Paul, but while listening to her father's commands to Paul to feel tired and "go to sleep" Joanne closed her eyes and went into a state of hypnosis.

MacIver then switched his attention from Paul to his daughter. He suggested to Joanne that she was going to see herself and remember herself as she was on her fifth birthday. To his surprise Joanne responded by pronouncing completely unfamiliar names unrelated to the family history of the MacIvers—Reuben, Tom, Susie. MacIver then suggested that she see herself at age sixteen. In response to questioning it appeared that Joanne was replying as a "Susan Ganier," living on a farm in Ontario, Canada, in 1848. This was extremely interesting to MacIver and in subsequent weeks he hypnotized Joanne regularly to get more details concerning her life as Susan Ganier. In 1965 the case received radio, television, and press publicity. In 1966 Jess Stearn spent some days in Orillia and went with Ken and Joanne MacIver to the area where, according to Joanne under hypnosis, Susan Ganier had lived and died. This was about ninety miles to the west of Orillia, just inland from Meaford, which is on the shore of Georgian Bay, a little to the east of Owen Sound. Stern called their quest the "search for the girl with blue eyes" because, like Joanne herself, Susan Ganier had blue eyes. It is unusual in cases of supposed reincarnation occurring in the Western world for the previous incarnation to have been located in a nearby area. However, cases of this sort are claimed in India and have been described by Dr. Ian Stevenson of the University of Virginia. (Dr. Stevenson was born in Canada; unfortunately space does not permit of his work being discussed here.)

In the course of many hypnoses by Ken MacIver and others a biographical sketch of Susan Ganier emerged. Susan Ganier was born about 1833 in St. Vincent township of Grey County, Ontario, the child of parents from Quebec, Catherine and Mason Ganier. The nearest settlement was Massie, to the south of where they lived. They kept cattle and raised pigs and had apple orchards. Her father's grain was milled by a Mr. McKelver. Joanne, speaking as Susan, spoke of MacGregor and Milligan as storekeepers in Massie; she referred to a farmer as Old Man MacGregor—a kindly person whom she liked. There was a neighbor named Urket (or perhaps Urquhart) and a Watson. Susan had a brother Reuben, who married a Rachel Brown.

Susan at age seventeen got married in 1849 to a young neighbor, Tommy Marrow, aged twenty-one, who had a small farm in Sydenham township that he bought for a hundred dollars. The wedding ceremony was performed by a preacher called McEachern. A man called Yancey used to help on the farm. When speaking of him, Joanne, under hypnotism, in the personality of Susan Marrow, showed great dislike and even fear. In one session of hypnosis in the role of Susan she apparently relived a scene in which Yancey grabbed at her. She broke loose and hit him with a shovel.

Susan and Tommy's marriage was affectionate but childless. In

1863, after about fourteen years of marriage, Tommy died, cut in the neck and shoulders by the blade of a scythe that fell on him in the barn. A Mr. Brown was present. He fetched a Dr. Black but by that time Tommy Marrow was dead. Susan sold the farm and stock for about four hundred dollars. She retired to a small house or hut in the locality, and led an exceedingly quiet life until her death in 1903. She had a vegetable garden and was given a pig each year by a Mr. Thompson who used to help her with wood-chopping and bring her flour, sugar, and tea. MacGregor gave her eggs and chickens. She was also befriended by Mrs. Speedie, the postmistress of the village of Annan.

This life history of Susan Ganier was pieced together from many sessions in which Joanne under hypnosis thought of herself only as Susan and had only Susan's memories. Her twentieth-century life as Joanne seemed to be entirely forgotten until she was awakened from the hypnotic state. Were Joanne's memories as Susan truly recollections of another life or only a fantasy? To decide this Ken MacIver and later, Jess Stearn, studied old records and interviewed residents in the Meaford area.

On a map of 1860 showing landholdings in St. Vincent township, the name Ganier appears on lot 37 of Ninth Line. Over it have been written "Hartman" and "Hagerman." Four miles or so to the south and west an Archibald Marrow is shown as owner of lot 31 on the St. Vincent township line in 1840. Other records, however, show that he vacated his holding within a few years. The census of 1851 showed a Catherine *Granier,* too young to be Catherine Ganier, Susan's mother. In fact, no other Ganiers or Marrows are recorded in the district, although there are several Morrows and Graniers, as well as Browns. There were two doctors called Black. They did not live very close to Massie or Annan, but there were two other Blacks in Sydenham township. In Massie there was a blacksmith, Robert MacGregor, and a Joshua Milligan, who once kept a store, and then became a postman. The censuses of 1861 and 1871 reported many Thompsons in the area. Mrs. Margaret Speedie took over the general store in Annan after the death of her husband.

Their tombstones are in the cemetery at Annan. There were no Methodist churches in the area during Susan's infancy but Methodist services were held from 1840 onward. Several McEacherns farmed in the district; one of them may have been an ordained minister of religion able to perform marriage services.

A very old gentleman, Arthur Eagles of Woodford, when questioned by Ken MacIver and a local psychiatrist, Dr. F. Crawford Jones, said that he remembered the Ganier family and had often seen them in the company of other friends of his. He remembered Yancey as the name of a neighbor. He said that there had been a McKelver's Mill in an area now called the Tank Range because it is used as a proving ground for military equipment. Arthur Eagles's parents had told him that Tommy Marrow had died when Arthur was three years old. During his teens Arthur had got to know Susan Marrow, whom he remembered as a widow living in an old cabin in the Tank Range. He said that he sometimes drove her into Owen Sound.

Putting together such scraps of information as they had, Jess Stearn and MacIver took Joanne to the site of what Joanne, both in the waking state as herself and in the hypnotic state as Susan Marrow, believed to have been the farmhouse that she occupied in her former life with Tommy. The remains showed some features agreeing with Susan's memories, such as a terrace, but unfortunately only the foundations of the building were left.

It will be obvious to the reader that a great deal of importance attached to the evidence of Arthur Eagles. His is about the only direct testimony to the existence of Susan or Tommy Marrow. This does not mean that they did not exist. In the middle of the nineteenth century the Owen Sound area was settler country. Life was harsh and communications meager. Before 1879 there were no provincial birth or death records, and even after that date reporting of these events was liable to be erratic. But it is odd that no official record of Susan Marrow's supposed death in 1903 has come to light. In the absence of all documents of that kind we cannot really improve on the summing up of this case given by Allen

Spraggett in the *Toronto Star* of 6 February 1965. "The evidence for Susan as a previous incarnation of Joanne is tantalising but fragmentary."

If reincarnation is true, what does the soul do in the intervals between two lives on earth? Many readers will be familiar with the poetic and picturesque accounts of the time between death and rebirth given in some of the novels of Dr. T. Lobsang Rampa. The soul looks at the record of its past lives and in consultation with its friends and advisors decides what type of person it ought to be reborn as in order to make the most spiritual progress. This, of course, is in full agreement with the teachings of many groups who believe in reincarnation. It should be said that the Rampa books are novels rather than autobiography, but are very well written and pleasing to read. (As Dr. Rampa gives a P.O. Box at Fort Erie as mailing address he can perhaps be regarded as a Canadian author.)

Interestingly enough, Joanne under hypnosis remembered her death as Susan Marrow and how as Susan's spirit she had attended Susan's funeral in the graveyard of a local church. But just which church this was she could not remember. Until her rebirth as Joanne in 1948 Susan-Joanne spent the intervening time in "heaven." She found her Ganier parents there but not Tommy Marrow. Perhaps he was in an earthly incarnation; however, Susan-Joanne did not offer this explanation. Indeed, she provided almost no details concerning heaven as a state of being. Just prior to her rebirth as Joanne she saw her MacIver parents on earth, Mrs. MacIver already being well advanced in pregnancy. It was only at this stage that Joanne's soul entered the body of the unborn infant. Whether Susan-Joanne's port-mortem and prenatal experiences were true or merely fantasies we have no way of knowing, and cannot form a judgment.

Some spiritualist teachings contradict reincarnation doctrines because they envisage the soul as progressing after death on higher planes of existence without rebirth in this world. On the other hand, some spiritualists do believe that souls who have not attained a certain level of spiritual development are born again. Occasionally one encounters situations in which alleged spirit communications refer to a reincarnation. For example in a newly built house in Ontario not long ago there were some phenomena suggestive either of haunting or poltergeistery. Some visitors brought a ouija board to the house.

A ouija board, whose name is made up of the words for "Yes" in French (*oui*) and German (*ja*), consists of a board with an alphabet printed on it and also the words yes, no, and good-bye, as well as the numbers 0 and 1 through 9. The operators sit round the ouija board, which is usually on a table, with their fingers resting on a small mobile platform which has a pointer. After a while the platform will usually start to move and every now and again will come to rest with the pointer near a symbol. In this way questions can be "answered" and names and numbers spelled out. With the ouija board it is quite easy for one or more of the operators to cheat by consciously directing the pressure of their fingers. It is also easy to regulate the motions of the platform unconsciously without being aware that one is doing so. Occasionally the operators get the impression that an additional physical force over and above the one their fingers are supplying is present and chiefly responsible for the platform's movements, but it is almost impossible to prove this and I do not know of any case where it has been proved. Because the workings of ouija boards are so easily influenced by the operators, all "communications" received through ouija boards are highly unreliable. I think the communications obtained in the aforementioned house were no exception.

The ouija board at the house mentioned spelled out messages from "someone" who claimed to be the spirit of a Scottish soldier killed in that area (which is near the Niagara frontier) about 150 years ago. Curiously enough, he was not a casualty of the War of 1812, but, he said, the victim of a private crime, a murder. More interestingly, in later sessions with the ouija board statements were spelled out to the effect that the "communicator" had been the sweetheart of a previous incarnation (also Scottish) of a woman now resident in the house. The implication was that while she had been reincarnated, possibly more than once, he had remained an earthbound spirit. The possibility of finding historical facts to corroborate this story is, of course, almost negligible, and no such facts have as yet emerged. In their absence we really have no justification for considering the "communicator" and his story to be other than entertaining fantasies spun out of the daydreams, conscious or unconscious, of one or another operator of the board.

The foregoing negative conclusions are not reached lightly but on the basis of considerable experience which investigators have had with ouija boards. For example, a small group in Toronto who were playing with a ouija board got what purported to be a message from a man, whose name was given, who had been a schoolteacher and had on a specified date some years back been accidentally drowned in Lake Ontario, near Toronto. The message also asked that a "Charles" be told that the communicator was happy in his present condition. The little group of ouija board operators were sufficiently concerned to ask us about it. Efforts to trace a death certificate failed. A search through all the Toronto newspapers for the relevant period revealed no reference to the supposedly drowned person by way of news items, report of inquest, funeral, or In Memoriam notice. The address given for Charles did not exist, and no person of that name was listed in the telephone directory. After a while we began to feel as if we were scanning the *London Times* for Sherlock Holmes's obituary; we judged that duty had been done and that it was time to stop.

Is retrogressive hypnosis actually more reliable than the ouija board? By retrogressive hypnosis we mean the technique applied by Ken MacIver to Joanne—the hypnotized person is asked to retrogress, i.e., to go back mentally to an earlier time. It is an extension of age regression. When hypnosis is used medically in the treatment of physical or psychiatric complaints the patient is sometimes age-regressed, i.e., he is told to imagine himse'f just as he was at an earlier age. Often he is instructed, "It is your fifth birthday," and the patient will then appear to relive the events of that day and prattle in a childish voice about his toys and his birthday party. How reliable these memories are I do not know, as little has been written on this aspect of hypnosis. Obviously, if memories of the present life were to be proved unreliable we could hardly trust "memories" of former lives. In retrogressive hypnosis the age regression is carried a stage further and the subject is invited to tell the thoughts, feelings, and experiences he had at some date before he was born.

Retrogressive hypnosis has lately become almost a popular pastime. From what one hears, it seems that memories of past lives, instead of being rare, are produced with great facility. Verifications of the actual historical existence of the previous incarnations is, of course, another matter. It is difficult and laborious; it seems to be rarely undertaken—perhaps because it is a lot less fun than hypnotizing one's wife, daughter, or girlfriend in the presence of an admiring circle. The hobby has its dangers when conducted by unprofessional persons. For example, Ken MacIver once forgot to give Joanne the proper instructions when terminating a hypnotic session in which she had acted out an episode in the Susan existence. As a result, Joanne stayed for about a week in a dazed or "zombified" state in which she was neither Joanne nor Susan. It is the frequent occurrence of episodes of this sort that has caused many governments to ban all stage demonstrations of hypnosis. The law in Ontario is somewhat stricter. Hypnotism is legal only when performed for purposes of cure (medical treatment, anesthesia in surgery or dentistry, psychiatric treatment) or research by a registered doctor or psychologist, or a person with a licence from the provincial government. This is a more restrictive law than most countries have, but one can understand the reasoning behind it. Besides the inconveniences such as temporary "zombification" after inexpert hypnosis, there are more serious dangers. In retrogressive hypnosis the hypnotist is engaging in a general fishing expedition. Now all of us, even with reference to the present life, have painful memories that are normally suppressed. Occasionally, under hypnosis suppressed emotions can rise to the surface with explosive force and be very upsetting to the hypnotized person. I think this kind of reaction is much more common than amateur hypnotizers will admit. Certainly many amateur performances do end with the subjects weeping uncontrollably because they are suddenly inundated by emotions and feelings they can neither understand nor subdue. In some cases the reaction leads to a neurotic breakdown.

9

HEALING: ENZYME BREAKTHROUGH

Every human disease or ailment manifests itself both physically and psychologically, though very often the psychological aspect will be minor and secondary. In the case of an infection that responds swiftly to an antibiotic the psychological effects of the illness will be brief and transitory, and in treatment the doctor usually need give attention only to purely physical questions such as choice of medication. However, there are many medical situations, even when the disease is entirely physical in origin, in which psychological factors play a role in treatment. For example, the patient may have an infection that is immune to any known antibiotic. The only cure is by way of his own body's natural defenses. If these are adequate the patient's body will manufacture enough defensive substances in his bloodstream to exterminate the invading parasites, bacteria, or viruses. However, it may be a touch-and-go situation, in which case it depends on the patient's morale whether his defenses are sufficient for him to recover. Medical treatment will therefore consist of physical measures—rest, diet, and some medication—but will also have a psychological element aimed at diminishing the patient's worry and boosting his morale. A doctor's "bedside manner," his capacity for exuding confidence and communicating optimism to the patient, nowadays is recognized to be an important part of his professional skill.

Psychological factors play their part in encouraging rapid healing of wounds and fractures. This seems to have been well known to various tribes of North American Indians, who used to talk soothingly and encouragingly to patients who were undergoing bone setting (at which the Indians were rather good) or actual surgery. Only recently has white man's medicine realized the importance of what is said in the operating theater. Previously it was supposed that the patient, unconscious under a general anesthetic, did not hear remarks about his condition. Nowadays it is believed that although the patient usually has no conscious recollection of what is said, he does hear it and registers it unconsciously. Consequently, surgeons and operating staff are very careful not to let fall any remarks as to the seriousness of the patient's condition, or say anything which might be depressing or discouraging, or for that matter, derogatory, such as comments on the patient's figure!

There is practically no kind of disease or ailment in which the patient's morale and his confidence in the doctor are unimportant. If a patient has faith in a doctor and the doctor has a confident and authoritative manner, then whatever the treatment administered, it is likely to give the patient some relief of his symptoms, even if it may not actually cure the ailment. This is especially true of a large range of chronic but not fatal complaints which involve pain or discomfort but which do not threaten the life of the patient. Here we are speaking of complaints with an actual physical basis, i.e. an actual deterioration or malfunctioning of physical elements of the body—bone, nerve, muscles, etc. The alleviation of symptoms resulting from the patient's faith in the treatment is not purely a change in his psychological attitude to them, but an actual physical improvement. We are not suggesting that the illness is "all in the mind"; psychological factors can affect the body's physical state.

If a patient's condition can be improved by faith, does it have to be faith in a medical treatment or faith in a doctor? Indeed not— relief of symptoms often flows from faith in the healing power of the Deity, particularly if this faith is emphasized, reinforced, or initiated by an appropriate ceremony or service of prayer or intercession. This is why "healing circles" are often efficacious in relieving chronic complaints. These meetings seem to have much the same degree of success no matter what the religious denomination may be, provided that the patient is present at the service. He sometimes gets benefit when the service is held in his absence, provided that he knows this is being done; as a rule, however, this is less effective than direct participation.

Benefit can be had from healing circles even if the circle is not led by a dominant and outstanding leader, provided that the patient believes in the sincerity of the group and is convinced of their active sympathy for him. However, broadly speaking, we would expect better results from meetings led by a person of striking personality, authoritative manner, and fine speaking voice. This is because the situation is parallel to that of the patient, the medicine, and the doctor. It is from his confidence in the doctor that the medical patient derives his faith in the medicine. Similarly, in the "faith healing" situation it is the patient's faith in the leader that reinforces his faith in the "medicine," i.e. the power of prayer, divine intervention, or what you will. When the meetings are held under the auspices of a church the leader is not usually regarded as being himself the source of the healing power; the patients regard him, as he does himself, as performing the priestly role of helping the patient to contact the divine power.

Outside the church situation it is relatively easy for both the "leader" type of person who is interested in healing and the patient who longs to be cured, to mentally substitute the doctor for the medicine. Thus, the individual healer arises. Even though he may disclaim being anything more than an exceptionally gifted intercessor, his patients, friends, and acolytes will inevitably think of the healing power as residing in him rather than proceeding from a more exalted source. The practical results will be no worse, and may even be better. It is the fact of belief that counts, not exactly what is believed.

So far we have been speaking of cases where the results of faith or psychic healing are noticeable but relatively undramatic. The patient with a chronic illness or discomfort gets some relief as a result of a psychological boost. Occasionally the cure is complete, but usually the effect is temporary and there will be a relapse after some days, weeks, or months. Among the commonest ailments for which healers are consulted are aches and pains of arthritic or rheumatic type, often associated with stiff and "seized up" joints, such as knees, wrists, and ankles. Quite often the healer will introduce a touch of drama by telling the patient that he *can* move the joint and that it will not hurt (or hurt much). The healer will sometimes assist the movement by applying his own hands to the joint. As the mere fact of moving the joint will break up the solid deposits, it means that mobility will be restored, and pain diminished, at least for a time. Allen Spraggett in his book *The Unexplained* describes a spiritual healing mission conducted by the Reverend Alex Holmes, a minister of the United Church of Canada. At one point in the service Holmes, without warning, seized the ankle of an elderly woman—a sufferer from rheumatoid arthritis—and slammed her foot down hard upon the floor. The movement gave her very little pain. She was able to walk away from the meeting without using her stick. The ankle stayed better for several days but eventually started to ache again.

There is a whole class of ailments which are particularly amenable to actual cure by healing circles or other psychological means. This is because although they manifest themselves in physical terms their origin is entirely psychological. Included are various disorders of the functioning of internal organs which are described by doctors as being "psychosomatic illness." In addition, there is a large group of disorders which technically are called "conversion hysterias." Though the term hysteria is used to describe them, the connection with old-fashioned "hysterics"—attacks of weeping and laughing—is rather indirect. The disorders known collectively as conversion hysterias manifest themselves in a variety of physical symptoms: paralysis of any or all of the limbs, inability to walk or stand, lack of feeling in the hands or other parts of the body, blindness, deafness, skin conditions, asthmatic attacks, pains in the joints or the back, headaches, flexures of some of the muscles, drooping of the eyelids, nervous twitches of the face, and so on. The fascinating story of how conversion hysterias came to be recognized and understood has been given in my book *Hysteria, Hypnosis and Healing.*

The interesting thing about conversion hysterias is that although they manifest as physical disabilities their causes are entirely psychological. For example, if a person has a paralyzed arm as a result of conversion hysteria, no physical examination, however careful, will discover any actual defect in it. In this respect it will differ profoundly from the arm of a person suffering from a paralysis that is physical in nature. All the nerves of a hysterically paralyzed arm will be sound and also the related brain centers. The muscle will show comparatively little atrophy (i.e. wastage or enfeeblement). In the case of a physical paralysis, however, there is always some definite atrophy of the muscles and some of the principal nerves will be incapable of functioning because either they or the related areas of the brain or spinal column are damaged.

The person suffering from a hysterical paralysis must not be thought of as shamming or malingering. He actually cannot will the movement of his arm; he firmly believes that he cannot move it. The cause of his paralysis is entirely psychological. He has an unconscious motive for believing that his arm is paralyzed. As long as he so believes he will be genuinely incapable of moving it. We have cited paralysis as a simple and common example of hysterical illness, but the same explanation applies to all the other types of symptoms. Fortunately, a sufferer from hysteria usually has only one type of ailment at a time, or at most one or two symptoms. It is necessary to stress that a person with a hysterical symptom is *not* insane or even suffering from mental illness. He has a psychological disorder, it is true, but this is not what we can call a mental illness. A hysterical person can have a powerful intellect, be practically competent, and highly altruistic. His predicament deserves our sympathy. Though unconsciously he may have a motive for his apparent disability, consciously he is miserable and depressed concerning it and sincerely desires to be cured.

Since a hysterical symptom is psychologically caused it can be cured only by psychological means. This is true even when, as is sometimes done, a cure is effected by what appears to be a physical method, such as the application of a mild electric shock to the paralyzed arm or drooping eyelid. Here it seems that it is not the physical sensation but the associated psychological "shock" or impact that does the trick. A Canadian example suggests also that a physical ordeal may similarly be effective. One of the seventeenth-century Jesuit missionaries told of a Huron woman who suffered from attacks of dizziness and nervous spasms. We cannot say for certain that these symptoms were of hysterical or psychosomatic origin, but they could well have been. The assumption that they were of psychological origin tends to be confirmed by the fact that she cured herself by voluntarily submitting to a fire-walking ordeal. At her request, the town crier of her village proclaimed a feast. Three hundred ceremonial fires were lighted. Supported by two men the woman passed barefoot through the middle of each fire. She is said to have received little harm from the flames and afterward to have found herself cured of her symptoms. We do not know if the cure was permanent. Relapses are common with hysterical complaints. Sometimes the relapse takes the form of symptom substitution; the original condition does not recur but is replaced by a different symptom, e.g. a paralyzed hand may be replaced by a stiff knee joint. The Huron woman's healing has many of the features attendant on sudden cures of hysterical symptoms—strong conscious desire for cure, a period of elaborate preparation, and spectacular ceremonial.

It may be remarked in passing that the Canadian Indians in the early 1600s were much more aware than their European contemporaries of the fact that some diseases are psychological in origin. The Indians of Acadia (Nova Scotia) believed that one of the chief sources of disease was the presence of unsatisfied desires not consciously known to the patient. In this they went further than modern physicians would, who are well aware of the seriousness of confusing physically caused ailments with those of psychological origin, because the two types of disorder require entirely different kinds of treatment. The earlier Acadians, however, had the courage of their convictions; they called in shamans to determine by psychic means just what unacted desires were troubling the patients. The Jesuit missionaries do not record what treatments the Acadians applied in the light of the diagnosis. But their colleagues in Ontario reported an interesting facet of Huron medicine. When the normal remedies (poultices, emetics, potions, etc.) failed, the medicine men declared that the illness proceeded from the desires that troubled the soul. The healing of the patient then became the prime concern of the entire village. The villagers set themselves so far as they could to satisfy every reasonable or unreasonable need or craving that the sufferer might have. A festival was then declared with feasting, games and dancing, and much giving of gifts so that the patient at the end sometimes became quite wealthy. Often the original diagnosis proved incorrect and the patient declined and died. However, cures resulted frequently enough for the treatment to maintain its reputation for effectiveness. Indeed, this is what we should expect in view of the well-known tendency of patients to recover anyway. Also, the treatment was well adapted to give the patient a psychological boost; it made him the object of concern and sympathy; it relieved some of the pressures resulting from material wants and it was sufficiently dramatic and impressive to encourage spontaneous cure of hysterical and psychosomatic illnesses.

Psychosomatic and hysterical disorders provide the most dramatic and striking illustrations of the faith healer's art, because when it occurs, recovery is immediate and almost complete. It is very hard to resist the conclusion that most of the successes of faith healing are due to the operation of normal psychological processes. This is not to deny the value of faith healing. Provided that the patient takes the precaution of having his condition regularly checked by ordinary medical means, it is unlikely that he will be harmed by faith healing, and a definite chance that he will benefit by it. To be efficacious, faith does not have to be faith in God, or even in a person; it can be a faith in the "Odic force," in magnets or metallic plates, in a diet, in herbs, in flower essences, or whatever happens to strike the imagination of the patient. This is useful insofar as it results in cures which otherwise might not take place. However, it is scientifically unfortunate because it makes it difficult for any "real" physical effects these remedies may have to be distinguished from the workings of the all-pervasive power of faith.

Currently, it is acupuncture that presents this problem in a particularly obvious form. Acupuncture is intriguing to the psychical researcher because the acupuncture points, though lined up on the "meridians," do not appear to be located on any of the nerves of the body or be in any relation to the nervous system. If the acupuncture needles actually penetrated the nerves the successes of acupuncture would be easier for Western-trained physicians to understand, because we could suppose that by modifying the action of important nerves the needles succeed in altering various bodily processes. That acupuncture has successes cannot be denied; consequently an intriguing speculation has been put forward. It is suggested that the acupuncture points and meridians correspond to a definite structure in a nonphysical body—perhaps the astral body—a concept we have mentioned previously.

Be that as it may, acupuncture has certainly arrived in Canada and is here to stay. Acupuncturists are consulted not only by the Chinese Canadian residents of our great cities, such as Toronto and Vancouver, but increasingly by others whose ailments prove resistant to Western medical treatments. We would expect therefore that the conditions treated will include a goodly proportion of the kind already mentioned, chronic but nonlethal complaints. Consequently, just like any other system of treatment, acupuncture will have successes in this field, occasional complete recoveries and frequent alleviations of distress without radical cure. Very few formal studies of the cure rate in relation to type of ailment have yet been done. A small number of lay studies have been published in popular journals and, in the writer's opinion, tend to bear out what has just been said. Consequently, I feel that the essential qualities of acupuncture as a medical system will, for a long time to come, be obscured and overlaid by what are in effect faith cures.

At a recent conference on acupuncture an eminent acupuncturist from Hong Kong showed pictures of patients undergoing treatment. He himself had selected the cases to illustrate acupuncture in action. I was intrigued to find that they comprised two paralyses, one tic (i.e. uncontrollable twitching of the eye), a case of compulsively drooping eyelids, and one of persistent facial aching. If this had been a list of ailments deliberately selected to illustrate faith healing, it could not have been more representative.

In making these remarks about acupuncture I do not intend to dismiss it as only faith healing, but merely to point out that the ultimate truth concerning it is to be found only at the bottom of a particularly deep well. The proverb that truth lies at the bottom of a well is borne out by a discovery of first-rate importance which stemmed from the work done in Canada by Dr. Bernard Grad, a professor in the department of psychiatry of McGill University, Montreal. Dr. Grad is a biologist and biochemist. An expert on the biology of human aging, he has published more than fifty scientific papers on endocrinology (hormones), gerontology (the health of aged persons), oncology (the study of tumors), and general biology. Dr. Grad's work related to a form of healing which does not seem quite to fit into the ordinary pattern of faith healing. From time immemorial there have been a few people who relieve symptoms by the laying on of hands or "stroking." Quite often the "strokers" use little or no prayer or ceremony and perform their healing operation in private rather than in the setting of a prayer meeting. Some strokers actually place a hand on the ailing joint or limb; others merely pass their hands through the air near to the distressed organ. Patients often report that they feel a sense of internal warmth or an electric or prickling sensation. This type of healing is often called "magnetic healing" to distinguish it from the more ceremonial forms of faith healing. There is, of course, no evidence that the stroker produces a magnetic or electrical field. The term "magnetic" is used purely historically. Anton Mesmer at the end of the eighteenth century used to pass his hands over patients. He believed that this redirected their "animal magnetism"—a universal force which filled the cosmos and was important in the functioning of the human body. Strokers are recorded long before Mesmer's time.

Dr. Grad's interest was aroused when he met Oskar Estebany, a Canadian resident who in his younger days had been a colonel in a Hungarian cavalry regiment. When he was a cadet his brother officers noticed that his horse generally enjoyed better health than theirs, and when their horses were ailing he was often asked to stroke them. This seemed to accelerate the animals' recovery. Later in life, Estebany gained something of a reputation for healing by laying on of hands. Dr. Grad carried out a series of experiments to test Estebany's ability in as scientific a way as possible. (Accounts of his investigations are given in Dr. Grad's own papers and in the books by Allen Spraggett and Professor Mann.)

In one experiment small areas of skin were removed from the backs of mice. The mice were separated into groups which lived in separate cages. Each group was maintained as far as possible under identical conditions—food, water, temperature, humidity, etc. One group was untreated. The mice of another group were placed once a day in small cages which Estebany held in his hands for twenty minutes. Another group was treated similarly by people with no pretensions of being healers or strokers. Dr. Grad found that the rate of healing, as judged by size of wound, was fastest with Estebany by an amount which, though small, was statistically significant. In a similar experiment mice were used which had been reared on a diet deficient in iodine but supplemented by a special chemical. As a result the activity of their thyroid glands was below normal and they had developed goiters. Dr. Grad found that the mice treated by Estebany showed a retardation in the rate of growth in their goiters. Lest the effect should be due to the warmth received from Estebany's hands, Dr. Grad had two "control" groups of mice, one of which was maintained at room temperature. The other was exposed each day during the time that Estebany was treating his mice to a temperature equal to that of his hands.

In order to rule out the heat factor decisively, Dr. Grad varied the experiment in an interesting way. Instead of the mice being treated directly the healer held handfuls of wool and cotton cuttings. These were then put into the cages of the experimental mice, while untreated cuttings were put into the cages of control groups. Those mice that nested in the treated cuttings showed less thyroid growth than those who nested in the untreated ones. This strange result suggested to Dr. Grad that he try another experiment, this time with plants instead of mice. Barley seeds were planted in two sets, A and B, in peat pots. Each seed or seedling was watered daily with a standard amount of saline solution consisting of water with one percent of salt (sodium chloride). Although saline is adequate to irrigate plants it is not so good for growth as ordinary water. Dr. Grad wished to discover whether or not if Estebany "treated" the saline applied to group A, these plants would thrive better than those of group B, which were given untreated saline.

For such experiments to be scientifically valid neither the subject (i.e. Estebany) nor the experimenters (Dr. Grad and his assistants) must know just which saline is being applied to just which plants. This required the use of what is called a "double-blind" procedure, of the kind followed in all reputable medical or biological trials. It was achieved by an elaborate system of coding and recoding of both plants and the phials of saline. The treatment was applied by Estebany holding a phial of saline in his hands for a specified time prior to its being used to water the barley. Estebany did not know which seedling it would go to. Similarly, the assistants who did the watering did not know whether the phial was treated or untreated. The final result of the double-blind experiments was surprising. When the records were decoded and the plants of group A (treated saline) identified, it was found that on the thirteenth day of the experiment their mean height was 46 millimeters as compared with 36 millimeters for the plants of group B. The difference was statistically significant.

How this effect was produced remained quite mysterious. However, this research had a fascinating sequel. Dr. Grad's results came to the attention of a professor at Rosary Hill College, Buffalo,

New York. This scientist is Dr. Justa M. Smith, O.S.F., a Sister of the Franciscan Order, and a highly qualified biochemist who is the chairman of the biology and chemistry department of the college. Among the scientific fields in which she is especially expert is that of enzymology—the study of enzymes. Enzymes are special substances produced in the human body, which contains hundreds of them. They are catalysts; i.e. they are not of significance in themselves—they are not the actual constituents of bone, brain, blood, or other anatomical components of the body—but their presence is essential to life because they facilitate all the processes that occur in the living being. Without enzymes we could not utilize the oxygen we breathe, digest the food we eat, use our muscles, or even think. These enzymes are (in the most literal sense) of vital importance, and a very large proportion of diseases are caused by certain enzymes being present in the body in insufficient amounts. Dr. Smith thought it likely, therefore, that the "magnetic healer" produces his effects by increasing the activity of enzymes in the patient's body. She decided to test this assumption with Estebany. Interestingly enough, though "magnetic healer" is only an imprecise term deriving historically from Mesmer's ideas about magnetism, it happens that Sister Justa Smith is an authority on the effect of actual magnetic fields on enzymes. In fact she is the leading authority because it was her own doctoral research that first proved that strong magnetic fields have the effect of increasing the chemical efficiency of enzymes.

The experiment was performed under the auspices of the Human Dimensions Institute, which obtained financial grants to pay the skilled additional staff required from the Parapsychology Foundation of New York and the Shanti Foundation. The enzyme chosen was trypsin, the enzyme that helps us digest our roast beef and other items of proteinaceous diet. In each repetition of the experiment a solution of trypsin was divided into four equal amounts. Each was placed in a stoppered tube. One specimen was kept as an untreated control; another was damaged by an exposure to ultraviolet light sufficient to reduce its activity by about a quarter;

the third specimen was exposed to a very strong magnetic field; and the fourth was treated by Estebany. The treatment consisted of his holding the tube in his two hands for seventy-five minutes. To follow the course of any change that was happening in the enzymes as the result of proximity to his hands, a portion of it was taken out every fifteen minutes and its activity measured by giving it something to digest—presumably the laboratory equivalent of court bouillon.

The completed series of experiments brilliantly vindicated both Dr. Grad's earlier discovery of Estebany's talent and Dr. Justa Smith's enzyme theory. The activity of the specimens damaged by ultraviolet radiation was diminished by the amount expected, while that of the enzymes exposed to the magnetic field was boosted by the factor predicted by Dr. Smith's earlier findings. However, relative to the control, the activity of the enzymes treated by Estebany was increased to about the same degree as were the specimens put in the magnetic field.

This is a very remarkable result. The experiment was carried out with the most sophisticated biochemical and biophysical equipment. Unlike the studies of living patients, there is no problem of interpretation because there is no possible confusion of physical and psychological effects. Consequently, there is no adequate reason for doubting the scientific validity either of the experiment or of the conclusion to be drawn from it, namely that some healers transmit a force from their bodies that has a real physical effect on biochemical substances. This is the first time that such an effect has been demonstrated and it is a breakthrough of outstanding importance. Although the effect parallels that of a strong magnetic field, it does not seem that healers actually are magnetic; they do not affect compasses or magnetometers. All we can say is that some influence is propagated; it is a physical influence insofar as it produces physical effects; whether it can properly be described as physical itself is another matter. Whether it can, or should be, regarded as a psychic force or whether it bears any close relation to psychic manifestations is still an open question.

10

PYRAMIDS, ORGONE, AND COSMIC FORCES

In an earlier chapter we mentioned Mesmer's theory that a force called animal magnetism resided in the human body. Mesmer also believed that this force was a power possessed by all things in nature—animals, trees, and even rocks. This power could act at a distance. Also it was like a fluid; it could be transferred from one object to another, so that some objects could be "charged up" with it. The distribution of animal magnetism in the human body could be altered by actual magnets, or by making Mesmeric passes with the hands, or by stroking. This was the basis of Mesmer's system of healing—or so he thought: a shortage or maldistribution of animal magnetism in the body produced illness. In the twentieth century very similar ideas were put forward by Wilhelm Reich, who was born in Galicia, Austro-Hungary, in 1897, the son of a farmer. Demobilized from the Austrian army after the First World War, he studied in Vienna, received his medical degree, and entered psychoanalysis, where he made himself a reputation. His views were somewhat unorthodox and in 1934 he was expelled from the International Psychoanalytic Association. In 1938 after a spell in Norway he settled in the United States.

The rest of Reich's life was devoted to experiments on "orgone." According to Reich, orgone was a universal energy active everywhere, including the bodies of plants, animals, and humans. Being a vital energy it was fundamentally beneficial to health, but in certain forms and concentrations it could (like electricity) be harmful or dangerous. Reich's experiments, few of which are as clear-cut and decisive as a scientist would have wished, were, like his writings on orgone and other topics, almost innumerable. He made little headway with the scientific community and in his last years was forced, or drifted into, an extreme and isolated position. Falling foul of the U. S. Food and Drug Administration for selling devices called "orgone accumulators," in 1954 Reich received a court injunction forbidding the shipment of these pieces of equipment across state boundaries. The order was particularly hard as it also proscribed interstate transport of all his writings. After an involved legal battle Reich was sentenced to imprisonment for disobeying the injunction and died in 1957 after nine months in jail.

Wilhelm Reich's researches were so extensive and varied and so cross-connected with other fields of frontier research that it is not easy to form a unified picture of his ideas or to perceive all their ramifications. We have, therefore, reason to be indebted to a recent work of Canadian scholarship—*Orgone, Reich and Eros, Wilhelm Reich's Theory of Life Energy,* written by Dr. Edward Mann, professor of sociology at York University, Toronto. Professor Mann has collected together and presented with great clarity a vast mass of material with a very thorough set of references. He includes not only a presentation of Reich's theories and investigations but also all results from other fields of modern research which in any way parallel Reich's own findings or might be related to them. Dr. Mann deals with the orgone theory in all its ramifications and also with all previous theories of a universal life energy. He reports modern work on electrical force fields associated with living beings. Most relevant to the interests of psychical research workers are his accounts of theories of the human aura and of magnetic or spiritual healing and yoga concepts of health and life energy. Dr. Mann deals also with some very topical subjects—Russian theories of "bioplasmic energy," Kirlian photography, "pyramid power," and what appear to be effects of the sun and moon on living organisms.

Dr. Mann's personal researches into the effectiveness of Reich's "orgone accumulators," which he has pursued over several years, also deserve mention. Reich, as a result of his experiments, believed that if a layer of wool is put next to a layer of metal, the resulting structure has the ability to soak up orgone energy from its neighborhood. These orgone accumulators can be constructed in two forms—the orgone box, made of metal lined with wool, and the orgone blanket, which is a sort of eiderdown filled with a layer of ordinary wool and a layer of steel wool. According to Reich, an orgone blanket is helpful if put over an ailing patient for an hour or more, or over a painful limb; its accumulated orgone energy will be communicated beneficially to the patient. Dr. Mann in his investigations was well aware of the sources of error likely in experimenting with orgone blankets, namely psychological factors of the kind discussed in the chapter on healing, and the effect of warmth. Thus in his experiments he used control blankets lined with wool and newspaper as well as orgone blankets designed to specification with wool and steel wool. Professor Mann, as a true scientist, albeit an exceptionally well-educated and open-minded one, expresses his conclusions rather conservatively. He feels that his results suggest there is a case for supposing that orgone blankets have biological effects of a beneficial kind. However, he says rather cautiously, "After seventeen years of continually using the orgone blanket, I believe my observations have some value, but what is needed now is rigorous scientific checks using relevant instruments. Hopefully, qualified persons will soon come forward to undertake these."

Everyone who wishes to follow up an idea is not as prudent as Professor Mann. Recent years have seen the rise of an enthusiasm for "pyramid power." Journals are devoted to the occult powers of pyramids; prefabricated miniature hollow cardboard pyramids flood the North American market via mail-order sales or occult bookshops. Pyramid enthusiasts maintain that these model pyramids will resharpen one's used razor blades and also preserve portions of animal or vegetable food by a process of mummification. The origins of the pyramid craze are wrapped in obscurity. We can only guess how it came about. One clue is provided by the correspondence over the signature of "Colonel Musselwhite" which appeared regularly in the *Times* of London, England, in the years before World War II. It is now known, via the *Sunday Times* of London, that these letters on various scientific subjects were all hoaxes, written by Dr. Reginald V. Jones, now a Fellow of the Royal Society and professor of physics at the University of Aberdeen, Scotland. One of the Musselwhite letters advised that the performance of a razor blade could be improved if between shaves it were kept on a north-south axis so as to pick up the earth's magnetic field.

Otherwise, the "pyramid hypothesis" is supposed to have been originated by a Monsieur Bovis. Whether Bovis is an entirely legendary character or a real person is uncertain. However, it is said that when visiting the Great Pyramid at Giza in Egypt some years back, Bovis noticed that in the king's chamber were trash cans containing the bodies of cats and other small animals that had wandered into the pyramid and died because they could not find their way out. Bovis was struck by the fact that the corpses were mummified. He assumed that they had been preserved by the action of some force and that this force arose because of the shape of the pyramid. Bovis's theory was that the architects of the pyramids had chosen a shape which they knew would focus some kind of cosmic energy on a point one-third of the way up the pyramid. This energy, thought Bovis, would preserve organic matter from decay. It is said that Bovis made a hollow scale model of the Great Pyramid and successfully mummified a defunct cat by keeping it on a platform a third of the way up from the base.

This was the story as told to Sheila Ostrander and Lynn Schroeder when visting Czechoslovakia in 1968. Their principal informant appears to have been an engineer, Karel Drbal, who as early as 1959 obtained a patent from the Czech patent office for his pyramid razor-blade sharpener. Since 1970, when Ostrander and Schroeder's book appeared, pyramid enthusiasm has become rife in North America. The instructions given for constructing model hollow pyramids allow of any material being used, e.g., cardboard, sheet metal, or plastic. They insist that the dimensions should be strictly proportioned. They seem to be working from a specification laid down by Drbal which requires that the length of any one of the four sides of the square base of the pyramid shall be 1. 57080 of the vertical height. As I have shown in my article in *New Horizons,* these proportions do correspond to those of the Great Pyramid itself within the limits of error which apparently its builders (in 2600 B.C.) allowed themselves. This fact itself is very interesting. Twice the ratio mentioned, namely 1.57080, happens to be 3.14160, which is a very good approximation to the number pi, which, as every schoolboy knows, is the ratio of the circumference of a circle to its diameter. Whether the pyramid builders got their result by luck or by reasoning we do not know.

As our motto, like that of the Royal Society, is "Nullus in verbum," which freely translated means "Take nobody's word for it," we thought we would find out for ourselves what model pyramids did to food or to razor blades. The Toronto Society for Psychical Research organized a research team consisting of Allan Alter (B.Sc.Phm), Dale Simmons (Dip. Engr. Tech), L. A. Henwood, and Karen Perry, who built cardboard pyramids made to specification and acquired a commercially produced one of the same size. To test the alleged dehydration of food several test materials were used: hamburger, potato, bean sprouts, banana, apple, liver, and bone marrow. In all cases the test material was supported on a rigid platform of thin cardboard and placed with its center below the apex of the pyramid, which was oriented to the true north. Bean sprouts were laid in a small bunch, randomly oriented on the platform. Specimens of other material were used in slices, one-quarter of an inch thick and laid horizontally on the platform. Whenever the specimen was other than circular (as it was with bananas), the major axis was aligned to true north. The experiments were first done with the top of the platform at the one-third level in the pyramid, i.e. one-third of the height of the pyramid above the base. They were then repeated with the specimens at various other levels, one-half, three-quarters, etc., and also with the specimens in the bottom right-hand corner. Specimens were inspected at forty-eight-hour intervals over a period of two weeks. In each experiment a specimen of test material as similar as possible in composition, dimensions, and age to that in the pyramid was placed in each of various-shaped cardboard containers, of volume equal to the pyramid, in the forms of rectangular parallelepipeds, cubes, triangular prisms, and cones. This use of control groups seems to have been omitted in testing done by other groups.

In all tests the members of the research team, who performed their experiments independently in their various homes and offices while following the same agreed-upon procedures, were unable to discover any significant differences between material placed in a pyramid and material placed in the control containers. If anything, they had only rediscovered the "Cookie Jar Principle," that is, any substance placed in a container which keeps out air currents does not spoil as quickly as in the open air.

Specifically, they learned that hamburger and steak were bad test materials. A butcher explained that most commercial hamburger has preservatives added to it to prevent rotting, and good steak meat can be left at room temperature on a kitchen table for one week and still be good enough to eat.

Potatoes at first appeared to show less deterioration under a pyramid than in the other containers, but when the test was repeated with more care no difference could be noted. The explanation appeared to be that one slice of potato was somewhat thicker than the others. When care was taken to make all slices of equal quarter-inch thickness, there were no detectable differences. Results with apples and bean sprouts were also identical as between pyramids and other containers. Notably, bean sprouts are the easiest material to work with, as they dry out within twelve hours. Banana slices were no better preserved under pyramids than in the control containers.

In the cases of liver and bone marrow the control and pyramid specimens were tested twice: oriented to the magnetic north pole and then oriented to the true north. In every case the results were basically the same: the liver was hard and shiny with only slight odor; the marrow had no odor or change of color in either sample.

As a separate experiment potato slices were tested at different phases of the moon. Again no difference could be detected. (This experiment was conducted by D. Kimber.)

Our team concluded that although, for all that is known to the contrary, there may be a mysterious force within the Great Pyramid itself, there is no evidence in favor of the statement made by supporters of the pyramid theory that anyone can produce the effect in his own home.

Dale Simmons tackled the problem of the alleged sharpening of used razor blades by a very direct method. With the aid of a metallurgical microscope with an attached Polaroid camera he photographed the edges of blunted razor blades before and after they had spent time in the model pyramids. The resulting photographs made it obvious that the effect of sitting under a pyramid for even as much as a week was negligible. If there was any rounding off of the jagged protuberance it was no more than that which occurred with a control blade sitting in the open. However, it should be stressed that it was very difficult to see any change in a blade whether it had rested inside or outside a pyramid. Simmons carried out all the instructions laid down by pyramid suppliers very precisely and to the letter. He oriented his pyramids to the magnetic north. He did not think it worth repeating the experiments with orientation to the true north because in the dehydration experiments this had given no result. We may note that in pyramid literature there seems to be some confusion between geographical and magnetic north; some say one and some say the other.

11

WATER DIVINING, DOWSING, AND RADIESTHESIA

"Dowsing"—also called "water divining" or "well witching"—is a mysterious art, scoffed at by some but fully believed in by many practical-minded persons. The practice of dowsing certainly goes back to very ancient times; a Chinese engraving of A.D. 147 shows the Emperor Yu holding a forked divining rod. In both of the founder nations of Canada the tradition was strong. Even today in the drier parts of England such as East Anglia, it is common practice to call in a "water diviner" to find a good place to drill if one wants to sink a well. In Old France for centuries the village abbés and curés had paced their parishioners' fields with rods and pendulums divining for water. The practice of well witching must have been widespread in Canada. E. L. Marsh, the historian of Grey County, Ontario, says that in those parts the assistance of a dowser was regarded as the surest way of finding water. "The accuracy of the divining rod in finding water was proved over and over again. Indeed it was an indispensable method before the days of boring down through the earth and rock. Carrying a forked branch of witch hazel or willow grasped firmly in the hands and pointing downward, the water witch or wizard walked slowly over the ground. If water were present, the point of the stick would turn down toward the ground in spite of all efforts to hold it firmly. Early wells in the county discovered in this way produced a never-failing water supply."

The method of divining which Marsh describes is the one traditional also in the English countryside. The dowser cuts a forked twig freshly from a hazel or willow tree. Methods of holding it vary. The most usual one is for the dowser to pull the two ends apart so that the twig is in a V shape. He clasps the ends in his hands so that the twig, or "rod" as it is called, is horizontal. The ends which he is holding are then nearly at right angles to the direction (straight ahead of the dowser) that the V is pointing. Thus the two branches of the twig are both very much under tension and the twig is therefore rather unstable. The theory of dowsing is that when he is over water the dowser receives a kind of "signal" from it. Usually he is not consciously aware of this signal but in some mysterious fashion it is transmitted through his nervous system into the muscles of his arm and wrists. As a result his wrists make a slight involuntary movement. This is enough to upset the delicate balance of the highly stressed rod, which suddenly "flips" either downward or upward.

The method described is the most common way of holding the forked rod. However, some very famous dowsers such as Henry Gross have held it in quite a different way, with the V pointing downward and the two branches only slightly stressed. The dowsing reaction then takes the form of the rod moving bodily downward as if being operated on by a vertical force directed earthward.

Whether or not dowsing can be said actually to "work," the theory of dowsing is very interesting. As we have mentioned, it is assumed that the water transmits some kind of signal to the dowser, who usually is not consciously aware of it. The signal in some mysterious way induces a muscular reaction. The stressed rod, on this theory, merely plays the role of a sensitive indicator, a detector of slight muscular reflexes. On this theory it should not matter greatly whether or not the divining rod is made of fresh-cut hazel, and in fact many modern dowsers use rods of polythene. It will be seen that the reception of an unconsciously perceived signal that is translated into a muscular reflex is closely parallel to the idea put forward in an earlier chapter of this book with reference to psychic impressions. Psychic impressions, it would seem, are sometimes received unconsciously and fail to register in the mind as a consciously perceived message, but instead force themselves into consciousness in a disguised form, e.g. as a smell or as a "feeling."

Dowsers, in fact, differ amiably among themselves as to how dowsing works. Some believe that there is a physical field emitted by water, especially running water, and that it is this field or radiation to which the dowser is sensitive. Many students of dowsing have believed that the field in question is related to magnetism (i.e. magnetism of the ordinary, everyday kind, not "animal magnetism"). Interestingly, some dowsers claim to be sensitive to the earth's magnetism and to be able to map out the earth's magnetic field. Others believe that there is a radiation field given out by water and that dowsers are sensitive to it, but that it is not electricity or magnetism—some writers call it the "radiesthetic field." Other dowsers do not believe that there is any field, magnetic or radiesthetic, and say flatly that dowsing is a psychic ability, in fact one closely resembling clairvoyance. This theory gains support from the fact that dowsing operations can be carried out in a number of different ways. Some of these methods are very hard to explain by any physical theory involving radiation.

The form of dowsing described by Marsh, in which the dowser walks over the terrain and expects his rod to flip only when he happens to be standing above subterranean water, is called "field dowsing." Another method is called "directional dowsing." Instead of marching to and fro over the terrain, the dowser stands anywhere he likes and then turns himself slowly about. When the rod flips he will say, "There's water in that direction." He will then repeat the experiment standing at another point. This will give him two bearings and where the lines meet is (he hopes) the place beneath which water lies. The method closely resembles radio or radar direction finding, and if it is true that the method is successful, then it is conceivable that it can be explained by radiation.

When the dowser finds a spot over subterranean water his work is not yet finished because if it lies too deep it may be too costly to drill a well. Some dowsers say that they go through the following procedure. The dowser will ask, "Is the water below 200 feet?" If he gets a response from his rod, he then asks if it is below 300 feet. If he gets no response, he will ask if it is above 250 feet, and so on, varying his questions according to the responses until the depth of the water has been estimated within narrow limits. Some dowsers say that they can successfully apply this method of question and response to location of water without having to go to the actual site at all! They speak of the method as "information dowsing." Some practitioners of information dowsing claim that they can apply it to a variety of problems unconnected with well witching, e.g. finding lost objects or missing persons. These dowsers usually favor the theory that dowsing is a psychic ability related to clairvoyance.

Information dowsing is often carried out in conjunction with a map. By subdividing the area and asking appropriate questions the dowser will hope to pinpoint the location of the object that is being looked for. In "map dowsing" proper the dowser usually works over the map much in the way that the field dowser walks over the actual terrain. Sometimes, like the late John Shelley, Jr., who was president of the American Society of Dowsers, he will use a miniature polythene forked rod, but more usually a pendulum will be employed as "indicator." In fact, many dowsers use the pendulum in the field instead of a rod. Any kind of pendulum may be pressed into service, e.g. keys on a keychain. The pendulum is set into motion in the way that the operator prefers, usually so that the bob goes around in a circle, the chain being held in the fingers a few inches above the bob. Even if one is trying to hold the pendulum still it is rather uncanny how quickly it will get into motion, as anyone can verify who experiments with one. This is presumably due to the fingers involuntarily making tiny movements that their owner is hardly aware of. With the pendulum the dowsing reaction takes the form of a change in the type of motion that the bob is making; e.g. the bob will cease going around in a circle and will move to and fro in a straight line like that of a clock pendulum. With some dowsers it is the other way about, the dowsing response changes the motion from to and fro into round and round.

Besides water, dowsing is, of course, applied to finding oil and metals. It is common practice for the dowser who is looking for minerals to hold a sample of it in one hand—e.g. a phial of oil or a piece of gold, nickel, etc. The specimen is called a "witness"—it is believed that the witness helps the dowser to "tune in" on the substance he is looking for.

Does dowsing actually work? Occasionally formal experiments are done by scientists. Thus, in 1970, technical units of the British Army and Ministry of Defence carried out a series of experiments on map dowsing as a means of locating mines and on field dowsing for finding underground water and also for locating an assortment of metal, plastic, and wooden blocks which had been specially buried for the purpose. The results, as reported by the chief scientist involved in the research, were entirely the same as those that chance alone would produce. I do not have available accounts of all the experiments done by scientists with dowsers and cannot say whether this result is typical or not. The claims of dowsers therefore have to be taken with some reservations. However, I do not feel that such experiments necessarily prove that there is nothing in dowsing. There is no Canadian Society of Dowsers so that Canadians interested in dowsing tend, insofar as they are organized, to join the American Society of Dowsers or to subscribe to the journal of the British Society of Dowsers (Secretary, P. B. Smithett, High Street, Eydon, Daventry, Northamptonshire). It is the background of this society that makes one feel that dowsing may, in fact, have a degree of validity and practical usefulness. It was founded by, and has a membership well laced with, retired British Army officers, most of them with military experience in the Middle East. In such arid zones the finding of water for troops or villagers, and in earlier times for the army horses, has constituted an important part of the less glamorous side of military leadership.

When one comes on a brief reference to dowsing in geology textbooks the comment is usually hostile, and the prospector is firmly advised to trust only to geologists to find water or minerals. However, I have read a book on water engineering which remarks that, however good a geologist may be, the subterranean structure of the rocks cannot always be reliably deduced from what is seen on the surface and that the modest fees of a dowser will be money well spent if one really wants to find water. All geologists are not hostile to dowsing. I am informed that one of the foremost North American oil geologists never drilled a well without having the actual well site chosen by a dowser whose abilities he highly respected; he said that this dowser's ability to locate oil was almost 100 percent correct though he tended to underestimate the depth —a pardonable fault!

Dr. Grad, whom we mentioned earlier, did some interesting (unpublished) experiments with Romauld Morin of Ville St. Laurent, Quebec. For about thirty years Morin had been a spare-time dowser with experience in many Canadian oilfields and mineral-bearing regions; he had also had a number of psychic experiences—a combination of skills rather tending to support the view that successful dowsing is a variety of clairvoyance. In a series of experiments Morin was shown a number of paper bags, each of which contained a laboratory mouse. Some mice were healthy but others had leukemia. Without handling the bags Morin used divining rod and pendulum to ascertain which animals were well and which were sick. The double-blind method was used: neither the assistant who placed the mice in the bags nor the experimenter who brought them to Morin knew which bags contained the leukemic mice. A parallel series of experiments was carried out by Dr. Howard Eisenberg. In toto Morin had a remarkable degree of success in picking out the leukemic mice. The odds against his being right so often by chance were quite high, more than 2,000 to 1. It would seem that sometimes dowsing methods do actually work in the laboratory situation as well as in the field.

Dr. Grad told me that Morin made the determination in each case using dowsing rod, metal pendulum, and wood pendulum. These did not always agree so Morin would go either by the majority vote of the three instruments or by how he "felt about it." I have been told by some dowsers that, as a rule, irrespective of the dowsing response they form a conscious impression of the presence of the water or whatever they are looking for.

The pendulum, incidentally, is used by many people who are quite unaware of its connection with dowsing, but who use it to answer questions—i.e. they are doing information dowsing without knowing it. A popular question put to the pendulum is about the sex of an unborn infant. It would not be wise, however, to substitute the pendulum for a pregnancy test or to expect it to replace orthodox medical diagnosis.

Information dowsing would appear to be part of the large field of study called radiesthesia (or sometimes radionics) which has many adherents and a number of practitioners, some of whom are better than others. It is my own impression, for what it is worth, that the better practitioners of radiesthesia are also psychics. The theory of radiesthesia is broadly similar to the radiation theory of dowsing. It maintains that every substance or object of knowledge has a characteristic radiation, and the radiesthetic operator, like a dowser, can unconsciously sense the presence of this radiation. This unconscious sensing triggers off a subtle physiological reflex in the body of the radiesthetic person. The simplest example of this is the "sticking reaction." The radiesthetic operator will have his fingers on a semi-smooth surface (wood, metal, plastic, or what you will). Suppose you ask him to determine what allergies you have. He may hold your hand or some specimen (e.g. hair, nail clippings, or a spot of blood) that you choose to supply him with. He will then go through a list of allergies, e.g. eggs, ragweed, cat fur, etc. At each "call" of a name, which may, of course, be made silently to himself, the radiesthetic operator passes his finger over his "stick-plate" (the surface mentioned above). If it goes smoothly over the stick-plate he takes it as indicating a "no" answer and passes on to the next name on the list. If he experiences some resistance or "stick" he treats it just as does a dowser when his twig or pendulum yields the dowsing reaction; he regards it as a "yes" answer.

In my opinion, for what it is worth, offered quite undogmatically and with complete willingness to be corrected if contrary evidence is forthcoming, radiesthesia of the very general kind described is unlikely to be explicable in terms of radiation theories but is

akin to pure clairvoyance, i.e. direct knowledge of facts unknown
to any embodied intelligence. More precisely, the effective radiesthetic operator is a psychic person who receives the psychic impression unconsciously. The psychic impression causes an alteration
in the dryness of the fingertips so that they tend to move less
smoothly on the stick-plate. The change in surface moisture of the
skin could doubtless be shown by measurement of skin resistance.
One very talented woman we know, who is highly qualified in
medical technology, studied radiesthesia in her spare time and found
she had the radiesthetic ability. She is also a psychic person and
her own view is that radiesthesia is just a special manifestation of
extrasensory perception, and the indicator, whether pendulum, rod,
or radiesthetic instrument, functions only as an aid or as she says,
"a crutch to lean on."

In radiesthesia proper (as opposed to mere dowsing) the rod,
pendulum, or simple stick-plate is often replaced by a machine of
complicated appearance with many dials. Except for the dials, which
can be set to numerical values, the machine has no moving parts.
It contains electric wiring but offers no battery or power supply.
As a machine it is not unfair to say that it is a "nonsense machine"
—an expression that is likely to puzzle the average person. In
England there was a famous libel action brought by Mr. Delawarr,
who marketed such instruments, against someone who had publicly
denounced one of his machines as a swindle. The action was successful; the court found Mr. Delawarr had made no misleading
statements and that there was no reason to impugn his good faith;
substantial damages were awarded him. The typical Delawarr
machine has a stick-plate and dials and a little metal-lined bowl in
which is placed a specimen as witness. If the information dowsing
which is to be done concerns a person he can put his finger in the
bowl; more usually the person is absent and a piece of his hair,
or a blood spot on filter paper, is used. Suppose, for example, the
questioning aims at discovering whether the person is suffering from
a vitamin deficiency. The radiesthetic operator will work through
a list provided by the makers of the instrument. I have a typical

list in front of me. It starts A_1, 2344; A_2, 2404; B_1, 2455. To ask the question whether vitamin A_1 is deficient the operator sets the dials to 2344 and rubs the stick-plate. If he gets the sticking response, he will conclude that there is a possibility of A_1 deficiency. If not, then he works his way through the list.

The significance of the dial settings is hard to understand. According to the radiation theory of radiesthesia, this is the figure which tunes the machine into the substance, e.g. vitamin A_1, which is under discussion. But since what is being looked for is not the A_1 itself but a deficiency of it, then obviously the situation is quite different from that in the radiation theory of dowsing. The whole matter is so highly abstract that if it is a fact that radiesthetic machines do work, then one is forced to conclude that they function merely by helping the operator to use his ESP. We did an experiment with a radiesthetic operator and a Delawarr machine. The operator was given three blood spots from persons under medical treatment and a list of ten ailments from which they might be suffering. The actual state of the patients was, of course, known to their physician, Dr. A., but to no one else. The specimens were merely numbered and otherwise totally anonymous. The purpose of the experiment was purely theoretical, to see if radiesthesia worked and *not* for diagnosis. In any case the patients had already been correctly diagnosed. In the event our operator correctly gave the ailments the three patients had. The odds against this being a pure fluke or stroke of luck are 720 to one, which certainly suggests that radiesthesia can work, sometimes at least. Our operator was, however, less successful with two sets of ten blood spots supplied by Dr. B. and Dr. C. In this part of the experiment no ailment was correctly assigned to a patient. This, of course, does not disprove radiesthesia. It might be relevant that the operator had met and liked Dr. A., but had not met Dr. B., and had met and disliked Dr. C. Possibly an element of psychological rapport with the physician is helpful in establishing an adequate "psychic channel" for the flow of information.

Returning to the apparently simpler problem of dowsing, it is

interesting to note that it seems to be used extensively by public
utility companies for the purpose of finding buried cables, telephone lines, water pipes, and natural gas conduits. Utility workers
are concerned not only to locate their own cables, but to avoid
damaging other people's. A few years ago at my house in England
a team from the natural gas company arrived to replace the existing
main pipe to the house with a larger one which would take natural
gas, which was just being introduced. The line lay under the front
garden and as is often the case there were no accurate plans
available. The foreman was unperturbed. "It's all right," he said.
"Young Fred will find it." We were intrigued and watched young
Fred's operations with interest. He used a simple dowsing equipment appropriate to an engineering environment. He had two
L-shaped rods of the kind that are easily made by bending pieces
of mild steel. He held the shorter part of each L vertically in each
of his two hands so that the longer section of each rod was horizontal and pointing directly in front of him. Fred then walked
slowly and calmly across the grass with an abstracted expression on
his face. Suddenly both rods swung outward. Fred stopped. "Here
it is," he said. And it was, as an experimental dig verified a quarter
of an hour later.

In dowsing parlance the L-shaped rods used by Fred are usually
called "angle irons." Any metal will do—copper, steel, aluminum.
Usually the short vertical section is kept in a sleeve of metal or
plastic, and it is this sleeve that is held by the dowser. The theory
is that the dowsing reaction consists of a slight involuntary turning
down of the hands. As a result the rods swing outward under the
influence of gravity. I am told that with about 10 percent of dowsers
the rods swing inward so as to cross one another. In 1971 it was
revealed that employees of Ontario Hydro often use angle irons to
locate buried cables or even the precise position of faults in cables
(Hopkins). Two noted practitioners are Leonard Bradowich, a field
technician now at the Bruce plant, and Aubrey Leask, an area foreman in Orillia. The Scarborough Public Utilities Commission has
Vic Clague, a line-construction superintendent. About ten years

ago he took up the practice using bent welding rods to find buried cable. Since then a piece of cable-detection equipment has come into service. This is the Time Domain Reflectometer, or TDR, which works somewhat like a radar set to find the location of a fault in a cable. Clague had not tried his hand at locating cable faults but, in an experiment done in collaboration with Craig Gartshore, who operated the TDR, he found that his angle irons would do this job also.

A little-known application of dowsing came to light only recently. A student, Mr. F., of the University of Toronto was employed as a gravedigger at Streetsville during the summer vacation of 1973. There an old gravedigger taught him to detect unmarked burial sites by use of angle irons. These were made from coathanger wire, the long arm of the L being about 22 inches long. The short arm of the L, about 5 inches in length, was inserted into the hole of a wooden spool that was long enough to serve as a handle. Mr. F. would hold one of these in each hand with the spool vertical and the long arm of the L extending horizontally in front of him. If he walked over a grave in a direction parallel to its short side, the rods would swing inward and cross; but if he proceeded to undisturbed ground, the rods would quickly uncross and return to their straight-ahead position. On learning of this, four professors of the University of Toronto were so intrigued as to wish to look into the matter for themselves. One September evening they drove with Mr. F. to a cemetery near Tiverton, Ontario.

They found that Mr. F., using his angle irons, could locate unmarked graves. The four professors, none of whom had been a "believer," were then tempted to try their hands at detecting graves. To their surprise they found that although one of them exhibited only a low ability, three of them showed high ability. One of them was very good indeed. His irons would swing inward when he was over a grave even if he made a conscious though weak effort to prevent the motion. The strength of the movements seemed to be the same regardless of whether he was traversing an old grave or one newly dug. He noticed also that the strongest response occurred when his body, not the apparatus, was directly over a grave. With this operator both rods swung inward, but when either of the other two successful operators crossed a grave, only one rod would move. It would swing inward until it was nearly at right angles to the operator's outstretched arms.

This experiment in dowsing for graves was carried out in a casual way—a "spur-of-the-moment" impulse. But the results were sufficiently striking to convince the professors (all of whom, as befits their profession, are sober-minded people with a considerable degree of objectivity toward natural and human phenomena) that there is something in dowsing. One of them decided to do a more formal experiment. He equipped himself with a set of drawings that showed the buried utilities on one of the campuses of the University of Toronto, and without giving Mr. F. any idea as to their location, he took him over a course he had laid out. This course was such that Mr. F. would walk at right angles over:

1. a water main six feet deep
2. two closely-spaced pipes about ten feet deep (another water main and a storm sewer)
3. a plastic tube about three feet deep, containing an electrical conductor and a ground wire
4. a small-diameter sewer pipe

As we have said, Mr. F. was quite unaware of the location of these buried objects. On the first traverse of the course he obtained strong responses at targets 1, 3, and 4. Only a weak response was had for target 2. They repeated the experiment using rods of different compositions—aluminum, copper, brass, mild steel, stainless steel, plastic, and wood. So that Mr. F. could not exploit his memory of where he had got responses with the original coathanger irons, he did these latter walks with his eyes closed. The professor says that all the rods seemed to work equally well, though wooden rods showed a weaker response which, paradoxically, occurred sooner than that with metal or plastic rods. It is hoped to continue experiments of this kind in Toronto. The subject is of such potential practical importance that it merits the attention of serious scientists.

Angle irons as well as the other appurtenances of dowsing—pendulums or polythene forked rods—can easily be made up oneself or obtained from the Dowsing Supply Company of America (Box 66, East Kingston, N.H. 03827), which appears to be associated with the American Society of Dowsers (Danville, Vt. 05828). At its annual convention, which takes place at Danville, near St. Johnsbury, which is quite close to the Canadian border, Canadian visitors are made welcome and can acquire a remarkable amount of lore and practical tips about dowsing. A highlight of the convention is the treasure hunt in which a multitude of dowsers ranging from children to aged countrymen, but all equipped with rods or irons, race one another to see who can first dowse out the prize—twenty dollars concealed somewhere in a defined area centered on the village green. On the occasion I was there it was all over in a few minutes. This may have been luck, on the other hand it may have been the demonstration of the practical efficacy of dowsing.

If dowsing is so good why don't dowsers become very rich men? Of course, a few may have done so and then retired to live inconspicuously as oil magnates or holders of lucrative mining concessions. So the question is why don't all dowsers get rich? It was at the dowsers' convention that I heard a very convincing explanation of this. The dowser is usually most successful when he goes out casually to help a friend or commercially for his expenses and a modest fee. But generally dowsers should not try to dowse for themselves if much is at stake. They will not be calm enough or sufficiently detached; their hopes and expectations will interfere with the dowsing reaction; very likely they will get the dowsing response prematurely.

There still remain more things to be said about dowsing. It is generally accepted that in the majority of cases movement of the dowsing rod is due to the dowser's own unconscious muscular reflexes. However, some dowsers maintain that a real physical force operates directly on the forked twig. This force, they say, does not result from the twig's own stresses nor from the movements of their own wrists, but comes from outside. In the case of the famous U.S. dowser Henry Gross it is said that the force was sometimes strong enough to break the twig.

In view of the unusual way in which Gross held the forked rod, it seems unlikely that he could cause this by normal means. Two years ago a senior and highly qualified physicist carried out some experiments at Ottawa with an elderly gentleman whose dowsing abilities are highly regarded in his home province of Alberta. According to the physicist, this dowser went out into a field and hacked off a forked branch from a nearby tree and then paced out the ground. Suddenly he got the dowsing response. At that moment the bark abruptly peeled itself off the divining rod as if stripped back by an external force. The physicist was genuinely puzzled by this occurrence.

Another peculiar thing alleged by some dowsers is that when they are above the water or mineral deposit that they are looking for they can "see" a force field around the rod. This may be connected with some discoveries we made with an angle iron a year or two back which we shall discuss in the next chapter, where we concern ourselves with the strange ability possessed by some people of being able to "see" auras and force fields.

12

AURAS AND FORCE FIELDS

In religious art saintly persons are depicted as having around their heads great circles of radiance. These haloes are also called aureoles, from *aurum*, the Latin word for gold. In the annals of Catholic mysticism there are many reports (some of them from comparatively recent times and which seem to have a reasonable degree of credibility) of very spiritual persons being surrounded at times by a bright radiance. Thus the auras of the saints may, possibly, derive from actual observations. In the rock paintings of Ontario we sometimes encounter little men with sunflower heads. Whether these were intended to represent spirits or mighty shamans girt with the aura of uncanny power we cannot tell.

Oddly enough the term "aura," which appears in many modern writings with a meaning rather similar to "aureole," is not derived from the latter word but comes ultimately from a Greek word which meant "breeze" or "breath" and then was used to mean a subtle emanation (as from flowers) and later on a kind of atmosphere (e.g. of power, authority, or holiness) surrounding a person.

For about a century it has been claimed by various investigators that around every person there is a kind of force field or energy (Mann, 1973). Many names have been given to it, but "aura" is the one most used. Most modern writers accept the definition of the aura which was given by Dr. Walter Kilner, a physician at St. Thomas' Hospital, London, England (1911). He said:

Hardly one person in ten thousand is aware that he or she is enveloped by a haze intimately connected with the body, whether asleep or awake, whether hot or cold, which, although invisible under ordinary circumstances, can be seen when conditions are favourable. This mist, the prototype of the nimbus or halo, constantly depicted around saints, has been manifest to certain individuals possessing a specially gifted sight, who, in consequence, have received the title "clairvoyants" and until recently to no one else.

Kilner however did not believe that only clairvoyants could see the aura. He believed that anyone could see it if the lighting was right and vision aided by looking through certain transparent colored screens which he had invented. Kilner thought that the aura would be seen by ordinary physical vision without the help of any psychic faculty, and that in fact it was ultraviolet light given off by the human body. People who saw auras were not clairvoyant but could see farther into the ultraviolet than others. In any case he thought most people could be trained to see the aura with or without screens. Kilner's interest in auras arose because he believed that they could be used in medical diagnosis. He thought that one's aura varied in size according to one's state of physical health and vitality. He also thought that injury or disease in a part of the body would cause a defect of some kind to show in a neighboring part of the aura. The color of the aura was also affected by the state of the person's health. Since Kilner's time there has been a great deal of teaching about auras; it is said that the color and shape of one's aura depend on one's health, character, strength of mind, and the intensity of one's thoughts and feelings. Some people maintain that only clairvoyants can see auras; others claim to be able to teach one to see auras. There are healers who assert they can cure or alleviate illnesses by "manipulating" or "adjusting" auras. Thus the problem of auras is certainly interesting and may be important.

In the Toronto Society for Psychical Research we have not answered all the questions about auras, but we have done some very simple but careful research which we think is important. We feel that we have for the first time properly done the preliminary work necessary if the problem of auras is ever to be placed on a secure scientific foundation. The work started with some pilot experiments in which various observers looked at people's auras under various lighting conditions. To get lights of various colors and brightness we used an ingenious machine devised by a member, William Osborne of Thornbury, Ontario. During these experiments I noticed that a number of people when viewing target persons in a subdued light definitely saw a kind of narrow halo around the heads (and often the necks, shoulders, and arms) of the targets. (A "target person" is one whose aura is being looked at.) This halo was a kind of misty band, usually about an inch wide, primarily gray or colorless and sometimes seeming mildly luminous. Some of the observers who saw this band or halo had attended lectures elsewhere on aura viewing and they called it a "rim aura" or "prana aura."

The Sanskrit word *prana*, which means "breath," is interpreted by Theosophists and others as "life energy." According to theosophical doctrine one's physical body is permeated by a more rarefied body called the "etheric double," which is supposed to be the vehicle for the prana, which sustains life. Dr. Kilner believed that the etheric double was very slightly larger than the physical body so that it protruded a little and could be seen as a dark band between one-sixteenth and one-eighth of an inch wide following the contour of the body. What Kilner called the "true aura" is seen outside the etheric double. According to Kilner, the true aura consists of two distinct regions. The "inner aura" is the one nearer to the etheric double and, said Kilner, is about three inches wide. The "outer aura" commences at the edge of the inner aura and is several inches wide. Although our observers described it as a "prana aura," it is clear that the rim aura which they saw cannot be the etheric double. Also, the rim aura seemed rather too narrow to be identified with Kilner's inner aura. We therefore decided to investigate the rim aura on its own without trying to fit it in with anybody else's theories (Owen, 1974).

I had noticed that our observers saw the rim aura best when the target person was a foot or two in front of a uniform background which could be of any color so long as it was fairly uniformly lighted, but not too brightly. I also noticed that they saw the rim aura most clearly when the target person had a smooth-lying head of hair without waves or curls or projecting wisps of hair which tended anyway to produce a hazy appearance around the head. I therefore looked at the heads of people sitting in front of a suitable background and who had smooth heads of hair. My method was to look at the top of the head, then to look beyond it toward the wall, beyond the person. I did not, however, focus my eyes on the wall to the exclusion of the target head, whose outline I saw sharply defined. Every time I tried this I found that after a few seconds I would see a band about an inch wide adjacent to the target person's hair and following the outline of the head. Sometimes the band would extend around the side of the head and down the neck. Once I had got this band into view it was fairly stable; it would disappear only momentarily before returning. The band is essentially colorless but has a kind of luminosity which is surprising and hard to describe to anyone who has not yet seen it. After being observed for a minute or two it can become very bright indeed. The experience is astonishing.

As I am a "psychic moron," i.e. have no psychic powers of any kind, I thought it rather unlikely that I was seeing auras of the kind that clairvoyants speak of. I thought it was of the nature of an optical or visual illusion, though not one of the better-known ones. Indeed no one seems to have drawn attention to it. It seemed to me that the illusion depended to some extent on contrast. This conclusion was reinforced by the fact that when I looked at fair-headed persons seen against a darker background a thin dark band interposed itself between the outline of the head and the lighter rim aura. Possibly this may explain Kilner's observation of the etheric double as he looked at his patients undressed in front of a dark background. To test the assumption that the rim aura was an optical illusion I chose as a target a large toy panda bear with nylon fur. The forehead and cranium are a very pure white and the ears large and black. If contrast played a part in generating the rim-aura illusion this experiment was well adapted to show it, as in fact it did. The rim aura around the bear's black ears was about an inch wide and particularly bright. However, next to the pure white cranium was a narrow band of colorlessness that looked dark and gray in comparison with the neighboring rim aura, which was luminous and about an inch wide.

I found I could also see the rim aura around black squares or picture frames provided the lighting was right. This proved that I was not hallucinating or projecting an aura on Hopewell (as our bear is called) just because, as a family favorite, he has a "personality." It is sometimes said that if people handle objects they leave some of their own aura on them. If this is true, then perhaps the aura around an inanimate object could be a "contamination aura." Admittedly, Hopewell does get cuddled by visitors, including members of the society, during the more lengthy and tedious experiments, and so could be contaminated with relic aura of humans. However, the rim aura on Hopewell's ears was actually brighter than I saw on human heads, which is not what one would expect if it was merely due to a relic of vital energy which had rubbed off on him, as it were. More conclusive still was the brightness of the rim aura around black picture frames which are not handled from one year's end to another. The rim aura also agrees with optical illusions in being just as striking when viewed in a mirror. Indeed, this is a very good way of seeing one's own rim aura.

Kilner believed that the aura was a real physical energy—a kind of radiation given out by the human body. He recommended that in training oneself to see auras one should look at one's hand held out in front of a dim background. Aura would then be seen around the edge of the hand and "filling in" the angles between spread-out fingers. He also suggested a simple experiment which anyone can do, as follows. Spread out your hands with palms facing you and the fingers separated. Place the tips of corresponding fingers of the right and left hands together, middle finger to middle finger, ring finger to ring finger, etc. Now draw the hands slowly apart. It is very likely that you will see grayish bands stretching between the tips of corresponding fingers. If the distance between the two hands is slowly varied the bands very much resemble elastic bands made of colorless nothingness. I found I could see all these Kilner effects, so to test whether they too were visual illusions, I made myself two cardboard profiles of hands and found that the aura and bands were just as vivid with them as with my real hands.

In order to find out whether or not there was something wrong with my eyes or with my head, making me see things differently from other people, I invoked the aid of members of the TSPR. In all, twenty-two of them kindly acted as observers of auras on people and on the panda bear. In such experiments one has to be very careful not to "lead one's witnesses," i.e. to suggest to them what they ought to see. I merely told them my method of looking at the tops of the heads of people or bears and asked them to make little sketches of what, if anything, they saw. The sketches were drawn on prepared sheets having a human outline printed on them. I found everybody could see the rim aura on Hopewell except one person who practically refused to look, saying briskly, "That's dead; there's nothing there." I felt that Hopewell had not been given a fair chance. One subject saw only the rim aura on the bear and described it much as I have above. However, on the target people her experience was quite different. She saw complex masses of varied color both on and around them. This woman made no claim to psychic talent though she had had several spontaneous experiences that she thought were psychic ones. So far as I could ascertain she did not seem to be acquainted with any of the various theories concerning auras, but is interested in finding out what the experience of aura viewing means because she regularly sees people with patches of color on them.

Our other observers each looked at several target persons. All of them saw the rim aura much as I did. However, four of the observers, while seeing only the rim aura on most of the people they looked at, did see a larger, colored aura around at least one of the targets they observed. I am sure that these were sincere persons

who were not making it up. I do not think they were at all suggestible or versed in the lore about auras.

From this work I drew two main conclusions. As soon as their
attention is drawn to it, anyone can with minimum training or effort
see the rim aura. The fact that most people do not usually see it
is neither here nor there; to see it they need to have their attention
drawn to it. It is surprising what things we do not usually see
unless we are looking for them. Andrienne Henwood showed us a
simple experiment which is highly instructive. She told us to look
at a lighted candle and see what we could see. Everyone present
saw a magnificent aureole of light about two feet in radius surrounding the flame. This is something we do not usually see. The
same holds for rim auras. When someone tells us that he sees an
aura we have to treat the statement with respect. We cannot assume
that he is just romancing or having hallucinations. He may be
speaking the literal truth, as will be the case if he sees rim auras.
What then about the people who say they see large colored auras?
We have to treat them with equal respect. The fact that you or I
perhaps cannot see them means nothing. We have to approach the
problem without preconceived ideas and try to find out what it
means. Is it a defect of vision, a form of psychological projection,
or a real and strange talent?

What have auras to do with psychical research? Well, it is very
difficult to be sure, but it does seem that a significant proportion
of the people who see auras do, from time to time, have psychic
experiences. Similarly, many psychic people claim to see auras.
How they see auras is a mystery. James Wilkie, the celebrated
Canadian psychic, tells me that he sees the aura as a very narrow
band pulsating with color. The color varies with the person.
Douglas Johnson, the renowned English psychic, sees larger auras
but not in color. Clearly, their experiences are quite different. They
were both kind enough to let me test their color vision. Oddly
enough, though neither psychic is color-blind in the ordinary sense,
they both have a minor anomaly of color vision which, incidentally,
I have too, though I see only rim auras. The subject of auras is

extremely complicated: Douglas Johnson tells me that when he
sees auras in the usual way they are colorless, but if he sees them
clairvoyantly they have color. One is at liberty to wonder if when
a psychic person sees an aura he is not just receiving a psychic
impression that is translated into a pattern of color around the
target person. If perception of large colored auras occurs by
clairvoyance and not via the actual eyesight, then one would expect
that the psychic aura viewer would be able to see them in the
dark or with his eyes closed. Some psychic people have told me that
they can actually do this. The whole subject is extremely intriguing
but as yet has hardly been explored scientifically.

However, we came inadvertently on a clue, which suggests that
whatever the truth about the aura may be, human beings can sometimes generate energy fields in their vicinity. This discovery was
made almost by chance in January 1971 when a number of us had
gathered at my home for an informal program of experiment and
discussion. The group included several medical doctors and other
scientists. The guest of honor was a remarkable young Canadian
named Jan Merta. He was born in 1944 in Moravia, Czechoslovakia. In 1968 he obtained a degree in social work from the
University of Prague, but shortly after that he emigrated to Canada
and studied at McGill University, obtaining a degree in science.
Though he was orphaned early in life and has experienced many
vicissitudes Jan has a very buoyant and happy nature. He goes
around bursting with ideas and good humor. He is also a psychic
person.

The day prior to the episode I shall shortly describe Jan had
told us that he had become interested in ESP in Prague many years
before, when he had participated in the work of a psychical research
group and benefited from knowing Dr. Martin Rysl, an eminent
psychical research worker who has since also come to North
America. Jan then outlined his own theories about human energies
and psychic ability. He believes that the existence of the aura is
evidence that there is a certain energy field around the human body.
Jan also thinks that this field is part of the body's natural defenses

and reacts protectively if the body is threatened. He believes that one can, by conscious effort, control one's own energy field to some extent so that one's skin is protected from burning or blistering when touching hot objects. This is a possible explanation of the feats of Canadian Indian fire-walkers. However, when we met next day we had forgotten all about auras and the like and were thinking about something quite different.

We were doing an informal experiment with an angle iron obtained from the American Society of Dowsers. It was made of mild steel rod; the horizontal section was 14 inches long; the vertical section 6 inches and able to turn freely within a sleeve of plastic. In this experiment the iron was being held, dowser-fashion, by one of the doctors whom we shall refer to as "T53," as we did in the original report (Owen, 1972). There is some evidence that T53, like Jan Merta, has psychic ability. T53 challenged Jan to force him by a mentally transmitted command or suggestion to cause the iron to turn either to right or to left. The logic behind this experiment need not concern us, because events took an unexpected turn.

The iron stayed still in T53's hand but, after about a minute of concentration by himself and Jan Merta, T53 said in a tone of considerable interest, "Look at the aura around the thing [the iron]. It's fantastic, look at the aura." My wife, Iris Owen, immediately exclaimed, "I saw it too, the aura around the rod. . . . I saw it a shimmering silver." About then the aura faded. Five people in all had been looking at the iron at the moment in question. Before speaking further about the event they all retired to separate corners to write down their descriptions of what, if anything, they had seen. Jan Merta found it difficult to describe it; the best he could do was to compare it to hot air as seen over a road surface or a hot stove. T53 did not compare it to the appearance of hot air (a well-known effect explicable by optical refraction of light) but said that the shape of the aura was like a circular cylinder occupying all the space within about one inch from the iron (i.e. its form was like that of a giant cigar tube two inches wide). The aura was also active, said T53; gray in color, it streamed out from the longer horizontal part of the iron and was brightest while he and Jan were concentrating on the iron.

Iris Owen wrote that the aura stuck out about one inch all around and covered the last four inches. It was like hot air, but there was also a swarm of "sparks" like those given off when metal is welded; they were silvery in color. Dr. V. saw it as extending about one inch in all directions from the end of the iron and several inches back along its length. It was both like hot air and shimmering and silvery. Dr. Z. likened it to a "heat wave" and otherwise described it exactly as did Dr. V. None of these witnesses had seen a human or any kind of aura before and are not, in my opinion, suggestible or sensation-seeking by nature. I regard the similarities of their independently given descriptions taken in conjunction with those of T53 and Jan Merta as very strong evidence for this having been a genuine happening.

Was it merely an unusual electrical phenomenon? If so, I have never met it or heard of it. That afternoon the climate was that of a typical Canadian winter's day. The indoor temperature was about 70°F. The floors were covered with wall-to-wall nylon carpet, which tends to amplify the normal tendency, with which Canadians are very familiar, to charge oneself up so that on touching a metal object or a grounded point one triggers an electric spark. Was the aura around the iron then merely something like the corona sometimes seen around high-tension hydroelectric power lines? If so, it is a little difficult to see how, even if T53 had involuntarily charged himself up, the charge had got localized in the rod. More research admittedly needs to be done on manifestations of electric charge on people, but provisionally one would think this type of manifestation somewhat unlikely. If it were the explanation it would, of course, be a very interesting phenomenon in itself. The electrical explanation is not put out of court but is rendered somewhat implausible by the fact that in the following April we successfully repeated the experiment. This was done in pleasant spring weather, dry but with no domestically generated electricity or sparks in evidence.

To do this repetition without implanting suggestions in the minds of the witnesses that they might see something needed a certain amount of innocent but artful maneuver (Owen, 1972). Again, T53, Jan Merta, Dr. Z., and Dr. V., who had been present before, saw the aura very much as they had previously though not quite so large or striking. Two other witnesses who had been kept deliberately in ignorance of the earlier happening testified independently as follows. Dr. B. saw it like heat and silver-gray or white depending on the background against which he saw it as he moved his head. Dr. C. saw something "purple-blue" along about two-thirds of the iron. I myself was surprised to see a "hot-air" appearance as I am not given to seeing things. Douglas Johnson, a highly psychic person, happened to be visiting. He saw an aura of influence extending "spaghetti-like" from Jan Merta's fingers toward the iron. So far as it goes, this suggests that the appearance *might* have been related to some kind of interplay of a mysterious force field between Jan Merta and T53 or the iron.

If we feel ourselves at liberty to believe that an unusual phenomenon occurred repeatedly it opens up an interesting area of research. Only the simplest apparatus is needed. But it may be difficult to find suitably endowed human participants like T53 and Jan Merta, who are very "psychic" people; these are in shorter supply than angle irons. However, others of their ilk may be blushing unseen in the wide expanses of Canada; also, as we shall see in a later chapter, it is possible with sufficient enterprise to generate remarkable physical phenomena with people of modest psychic talent. Whether the aura formed around the angle iron has anything to do with the human aura or is a special kind of force field that these people can generate is not at all clear. But so far as it goes it tends to support the idea that humans may have strange auras or force fields around them. Of course, if later we prove that it was a freakish electrical effect, it would still be interesting.

13

ASTRAL PROJECTION
AND PSYCHIC PHOTOGRAPHY

Photography first became an inexpensive and easy process in the closing years of the last century. Before long "spirit photographs" started to make their appearance. These are photographs which on processing show additional features not visible in the original scene. Sometimes these are readily explicable as due to faults in the camera or development of the negative—scratches, blobs, fogging, etc. Sometimes, however, they show human faces or figures. Many such photographs that were hawked around in the old days were shown to be fakes; sometimes the newsprint on the back of newspaper photographs that had been artfully reproduced in the finished product manifested itself on enlargement and viewing against a bright light.

Occasionally one encounters photographs whose history is known and which are sufficiently odd to be intriguing. Thus one of our groups visited a house in Ontario where some poltergeist happenings had been reported and one of the children, a boy aged five, had seen a man in the basement. As a matter of routine our team took photographs in the basement and other rooms but with no thought of getting spirit or ghost photos. The camera was an ordinary Kodak Instamatic loaded with cartridge film for color slides. All the slides were normal except for two—those of the basement and the living room, which showed large irregular patches of what as much as anything resembled white mist. The Kodak processing laboratories at Toronto said that they could not provide any explanation except perhaps reflection as from clouds of smoke. Our investigators had seen no smoke or steam there, of course. Perhaps, despite what Kodak said, there was a failure in the processing. If so, it was something of a coincidence that it should happen in an allegedly haunted house. Still, according to the laws of probability, pure coincidences must happen sometimes— an undoubted fact, though an irritating one for psychical research workers.

If the blemishes on those slides had been in a human likeness instead of just misty patches the problem of interpretation would have been more acute. The most intriguing cases are those when a good portrait of a real person who is deceased or absent from the scene appears in the picture. Some years ago a family in Mississauga gathered outside their house for a family reunion picture. When the print was made it showed an extra face—that of an elderly woman apparently inside the house and looking out a window. This addition really does look like an old lady's face. The family says it is in fact a good likeness of a grandmother who had died some years before the picture was taken. They were quite sure that there was no one inside the house while the picture was being taken.

One of the tourist attractions in the parliament buildings at Victoria, B.C., is often called a "ghost picture," though this is something of a misnomer. Taken on 13 January 1865, it is a photograph of the first legislative council of British Columbia. One member of the council, Charles Good, was unavoidably absent on account of serious illness. Yet to the surprise of himself and everyone else, when the photograph was printed the face of Good distinctly appeared in the vacant place he would have occupied had he been there. It looks somewhat transparent or ethereal and, as Allen Spraggett points out (1967), photographers might be tempted to explain it by saying that Good arrived late, and so was underexposed. However, there seems to be little doubt of the historic facts that Good was critically ill, did not come to the meeting, and was very astonished to see his own face in the picture.

Some people would regard this episode as an example of astral travel. On this theory, the astral body or etheric double of Charles Good, actuated by his strong desire to be present with his colleagues on their historic day, left his physical body—perhaps while he was asleep or in a coma—and was "projected" to the council chamber, where its presence was registered by the camera, though it was unobserved by any person in the room. We met the idea of astral travel previously when we were looking for explanations of crisis apparitions. If Charles Good did travel astrally to the council chamber he was unaware of it, as have been the great majority of people whose apparitions have been seen at places remote from their physical bodies while they were still alive. In only a very small number of cases has it been claimed that a person who is seen as an apparition has simultaneously had the experience of seeing the place where his apparition appears or felt that in some mysterious way he was there at the distant place. I know of no Canadian examples.

Many people do have what are called "out-of-the-body" experiences. These seem to occur as frequently in Canada as anywhere else. I have the impression that it is not necessary to be psychic in order to have these experiences. In the commonest form of episode of this kind the person concerned is in bed at night and is either in process of falling asleep or has actually been asleep. Suddenly he is aware of being high up in the room—floating as it were—and looking down at himself in bed. In the Canadian cases I have been told of, my informants say that after a few seconds of wonderment at their situation panic sets in with an urgent desire to get back to their body. At this stage they suddenly find themselves lying normally in bed and awake but with rapid breathing and pounding heart. This is completely typical of reports from all over the world. It seems to happen sufficiently often to be counted a normal type of human experience. Whether it is a psychic phenomenon and connected with the etheric double is quite unknown; the causes of the experience are just not understood. I have not met any Canadian instances but there is a variant reported sometimes by people in other countries who instead of panicking find themselves gliding out of the room and going on an extended flight through the neighborhood. This experience is often said to be a pure dream. Space does not permit us to discuss it here. One Toronto woman told me of an incipient out-of-the-body experience that came on her during meditation. She felt herself leaving her body. She was alarmed and immediately found herself back in her body. After this she gave up the practice of meditation.

Another form of out-of-the-body experience occurs in situations of physical trauma, e.g. when the person is in the operating room having surgery under general anesthesia or is lying severely injured by an accident. The latter cases are essentially the same as the operating room cases, which are slightly better known. Some interest in the operation cases was recently aroused by the *Journal* of the Canadian Medical Association publishing an account by a Toronto businessman of an out-of-the-body experience he had while under general anesthesia. He found himself up near the ceiling of the operating room looking down on himself on the operating table. From the vantage point he watched the progress of the operation and listened to what was said by the surgical team and supporting staff. Afterward he recorded an account of what was done and said. The surgeons themselves confirmed that his account was accurate. The striking thing about this case is that for part of the time the patient was medically dead. His heart had to be restarted.

Like the night-time ones, the operating room experiences occur sufficiently often to be counted a normal type of human response. When the patient is *not* medically dead, it is not at all clear that there is anything especially psychic about it. We now know that patients under general anesthetic can hear and sometimes actually remember things said by the bystanders. It is possible that some people with this ability organize their memories into a mental dramatization of the sequence of events. If, however, they were proved to have accurately visualized events that could not have been deduced from the sounds in the operating room we should have to think again, and either admit that they must have been out of their bodies or had gained their knowledge by ESP.

Here we fall foul of a notorious dilemma which arises when we try to evaluate an alleged phenomenon somewhat akin to the out-of-the-body experiences. This is what is called "traveling clairvoyance." Often a person gets genuine and accurate information in the form of a psychic impression; the fact just comes into his mind as a mere thought unaccompanied by any visual picture. Sometimes, however, the person sees a distant scene. Whether this occurs by telepathy or clairvoyance need not concern us. Usually, however, he sees the scene as a mental picture (or more rarely as a vision) without having any feeling of having actually been at the place or having left his body. Most rarely of all, the psychic person will feel he was in some sense or other actually present at the distant place. This is called traveling clairvoyance. The percipient may or may not have a recollection of actual traveling and he may or may not see himself on the scene or feel that he is present there in a body actual or etheric. Where there is no impression of an actual journey or of a body, it is very difficult (indeed, strictly speaking, impossible) to decide whether this is a case of astral travel or one of pure ESP.

A few of my friends claim on occasion to have visited the apartments of one another by astral projection. Unfortunately, we have not yet had time to research this or set up appropriate experiments in the hope of finding out just what is involved. A woman of considerable psychic gifts claims to do traveling clairvoyance and regards it as astral projection. At present her ability to see objects in New York while she is at home in Toronto is being investigated by Dr. Karlis Osis, Director of Research at the American Society for Psychical Research. We must await his report; however, he was impressed by her ability to describe complicated arrangements of objects set up at the society's premises. This research program resulted from a bequest by a gold prospector who actually found gold in the west: whether by dowsing, ESP, luck, or ordinary professional acumen, I do not know. However, he left his money to go to whatever organization was best qualified to prove that man has a soul. After lengthy court hearings the bequest was awarded to the ASPR, who thought that out-of-the-body experiences provided as good an approach to this problem as would any other.

In her *Folklore of Nova Scotia* Mary Fraser describes an apparition that appeared to her own father. Lambert cites it as a case of astral projection. Mary Fraser's father as a young man was in California negotiating to buy a ranch stocked with cattle. One night a complete stranger came in and stood at the foot of his bed. She was a young woman in a black dress with a white ruffle around her neck. Three times she said, "Don't buy those cattle or you'll be sorry for it. Come home!" She then vanished. Next day he set off for the family home at Antigonish Harbour. There his mother persuaded him to buy a farm that had just come on the market. Visiting a neighbor's home soon after, Fraser was astonished to recognize one of the daughters of the house as the original of the girl in the dream. Like the vision, she was dressed in black with a white ruffle around her neck. Put out by being stared at, she left the room in a huff. Eventually he made his peace with her; and they got married. Just how Mary Fraser's mother could have been astrally projected to a man she did not know of and had never met is not at all clear. If any sense is to be made out of this very strange episode it would seem best to regard it as a precognitive vision or dream. Only the appearance of the future Mrs. Fraser was precognized; it was not a case of an actual future event or scene being literally and accurately portrayed.

It would be unwise to speculate much about spirit or astral projection photographs without giving consideration to the subject of "thoughtography." For many years claims have been made by various investigators such as Fukurai in Japan and Dr. Jule Eisenbud in the United States that certain psychic people can by exerting thought alone and without using a properly functioning camera so modify photographic film that when it is developed it shows a picture. This is, of course, a very fantastic claim and no one would, or should, consider accepting it without very strong evidence.

Fukurai claimed that his psychics could put images (in the form of abstract patterns or of characters occurring in Japanese writing) on film sealed in its original wrappings. If this was so it was done in the absence of any light and involved a direct effect on the chemical coatings of the film. We can call this psychokinesis if we like; but it works at the molecular level, because new chemical compounds have to be formed; perhaps it ought to be called psychochemistry.

Dr. Eisenbud's work has mostly been done with the famous Ted Serios. Assuming, for the sake of argument, that Ted's effects are genuine and not the result of fraud, it is not easy to see exactly what it is that he does. Often he works with a normal camera and looks into it, so that when the (Polaroid) print has been developed it should, if anything, show a picture of Ted himself. Often, however, it does not. It may for instance show what, though distorted, is recognizably a picture of the Empire State Building or of some other edifice. Sometimes these pictures though quite recognizable do not seem to be identical to any existing photographs, because of the curious distortions, and because often the photograph resembles one taken from a very unusual viewpoint. This peculiarity is a strong argument against its being done by trickery on the part of Ted Serios or any accomplice. Anyhow, when Ted makes pictures in this way the camera is receiving light so that we do not know if he is doing direct psychochemistry on the film or is bending the light rays so that they make an image. Sometimes Ted got precisely similar effects with a camera from which the lens had been removed. Occasionally results were obtained with a camera rendered lightproof by an opaque sealing of the lens.

One of the most brilliant and fraudproof demonstrations of Ted Serios's abilities was in an experiment on 13 August 1963, organized by Allen Spraggett. It took place in a Toronto television studio in the presence of Allen Spraggett, the studio staff, and two specially invited witnesses, Professor Benjamin Schlesinger of the University of Toronto and Barry Black, manager of the well-known Toronto firm Black's Cameras. Both were highly skeptical of Serios's powers and previously unacquainted with psychical research. Ted was seated under bright lights in a chair in front of the studio's movie camera under the close observation of Black, Spraggett, and Schlesinger. Black had brought a brand-new Polaroid camera, which he loaded himself with fresh film straight out of stock. Black himself, closely watched by the other two witnesses, made up the "gismo" which Ted used as a finger rest to prevent his fingers from inadvertently covering the lens when the shutter was sprung. This was merely a cylinder of cardboard an inch high and three-quarters of an inch in diameter fastened with cellulose tape. The witnesses could see that it contained nothing capable of yielding a fake picture.

Ted was given the camera and asked to get a picture of the old Toronto Armories, then in process of demolition—buildings Ted had never seen. Ted set the camera on his lap, with the lens upward. With his right hand he held the "gismo" over the lens. In his left hand was a rosary. Perspiring, and with his breathing becoming rapid and shallow, he concentrated intensely on the camera. At length he released the shutter. Barry Black took the camera from him. The resulting print was totally black, as was the next attempt. The next four prints were also black, but had on them what seemed to be light fog patches. Ted said this was a picture trying to build up. The seventh attempt caused everyone present to gasp with surprise. It was not a picture of the old Armories, and fuzzy in places, but an undoubted picture. It was a city scene showing a vast fortresslike building reminiscent in style of Byzantine architecture. Next to it was a huge domed structure somewhat resembling the Mormon Temple at Salt Lake City. In the distance was a row of high-rise apartments. The picture resembled an aerial photograph. No actual scene of this kind has ever been identified although the fortresslike building had some resemblance to the Armories.

The witnesses were quite sure that Ted perpetrated no fraud. The picture and the "gismo" were examined by an independent research laboratory in Toronto, whose staff said in writing that there was no way in which the finger rest could have been used to produce the picture. During the experiment Ted's every action was recorded by a movie camera. This intrigued Ted, who declared that he was trying to "mark" the film. When it was developed peculiar markings were found at various places both on the exposed and unexposed sections of the film. These markings, which the puzzled technicians called "unidentified radiation patterns," looked like bursts of forked lightning. The film makers said they had never encountered anything of that sort before.

In 1970 we were invited to the Human Dimensions Institute at Rosary Hill College, Buffalo, to meet Joseph Veilleux and his two sons, Fred and Richard. The Veilleux family are of French Canadian descent, but citizens of Waterville, Maine. They told us that some years ago they had a ouija-board session at their home; a message was spelled out directing them to go to the neighboring cemetery and take some photographs. Intrigued but mystified they took their camera to the graveyard. To their surprise some of the resulting prints turned out quite unexpectedly. Some of them showed the actual scene that had been photographed but had additional luminous patterns superimposed such as great spheres of light, or crosses, or human faces. Repeating the experiment many times, in a few months they had built up a remarkable album of pictures. Occasionally almost all of the actual scene was absent and a totally different one substituted for it. Thus one photograph is occupied almost entirely by the façade of a Roman temple.

This early work was done on their own without supervision. However, everyone who had met them since had been impressed with them as very straightforward, honest people. It is also a fact that they have received no personal gain from their photography either in the way of money or fame. Unlike Ted Serios, they use no "gismos" and do not point the camera at themselves. They merely aim an ordinary Polaroid camera at an ordinary scene, which does not necessarily have to be a cemetery. All three, Joseph, Fred, and Richard, have produced paranormal pictures. According to their diary, the effect is seasonal; the majority of the strange photographs occur in the spring.

A few years back they came to the attention of Dr. Eisenbud. He was impressed by some of the photographs they took under his close supervision. At his suggestion the Toronto SPR and Human Dimensions decided in 1970 to invite them to Toronto and Buffalo for some experiments, which the Veilleux agreed to, actually at some inconvenience to themselves. The precautions against fraud were quite elaborate and have been fully described elsewhere (Rindge, Cook and Owen, 1972). During the experiments in Toronto on 14 and 15 May, the weather was dark, rainy, and depressing. No fewer than ninety-six photographs were taken in our home in Toronto. We were disappointed, as were the Veilleux, by the fact that no spectacular pictures resulted. However, one peculiarity was observed. As I have implied, the lighting in the room could only be described as dim, the feeble daylight being supplemented only by some 100-watt ordinary standard lamps without any photographer's lights. To our surprise five photographs (all taken as it happened by Fred Veilleux) showed the scene as if it had been taken in a much brighter light than was actually available, or as if taken with a much longer exposure than that which the camera (our own Polaroid 3000) might have been expected to provide for automatically.

During the next two days, when the weather was even worse, Fred Rindge and Jeanne Rindge of the Human Dimensions Institute carried out experiments with the Veilleux at Buffalo. One hundred and twenty-six photos were taken with the Rindges' own Polaroid 360 camera in a variety of situations. Four were taken at the grave of Chief Moses Shongo, an eminent Seneca medicine man, to which the party was escorted by his granddaughter, Twylah Neitch. Curiously, though the scene was as dark as could be while heavy rain was falling, these photos showed bright white patches. In a fifth abnormal picture taken at the Rindges' home there was a bright patch, though control photographs taken simultaneously showed nothing unusual there.

In February 1971, William Cook, of the Research Association for Parapsychological Study of Portland, Maine, visited the Veilleux at their home. With him Fred Veilleux produced a number of dark pictures, totally black, as if highly exposed. Cook, who is a professional photogrammetrist and has also worked with Ted Serios, is of the opinion that the overexposures got by Fred at Toronto and the underexposures at Waterville are the results of effects produced by Fred directly on the light-sensing elements in the Polaroid cameras (Cook, 1972).

The term "psychic photography" is generally used as a blanket phrase to cover all the various kinds of unorthodox photographs that turn up from time to time: the "thoughtography" of Fukurai's psychics and of Ted Serios, the strange composites produced by the Veilleux in their early days, and the intrusion of the likenesses of deceased persons. So far few practitioners of thoughtography have been found. As a happening thoughtography is mysterious indeed. What is fantastic is the minute precision of the process which, it seems, can guide the chemicals of photographic emulsion to recombine and arrange themselves in subtle patterns. For want of a better way of speaking of it we have to ascribe it in some way to a power at present totally mysterious but possessed by thought itself.

14

MIND OVER MATTER:
JAN MERTA'S BREAKTHROUGH

When Sheila Ostrander returned from her visit to Russia in 1968 she brought with her two short motion pictures on the phenomena of Mme. Nelya Mikhailova (née Kulagina) which had been made by Edward Naumov, a biologist who, Ostrander and Schroeder (1970) say, was then in charge of a special laboratory for "technical parapsychology" at the physics department of the State Instrument Engineering College in Moscow. These two movies have since become quite famous in North America because they show Madame Mikhailova seated in front of a coffee table on which there are several small objects. After a little concentration these objects are seen to move, apparently in response to Madame Mikhailova's willpower. Since then she has exhibited this phenomenon several times for visitors from the West who have provided their own objects for the experiment so that they could be sure that no simple trick was involved such as using iron objects that could be moved by concealed magnets.

Some years ago Madame Mikhailova came to the attention of Professor Leonid Vasiliev, an eminent physiologist who was interested in psychical research, because she was a poltergeist person of the kind we described earlier (domestic utensils would slide off shelves and fly around). She is especially interesting as an example of a poltergeist person who has learned to control her power of psychokinesis and operate it voluntarily.

Visitors who have returned recently from Russia say that some

Soviet scientists are seeking to train poltergeist people to do voluntary psychokinesis, and claim some success with this venture. To
give their trainees confidence the Russian workers let them practice
a kind of "electrostatic pseudopsychokinesis." Small cylinders of
glass, cardboard, or metal (a cigar tube will do) are laid on a
Plexiglas table. We have seen a film brought from Russia which
shows a woman putting her hand some inches away from such a
tube. The tube will then roll briskly on the table top following her
hand, but without contact. When she stops moving her hand the
tube stops itself also. Many who saw this movie must have thought
that they were seeing PK (i.e., psychokinesis) as it was not made
completely clear that the effect was electrostatic. As we happened
to have a Plexiglas table we were soon able to verify that anyone
can produce this effect, and that it is entirely due to static electricity.
The trick is to charge up the Plexiglas top by rubbing it energeti-
cally with a woollen scarf, preferably one of the fluffy kind. We
found that a cardboard tube about four inches long and one and a
half inches in diameter performed best. Our table was a very cheap
one with a somewhat corrugated surface but, even so, it worked
quite well. It is not easy to predict whether one's hand will repel or
attract the tube. These experiments do best in the dry Canadian
winter when there is little or no leakage of static electric charges.
After we had discovered the effects we were told that the Soviet
scientists sometimes charge up their PK performers to a high
voltage.

More interesting to us was the work of Jan Merta. As we have
said, he is a "psychic" person. But he has also had poltergeist
events of a mild kind happening in his presence, so that he can be
considered a potentially psychokinetic person. A few years ago he
interested himself in the problem of voluntary PK. It was through
this work that we got to know him, as Dr. Bernard Grad, in whose
laboratory Jan was working, drew Allen Spraggett's attention to it.
Jan evolved a theory that he could build up his personal force
field by eating only a special diet which he designed for himself,
and also doing some yoga training. As far as we could gather the

diet consisted mainly of European-type sausages and rye bread, and the yoga was more of the meditational kind, though Jan attached great importance to breath control. He said that in order to move his PK object he first put himself into a relaxed state of mind. He then let the thought of moving the object in a particular direction (e.g., to the right) come into his mind as a conscious intention, and be passively held there without striving or concentrated willing of the desired result. At the same time he regulated his breathing so that his mental intention would coincide with an appropriate stage in his breathing cycle. Jan's state of mind for psychokinesis much resembled that which Eugen Herrigal, the author of *Zen in the Art of Archery*, recommends for taking aim with bow and arrow.

Jan's choice of an object to be moved by psychokinesis was also quite original. He believed that it would be easier to move substances of organic origin, i.e. things that had once been part of living beings. Thus, wood ought to be superior to metal. He therefore made up a simple mobile out of two chicken feathers whose quills were joined. This was hung by a nylon thread inside a thick glass jar two feet high and one foot square. The thread was taped to a glass plate which covered the opening of the top of the jar. Air was excluded by greasing the contact between the plate and the rim of the jar. Even in the closed jar the mobile has a certain amount of random motion, but this dies down after a period of waiting and the mobile then usually stays at rest.

In January 1971 Jan gave the Toronto Society many demonstrations of what seemed to be psychokinetic movements of the feather. In a typical session when the mobile had ceased any random motion and was at rest, Jan stood about six feet away from the jar. He raised his right hand; the mobile started from rest and swung to the right. Demonstrations of this kind were repeated many times. In each case the feather was allowed to come to rest before giving it another command. Commands "right" or "left" were also given as directed by the observers and not at the choice of Jan Merta. Also, a series of movements was executed with Jan's back to the apparatus to ensure that he was not observing slight incipient motions of the mobile and adapting his instructions accordingly. Throughout, Jan was not only remote from the apparatus, but also physically quite passive. In one series of demonstrations he did not move head, body, or hands, and did not himself announce the expected direction of movement. The feather moved to right or left according to the requests of the observers, which they made to Jan. On some occasions when the feather had just completed the movement which it had made according to instructions, Jan was asked to continue swinging it in the same sense and it picked up speed again. On other occasions Jan was asked to stop or reverse the motion just after it had started, and this he successfully did. In a final series Jan sat, completely passive, about twenty-five feet away from the jar with his hands clasped behind his head. The responses of the feather were no less definite than the ones at closer range (Owen, 1972).

It was the opinion of the group of doctors and professional men who participated in the session described that a very unusual physical effect had been shown in operation. Precognitive anticipation of random movements of the feather seemed to be clearly excluded by the fact that instructions had been given not just by Jan Merta but also by several different members of the audience, who did not claim to be precognitive. Nor did these observers see any reason to suppose that the effect was electrostatic. The times when Jan was passive and several feet away seemed definitely to tell against this interpretation. This was also felt by observers at other sessions with a very small number of exceptions; these latter felt very firmly that somehow electrostatics must come into it, though they did not find it very easy to explain just how. They spent some time standing very close to the jar, rubbing fountain pens briskly on their sleeves and hopefully waving them at the feather, which could not be said to have been particularly responsive.

Unknown to Jan Merta and all of us at that time was some work done by Mayne R. Coe, Jr. in the United States about 1958. Coe found that he and members of his family could cause strips of aluminum foil balanced on needles to rotate when they brought their hands near them (Gaddis, 1967). He thought this was due to static electricity. His interest being aroused, he studied instances of electricity generated by marine animals such as catfish, electric eels, torpedoes, and the like and concluded that human muscle can generate electric currents. Then he studied yoga, putting himself on a rather strict regimen of fasting alternated with a light diet and breathing exercises. One evening during this period while sitting relaxed he felt what he described as "a powerful current" passing down through his body. He thought it was bioelectricity generated in his muscles. In due course he acquired the capacity either of voluntarily "switching on" this current or of knowing when it would switch itself on. As a PK object he constructed a large mobile made of a cardboard box seven feet long and seven inches square in cross-section. When his internal current was flowing, so he said, he could regulate the swinging of the object to right or to left. Coe also charged himself to 35,000 volts. (Readers should *not* imitate this unless they really know what they are doing, because any appreciable current through them at this voltage will kill them dead.) He found that he could move his mobile while he was charged even though he experienced no internal flow of current.

It is difficult to evaluate Coe's results without knowing exactly what was done. It could be that he was a psychokinetic person and the electricity was just a red herring. Or it might have been that he was in some odd way a more electrical person than most and the movements of his mobile did result, just as he thought, from electrostatic fields. I find Jan Merta's phenomenon hard to explain by electrostatics because he could influence his mobile at such long distances. I saw him do very impressive demonstrations in conditions very adverse to working with electric charges. This was at the dowsers' convention at Danville in early October 1970. The Vermont maple trees were in their full autumn splendor but the shine was rather taken off things by the persistent fall of heavy rain. However, Jan set up his glass jar on a desk at one end of the office of the school in which the convention was being held. Dowsers, having heard that someone was going to demonstrate something, enthusiastically flocked in. The atmosphere in the room was as damp as could be and most inimical to any formation of electric charges. However, the feather responded most decisively to Jan's commands, which at the end of the demonstration he was giving from about thirty feet away.

Jan Merta's PK force is admittedly rather small. But the importance of an unusual effect is out of proportion to its size. The interesting thing is that its size is not zero. However small the effect is, its ratio to zero is infinity. What is important is the mere fact that it exists. It is interesting to compare the force that Jan Merta applied at will to the feather with that which the Israeli psychic Uri Geller, now in the United States, can voluntarily apply to a delicate electric balance. It appears that Geller can exert a force of the order of one-twentieth of an ounce weight. It is easy to see that Jan Merta's force is of this order of magnitude and possibly is greater than Geller's. The poltergeist phenomena that accompany Geller obviously involve much stronger forces but this is not relevant to the comparison we are making. Why consciously directed psychokinetic forces should be much smaller than those that are released poltergeist-style is a mystery. But this is not what is remarkable about thought-directed PK. As Dr. Samuel Johnson said of a certain event that in his time was unusual, it is astonishing that it can be done at all!

15

PSYCHIC CANADIANS

Psychic abilities seem to be distributed very fairly among the nations of the world. Poltergeist outbreaks seem to take much the same form whether they manifest in Poona, Peking, Paris, or Pretoria. Similarly, each country has its psychic sensitives—Uri Geller in Israel, Croiset in Holland, Douglas Johnson in England. Canada too has great psychics like James Wilkie and very interesting people like Jan Merta. But to concentrate on the star performers would be to overlook the fact that psychic experiences befall a great many ordinary Canadians found in every walk of life. In 1961, in preparation for a series of radio programs, the Canadian Broadcasting Corporation advertised in newspapers for people who had had psychic experiences. They hoped for at least a dozen replies but received almost two thousand. Sidney Katz, then associate editor of *Maclean's* magazine, wrote (1961) that he was impressed by the intelligence and objectivity of so many of the respondents. They included businessmen, engineers, accountants, writers, actors, artists, and housewives. Some were university graduates or actively engaged in academic work. A high proportion of them seemed to be down-to-earth people free from crankiness or any unhealthy interest in the bizarre.

The more striking accounts were narrated in a series of CBC radio broadcasts but an interesting selection was published by Sidney Katz in *Maclean's*. This included several telepathic communications of the kind we mentioned in an earlier chapter, but also many precognitions and some interesting examples of possible clairvoyance. In one of these latter cases the chief designer of a construction company woke up in the middle of the night with a strong presentiment that a strut was missing from a particular section of a highway overpass that was under construction. He found no error in the blueprints. The next day he was assured by the engineer on the site that there had been no omission. But, still very concerned, he went straight to the section that had been indicated in his premonition and found that the strut was indeed missing. The designer had had other experiences of this kind which he felt amounted almost to possession of a sixth sense. Possibly this particular experience was merely coincidence and his concern merely the reflection of great conscientiousness. However, if it was ESP, then it may well have been pure clairvoyance or direct knowledge of the defect in the structure. But, as in many other instances of presumptive clairvoyance, it is almost impossible to prove that it must have been clairvoyance and not telepathy. One can argue that one of the site engineers or foremen, though not consciously aware of the omission, had noted it unconsciously and was being subliminally "nagged at" by the knowledge; the designer could have picked this up by a form of telepathy, because just as telepathic messages can be unconsciously received, so, it would seem, they can be subconsciously transmitted.

Katz's selection of precognitions was a very interesting one. Most of them, as he remarks, were presentiments of disasters or unpleasant experiences but they came to the percipients in different ways. Also, the time interval between the premonition and the event showed a remarkable degree of variation. For example, a man in British Columbia left a plane for Vancouver, which he had boarded at Kemano, because he was suddenly overwhelmed by a strong conviction that it would crash. En route it flew into the side of Mount Benson. Here the event followed the premonition by at most an hour or two. But in the case of Mrs. Andress of Brockville, Ontario, the time interval or latency was three days. On 7 July 1959 she dreamed that her son was lying trapped in a wrecked car by an uncompleted stretch of the MacDonald-Cartier Freeway near the

Thousand Islands Bridge. The accident actually happened at the precise spot three days later.

A Toronto housewife, Mrs. Forgie, used to have regular premonitions with a similar latency but in connection with a happier kind of subject matter. A few days prior to a horse race she would dream of the winner! Often these horses would have very long odds. Her dreams were, therefore, true precognitions and not rational predictions based on study of the form. A lady at Thornhill, Ontario, had a sudden hunch that her brother in England would soon be dead. It was ten days later that he became the one fatal casualty in a train crash.

In the case of a woman living near Halifax her premonition preceded the event by several months. Sitting at home with her husband one day, she experienced a sudden dizziness followed by a kind of waking dream. In the dream it seemed she was sitting in a fast train with her husband. He silently left the coach. She followed him through the train until he entered the luggage car, slamming and locking the door behind him. In the dream she banged desperately on the door shouting, "Let me in!" At that stage she awoke in her own living room, where she found herself beating the walls with her fists. The same dream was repeated twice; but when a few months later her husband suddenly died, it had faded from her memory. She took her husband's body on a long train journey back to his hometown for burial. En route, feeling a sudden urge to look at his coffin, she left her coach and went to the luggage car. The door was locked, and overcome with emotion, she found herself pounding on the door with her fists crying, "Let me in!" just as in her waking dream. This form of precognition, in which the percipient, as it were, lives through a future experience in advance, is a fairly common one.

A Hungarian widow living in Montreal told the CBC how she had had a dream symbolizing her son's death eight years before the tragedy occurred. When the child was three she dreamed of a priest standing beside a coffin. In the dream she knew it was her son at age eleven. In 1945 when Soviet troops advanced into Hungary she left her suburban house and took refuge in Budapest. Every night for two weeks she had the same dream repeated—she and her son were at home—suddenly the boy ran out into the garden (which in the dream she saw through a kind of haze) and lay down in a wading pool and died. Thinking the area was not under bombardment, in spite of the dream, they returned home one day to collect some of their possessions. A shell exploded in the garden and the boy's clothes were ignited by a splinter. He rushed out through the smoke and fumes, flung himself into the pool, and died. (Incidentally, it seems that this premonition would *not* have come true had the mother taken it as a warning and avoided going home.)

A woman in Vancouver, now a novelist and broadcaster, when living in England and only fifteen years old had a dream in which she found herself being held down in a bed of a hospital, which she felt was not in England, while she struggled to regain her sanity. She also awoke with a strong feeling that she would not survive her thirty-fifth year. She told the CBC that the dream was repeated at intervals, strengthening her foreboding of dying in a foreign hospital. The presentiment was so strong that she broke off several engagements to marry as she felt that she had no future. Though she came to Vancouver to do radio work she refused several good offers of posts in New York, feeling that the United States might be the foreign country of her dream. However, she eventually took a job in New York, which she held for five years. But, she developed a brain tumor and from March to June of her thirty-fifth year she was in a New York hospital fighting for both life and sanity. Fortunately she survived and has had no premonitions since.

Not all precognitions are concerned with disasters. One Toronto woman we know does often have genuine precognitions of deaths and illnesses of relatives and friends, and very upsetting it is. However, sometimes she has trivial precognitions about matters of no importance. Thus in 1967, whenever she reminded herself that she ought to get her car license, the number 100 came into her mind. When she finally lined up at the office to get the license, she checked to see what the number was likely to be. If received in order it would have been 487 083. In the event, the typewriter jammed and she got 487 100.

Often a precognition correctly reflects aspects of what will happen but the percipient receives no clue as to how it will come about. Carol Zmenak, wife of a Grimsby chiropractor, often has psychic impressions that come true. One night in 1970 she told her husband that if he went out somebody would be killed. She had had impressions of being awakened by a telephone call from the police and of a body without legs. Her husband went to a committee meeting in Toronto and before leaving spoke of this to two witnesses. On the way home all the electrical circuits in his car suddenly failed. Though a large truck was hard on his tail, he managed to park the car on the roadside near the Stoney Creek traffic circle and set out on foot for the nearest telephone. A police car stopped and when he learned what had happened the officer gave him a lift. They had hardly started when a car stopped on the other side of the road (Highway 8) and a man got out to ask the way. After receiving directions he started across the road toward his own car but was recalled by the police officer, who spoke with him again. The man set off across the road once more and walked in front of an oncoming car. He was killed instantly. Both of his legs were broken; his body was crumpled up so that only the torso was visible. Since the chiropractor had to stay as a witness, it was the police who telephoned his wife. Thus both parts of the premonition came true (Zmenak, 1972).

In the episode just described Mrs. Zmenak associated her presentiment with her husband's proposed journey to Toronto. This was correct, so that the time lag between prediction and realization was only a few hours. It is more usual, however, for the percipient to have no clue as to when the event foretold will actually take place. It may be days, months, or years later. This is equally true of highly endowed psychics. For example, on 13 September 1962, James Wilkie made a very striking prediction while making a recorded interview for *Tempo Toronto*, a nightly radio show. Present in the CKEY Studio were Norm Perry, Michael Hunt, Brad

Crandall, and Allen Spraggett. Wilkie said that total war was nearer than at any time since 1945. There would be a crisis centered on Havana. Disaster would be averted but only after a build-up of United States forces in Florida for an invasion of Cuba (Spraggett, 1967).

At that time no member of the public knew of the Russian missiles in Cuba, though it may be that the suspicions of the United States authorities had already been aroused. The missile bases were, of course, known to some Russians and Cubans, so that Jim Wilkie's prediction might possibly not have been a true precognition but have arisen from telepathy. However, what he had to say did refer to what was then the future and not to what was then the present. When the interviewers asked Wilkie when the crisis would occur, he said it was difficult to be precise, but he hazarded that it would occur in the first week of the "Christly month" (presumably December). The crisis was in fact more imminent: it flared up in October. However, Wilkie's guess was less in error than those made by many psychics in estimating the date of events they had foretold even though they may have accurately foreseen them in detail.

Some psychic people are able to recognize when a hunch is the "real" thing, i.e. a psychic impression and not a random thought, though usually they are unable to explain exactly what the difference is—it just "feels" different. Sometimes a hunch demands to be acted upon and if it is ignored the percipient will be punished by feelings of anxiety or even physical discomfort. For example, the woman mentioned above in connection with the 100 premonition suffers a severe headache if certain of her hunches are not immediately followed up.

However, sometimes a psychic impression cannot be acted upon, even when the percipient is convinced that it contains genuine information. This occurs when the meaning of the images which the percipient sees in a dream or in his mind's eye is obscure. For example, an Ontario high school teacher had a dream which he felt to be precognitive. In the event it was shown to refer to an accident happening to someone else and which was totally unforeseeable at the time. Among the images seen in the dream were two blue squares which the percipient could not interpret. However, on the basis of past experience he believed that the squares would, together with the rest of the dream, become meaningful. This in fact was so. A few weeks later he was attending a funeral service for victims of the accident. The blue squares of his dream were immediately recognizable: the members of the choir were wearing blue robes and blue "mortarboard" hats. Because psychic impressions can be so obscure, it is never wise to try to deduce logically what they refer to. Douglas Johnson, the English psychic, who visits Canada from time to time, says that he has to exercise great restraint not to attempt logically to deduce what an impression is really about, for the interpretation is all too likely to be mistaken.

Some people get psychic impressions but cannot reliably distinguish them from their other random thoughts or dreams. Consequently, they cannot be sure if their premonitions are genuinely prophetic or not. This makes it especially difficult for them to act on the basis of their hunches or presentiments. For instance, should they issue warnings of catastrophes? No one wishes to look a fool or be regarded as slightly mad. We run a Premonitions Bureau in Toronto. If you have a presentiment you are invited to send it to Box 427, Station F, Toronto. Public events are easier to evaluate than private ones and our correspondents tend to predict these rather than happenings in their own lives. Confidentiality is maintained and nothing concerning the person or his or her premonition is published without written permission. We are sometimes asked whether we would warn a person of a danger which had been psychically foretold. Our answer is that the person who has the premonition must do this himself if he has sufficient conviction in the truth of his prediction. This is not to say that if we had several detailed predictions of the same thing from different sources we would not act, but so far this has not happened.

It is sometimes very difficult for a person to decide whether to give a warning or not. One man we know had had some experiences which turned out to be true predictions and others which were not.

Last year he had an impression that a woman at his place of work was going to be killed in a street accident nearby, and in the lunch hour. He did not know her very well. After some thought we decided on a compromise solution. He would visit her office on some routine pretext and in casual conversation complain of the prevalence of street accidents and stress that it behooved everyone to be very careful, especially in that district. A few days later the woman was struck by a vehicle in the neighborhood during the lunch hour. Happily the premonition was not quite exact; she was injured but not killed. Precognition is rarely one hundred percent accurate.

If one deals much with psychic people one is always at risk of having predictions made about oneself. If possible, I always refuse them on the simple principle that if one is professionally concerned one should not allow oneself to get emotionally involved in the question of whether the psychic sensitives one is working with are right or wrong. This is not to say that I would ignore a very specific warning given me with great conviction by a psychic of high caliber like Douglas Johnson or Jim Wilkie. If told, for example, to avoid a certain plane flight on a specified day, I would probably do so. But vague warnings from lesser psychics are, I have found, not sufficiently reliable to burden one's mind with. Incidentally, we did once accept a prediction but this was from no less a person than Douglas Johnson. We were setting off to address a group at Port Credit on the subject of "Prophecy." Douglas said we would win a prize in a raffle and we did! We have won nothing else before or since.

Many people nowadays, especially in the big Canadian cities, have "psychic readings" from psychic sensitives. They often go to the reading with only the faintest idea of what to expect. At the worst, with the lowest class of professional psychic they will be shrewdly looked over. This psychic will make intelligent guesses as to their profession and character and will fish for information. The client's responses will often give away a great deal of knowledge about him without his realizing it. The better type of psychic will genuinely get a great deal of information about the client via telepathy or clairvoyance and will be able to discuss his particular problems, and if the psychic is a responsible kind of person (as the better ones usually are) he will get quite good advice. Indeed, some of the top psychics, in my opinion, successfully perform a role akin to that of the psychiatrist or social worker.

What people do not always realize is that most psychics, though they may be telepathic and even clairvoyant in some degree, are not necessarily precognitive. It is extremely unwise to regard the psychic as an inspired prophet, whose statements about the future are to be taken as gospel. Of course the best psychics do have flashes of genuine precognition and sometimes make remarkably detailed predictions which come true. But unless the client has had similar predictions previously from that particular psychic how can he put reliance on what is told him? The statements of some self-claimed psychics are indeed worthless and on a par with the "fortunes" vended by automatic machines at fun palaces. However, the better psychics will often give excellent advice. Sometimes this is just good advice, such as one might get from any experienced and wise person. At other times it may probe fairly deep. A psychic may say something like this: "If you overcome your tendency to indolence, stop quarreling with your boss, and cease resenting your wife's abilities, you will get a promotion and have a happier family life." When this is not based on what the client has inadvertently told the psychic, it may yet be true because it follows from a knowledge of the client's circumstances and character which the psychic has acquired by ESP.

Even with a great psychic it is not always easy to decide whether he had a genuine precognition or is making a projection into the future of present tendencies that he perceives by ESP. Thus a few years ago when Jim Wilkie was lecturing in Toronto he gave lightning readings on individuals in the audience. To one person he said, among other things, "I see you standing before a committee. Don't say too much. They will have all they need on paper. Just give token answers to their questions." Not long after, this person was interviewed for the post of school principal. His qualifications were excellent but he did not get the job because he did say too much—he put forward various educational ideas which were too innovative for the board at that time. Whether this was a precognition on Wilkie's part or a lightning summation of knowledge he had received by ESP is not really decidable.

The majority of psychics are less penetrating than Wilkie. However, those of good reputation will usually give advice which, if not especially pertinent, will be harmless and may be good. But, like all good advice one receives, it should be treated as merely one item among the many counsels and pieces of information one would normally draw upon when making a decision. On no account should one uncritically follow the advice of fortune-tellers whether they use playing cards, Tarot cards, palm reading, or scrying in a crystal ball. What they say is best totally ignored unless it is advice of the most platitudinous kind. This is not to say that some of the practitioners of the fortune-telling art do not have psychic ability. They may, on occasion, employ this talent to say something true and penetrating; but unless the client has already proved this as the result of much experience with this particular soothsayer he will not be in a position to assess the reliability of what is said.

A surprising number of people play (either singly or in groups) with the ouija board; and a surprisingly high proportion tend to take literally the messages or commands which are spelled out Usually there is little justification for this, and both spiritualists and psychic research workers issue warnings against developing an obsessive interest in the board's pronouncements. Dr. Albert Durrant Watson, who was president of a now defunct organization— the Society for Psychic Research, Canada—wrote to this effect in the early 1920s. "Howsoever we may waver in our theories of the source of matter communicated through ouijary [i.e. via a ouija board] we can be certain of the fact that continual use of the board is prejudicial to that end towards which all education should bend —careful and vigorous thinking" (Watson and Lawrence, 1923). It is possible that sometimes there is an ESP element in the "messages" spelled out on the ouija board, but usually they merely reflect the fantasies or wishful thinking of the operators.

The most experienced and gifted psychics have to guard against not fantasy but logic. If a psychic impression is received it may well be an isolated scrap of information and the meaning totally obscure. For example, I recall a woman of considerable psychic talent giving an experimental reading on another woman, who was completely unknown to her. At one stage the psychic lady said with some irritation, "I get 'Aggie,' and I get 'bandit.' What's bandit got to do with it?" Actually, Aggie is the second lady's mother, and Bandit is the name of Aggie's cat! One can easily imagine a puzzled psychic trying to reason out the meaning of "bandit"—was Aggie about to be captured by bandits, etc., etc? Douglas Johnson says that he has to take care not to try to deduce logically what some of his psychic impressions mean. They are best reported in their raw form without attempting interpretation.

This may be one reason why some psychics like Jim Wilkie deliver their impressions at a very fast rate—a precaution against their being adulterated by conscious reflection. Wilkie has several modes of acquiring knowledge by ESP. Since the age of twelve he has been able to go into the trance state. Allen Spraggett (1967) has described how Jim goes voluntarily into a trance state by relaxing in an armchair, closing his eyes, and breathing steadily. After a while he slumps in a limp condition. After a further interval his muscles tauten and he sits up again in a dignified posture. Though his eyes remain closed his face takes on a somewhat imperious and authoritative expression with a somewhat Oriental look. He then speaks with a voice differing considerably from the one he talks with in his normal waking state. It is as if the mind of a totally different person occupies Wilkie's body. This person calls himself Rama and describes himself as an ancient Egyptian who lived by the Upper Nile about 2000 B.C. When he awakens from the trance Jim Wilkie has no recollection of what Rama has said. This is usual with trance mediums, as they are called. Douglas Johnson has a trance personality, Chiang, who describes himself as a Chinese of the medieval period. Like Wilkie with Rama, Johnson is unaware of what Chiang says during the trances.

What is rather unusual among trance mediums is for them to be able to communicate with their "guides" (as personalities like Chiang or Rama are called) when they are in the normal waking state. But Wilkie says that while in his normal conscious state if he wants to know something he asks Rama and "Rama tells me." Whether Rama is a spirit or a construction of Wilkie's mind is extremely hard to decide. However, Wilkie says that he does acquire a lot of information by ordinary ESP without the intermediacy of Rama. His ESP feats include hunches and sudden psychic impressions such as he described in his own book (Wilkie, 1971) and traveling clairvoyance, as well as extremely insightful readings given on sitters in his presence. Like Johnson and other distinguished psychics, he is also adept at the strange art of psychometry, which we mentioned in an earlier chapter.

Jim Wilkie also has a method of working which does not seem to be psychometry but resembles psychometry to the extent that it exploits a kind of link or "ESP channel" by which information flows into his mind. He can get a very good impression of a person's character and circumstances from a quick glance at a sample of that person's handwriting, even though he is quite ignorant of handwriting analysis and makes no attempt to analyze the handwriting word by word or letter by letter. My wife and I did an experiment in which I showed Jim nine anonymous handwriting samples. Each specimen was a copy of the same text, which had been adopted on the advice of a qualified handwriting expert. The reading on each sample was dictated to me at great speed. Jim looked at the specimens very casually and briefly and I could not feel that he was actively analyzing the handwritings.

Jim had never met any of the people concerned; they were totally unknown to him. His readings were put away for a year and a half. I then gave them in random order to my wife—the only other person who knew all nine people—together with their names on separate cards in a different random order. Jim's descriptions were so good that my wife had no difficulty in matching them unequivocally to the names. On looking at the descriptions in detail we found also that Jim had correctly given the marital status of each of them and the sex of five of them, and picked out the only one of the nine who was born in the United States and not in the British Commonwealth. Statistically the results were so good as to leave no doubt that ESP had been at work and ESP of a high order (Owen and Owen, 1973). Of course the experiment had a flaw as Jim could have received the information from my mind by ESP. However, I respect his own opinion when he says that handwriting is a form of "link" to the person concerned which he finds particularly felicitous for establishing rapport, and my experiment certainly did nothing to contradict his belief. I may also have been wrong in thinking that he did not in some intuitive way analyze the handwriting, but the speed of his readings seemed much too fast for this to be a realistic possibility.

There are striking similarities and equally striking differences among the phenomena of leading psychic sensitives. Thus Douglas Johnson, like Jim Wilkie, while in his teens surprised his family by going into trance. Both have trance personalities or spirit guides (according to how one cares to look at it). However, Jim Wilkie's Rama will do ESP when Jim is in a trance, but Douglas Johnson's Chiang confines himself to moral teaching and answering questions about life after death and other philosophical topics. Both are capable, as we have found, of extremely high scores in readings on people directly or via psychometric objects. Each has, on occasion, scored one hundred percent in the sense that no statement made in the experiment is incorrect. Both have a minor anomaly of color vision, yet both see auras: Jim sees them narrow and in color, and Douglas sees them large but colorless!

Turning from eminent psychics to the average run of humanity, it would appear that the majority of us go through life without any striking psychic experience. This does not mean necessarily that we have *no* psychic talent. Many of us are "good guessers." This may result merely from natural shrewdness; on the other hand, many of us may have psychic ability in a muted or unobtrusive form. No one knows just how many psychic impressions are received unconsciously. Information obtained in this way, without our being consciously aware of it, could affect our judgments and course of action. What is called intuition may of course consist chiefly of subtle, rapid, and unconscious reasoning, but it may also involve some ESP. If, as I have often done, one addresses clubs or other groups on the subject of psychical research one will inevitably find that if there are thirty or more people present, then at least one of them will talk of some psychic experience he or she has had. It may be telepathy from a friend, a vision of a crisis apparition, a precognition, or involvement in a poltergeist outbreak. Therefore, at least three percent of Canadians must be expected to have had some "flashes" of ESP during their lives.

In between the rather small group of the very powerful psychics and the people who are psychic once in a lifetime come those who have repeated psychic experiences but irregularly and unpredictably. These may be telepathy, clairvoyance, or precognitions of the kinds we are already familiar with. Or they may be of a highly individual kind. Thus one Torontonian occasionally when he is reading a newspaper instead of seeing the actual page in front of him will briefly see what will be printed there in one or two days' time. There is a woman who sometimes sees not an aura but a kind of pall of blackness on a person. Each time that has happened the person has soon after been taken seriously ill or has died. This kind of vision would seem to be a premonition taking a symbolic rather than a literal form. Another woman sees a fleeting, shadowy kind of phantom a few hours before there is a death in her family. Some people do not seem to have psychic experiences as such but possess rather strange and individual talents such as an uncanny facility for finding missing objects or for making their way without the aid of maps or detailed instructions to obscure and totally unfamiliar places.

It may seem strange that nature has allotted psychic ability in such a capricious way. But though ESP is admittedly a strange faculty if we think of it as parallel to any other talent such as musical ability, then we should expect its distribution to be uneven and highly individual. Some can compose music and others conduct; some can sing beautifully, while others caterwaul; some have absolute pitch and others are tone deaf; some are congenitally incapable of reading a bar of music but can "vamp" on a piano, and so on and so on.

16

CANADIAN BREAKTHROUGH: TELEPATHIC WAVES IN THE BRAIN

In this book I have said almost nothing about experimental studies on extrasensory perception. Instead I have written a great deal about its spontaneous or free occurrences, mostly in everyday life. That is to say, I have been concerned with what can be learned from observation and description rather than from deliberately contrived experiments. There are several reasons why I have chosen this method of presenting the subject to the reader. Although experiments are an essential and vitally important part of psychical research, just as in any other science, the richness and wonder of psychic phenomena are shown far more adequately and strikingly by even a comparatively small selection of naturally occurring examples than by all the experiments that have been done in the ninety years that have passed since the foundation of the Society for Psychical Research in England. This is due in part to the fact that whenever we set up an experiment we are in effect restricting what we will observe: the experiment will yield information only on the particular phenomenon it was set up to test.

When we think of an experiment we tend nowadays to visualize white-robed scientists and their assistants in a laboratory busy making measurements of physical quantities—e.g. pressures or tensions, electrical currents or voltages, waves and vibrations, etc.— the results displayed on oscilloscopes, gauges, dials, or by computer print-outs. This is the popular idea shared by many scientists of what "real science" is. (Actually there is still a good deal of undoubtedly real science which is not done in quite this way—but I shall let that pass.) What would the ideal ESP experiment be like? For simplicity let us confine ourselves to telepathy between two persons—a sender and a percipient. The sender would be instructed to think a particular thought and would be attached to an appropriately designed machine which would register the electrical activity in his brain, corresponding to his having that thought. The percipient—preferably shut away incommunicado in a windowless, soundproof room—would be hooked up to a similar machine, which would register the electrical activity in his brain corresponding to thoughts he had. If the traces corresponding to the sender's thought and the percipient's thoughts agreed closely both in form and time of occurrence, then most people would feel that telepathy had been proved according to the methods of real science.

No one has yet done the ideal experiment, though I think now we are for the first time in sight of it. Later in this chapter I shall describe yet another Canadian breakthrough. We have reason to believe that the specific electrical response of the brain when a percipient receives a telepathic message can be exhibited. If this is confirmed by further and more elaborate experiments it will revolutionize that area of psychical research which is concerned with thought transference.

However, up to now the study of telepathy (and the other forms of ESP) has been to some extent handicapped by a feature that ESP experiments share with spontaneous ESP phenomena. In spontaneous happenings we have to assess whether the event was paranormal or merely the result of coincidence. If someone has a vision of a friend, previously in good health and not regarded as accident-prone, being hit by a truck at exactly the time that it happens this is unlikely to be coincidental and we can safely class the event as a psychic experience. On the other hand, if a person is concerned about a dying relative, a vision of that relative (unless it coincided very minutely with the precise time of death) would usually be regarded as possibly (though, of course, not certainly) a pure coincidence and would not be sound evidence for ESP.

Hitherto, all ESP experiments have had to cope with the problem of eliminating coincidence.

Though there have been exceptions, the vast majority of ESP experiments have been ones in card guessing. If we ignore all the necessary precautions which nowadays are built into the experiments to stop cheating, etc., a typical telepathy experiment will go somewhat as follows. In one room there will be a "sender" or "agent" with an experimenter. At intervals of one minute the experimenter will open a sealed opaque envelope and take out a card which has on it one of five possible pictures. The sender will contemplate the picture for, say, half a minute. In another room a percipient, supervised by a second experimenter, will try to guess just which of the five kinds of picture the sender is looking at. The percipient's guess is recorded either by the experimenter or by an automatic machine. It is important that until an envelope is opened no one at all (including the experimenters) knows which kind of picture it contains. Therefore the cards are put into the envelopes some time ahead. The envelopes are well shuffled and labeled with random numbers. The experimenter who is with the sender will then use a second series of random numbers to determine the order of presentation of the targets to the sender.

The kinds of pictures most used for targets (as they are called) have been five designs invented by Professor J. B. Rhine at Duke University in the early 1930s. Cards with these designs are called Zener cards. Zener cards can be bought in packs of twenty-five. Each pack contains five of each of the following somewhat abstract designs or diagrams printed black on white: a circle, a square, a Greek cross or "plus" sign, a star, a pair of wavy lines. The mode of presentation of the targets is usually so arranged that the chance of a target being a circle is just one-fifth; of being a square just one-fifth, and so on. Clearly if no ESP is operating the percipient will get about one-fifth of his guesses right. Correct guesses are called "hits." We say that the "expected proportion" of correct hits by chance (without ESP) is one-fifth. In fact, the percipient may get more hits than this (or fewer). If he gets vastly more than one-fifth hits we would feel very sure that he had got the extra hits by ESP. If he gets only slightly more hits than the expected proportion we would tend to say these extra hits were due just to coincidence or chance. There are various simple mathematical rules for deciding whether ESP is a more likely explanation than chance for extra hits. Instead of Zener cards some experimenters have used animal pictures, e.g. elephant, giraffe, lion, pelican, and zebra.

Now and again a percipient unequivocally demonstrates psychic talent by getting a very large number of extra hits. Sometimes the percipient is able to keep it up during very long experiments in which he guesses at hundreds or even thousands of targets. But this is rare; usually after a good run of success at the beginning the scores taper off so that the extra hits become too few to indicate more than the most rudimentary ESP ability. This phenomenon is so well known that it is given a special name—it is called "the decline effect." Two different explanations have been offered. One says that unconsciously the percipient fears ESP as something uncanny and disturbing to his view of the world; hence an unconscious mechanism acts to shut it off. The rival explanation says that the sheer boredom of the experiment inhibits ESP.

It is more usual for card-guessing experiments to show a very small ESP effect. The average percipient seems at best to be able to know one in twenty of the cards by ESP, all his other hits being due to chance. While I think that these experiments do prove the occurrence of ESP, some critics are of a different opinion and argue that these small effects are due to various imperfections in the experiment, such as a lack of perfect randomness in the presentation of the targets. Rightly or wrongly, this tends to put the experimenters on the defensive. This is entirely because the extra hits are few. In cases when the scores are really high the critics' arguments would fail.

In my opinion the card-guessing experiments that have been done in various places during the last forty years do show that a few people have strong ESP even in the card-guessing situation and that a large number of ordinary people do have a weak or rudimentary ESP ability. However, the majority of ESP experiments on record show only these weak effects, and in the study of ESP, as with other natural phenomena, we are at a disadvantage if we encounter it mainly in a feeble form. It is only from strong manifestations that we can hope to learn very much.

During the last few years investigators have been seeking new approaches in ESP experimentation. For instance, it was once hoped that psychedelic drugs might enhance psychic powers. Professor Duncan Blewett of the department of psychology at the University of Saskatchewan discussed this possibility in 1963. But this mode of attack seems not to have been proceeded with. What would be ideal would be to find some harmless substance that, added to one's diet, would give one ESP. It is often said that primitive people have more ESP than civilized men do. If this is true it is unlikely that it is due to any difference between our brains and theirs, which are quite big and work as fast. Conceivably it could result from diet, and perhaps we should start eating witchetty grubs or other exotic delicacies in the hope of releasing latent psychic talents! Another possibility is that psychic ability is not an endowment possessed by all primitive cultures equally, but is a result of genetic isolation; certain hereditary factors have been preserved in some cultures because they have not been lost by marriage outside the group and also are of some primitive advantage, e.g. in avoiding the dangers of the wild and in hunting and food gathering. A third explanation for the prevalence of psychic phenomena among primitives, if true, is entirely a psychological one. The argument is that in modern society any tendencies which children may have to exhibit psychic faculties are frowned upon so that these abilities become suppressed in early life.

This last explanation has been applied to explain the so-called decline effect in card-guessing experiments. It is commonly found that in such experiments people may do well for the first few hundred guesses but after that there is a marked falling off. It has been suggested that modern man has, either as an instinctive attitude or as a result of education, a fear of strange powers, and that should these powers be manifested the unconscious mind reacts so that before long they are repressed. This explanation has the advantage that it also tends to explain the phenomenon called "psi missing." Many percipients in card-guessing tests actually score consistently *below* chance, i.e. they make fewer correct guesses than they ought to by pure chance coincidence. It has been suggested that these people "know" by unconscious ESP what the targets are but are motivated, also unconsciously, to change their guess. This may seem to be rather farfetched, but it is the only explanation of "psi missing" that anyone has come up with, other than the hypothesis that it is a misleading appearance due to nonrandomness of targets and the percipients having preferences for some pictures rather than others when they make their calls.

Is ESP unique to the human species? If not, is it present in animals or even plants? Following on the work of Cleve Backster, which has been claimed to indicate a certain degree of psychic sensitivity among plants, particularly the philodendron and the rubber plant, the idea of plant ESP has been widely popularized. Some work on the skin resistance of plants when exposed to both physical and telepathic assaults is in progress in the Toronto Society for Psychical Research. It is, however, a difficult and delicate field of research and our results to date have been quite inconclusive.

Opinions differ as to whether animals may be expected to have extrasensory powers. Thus some writers suggest that ESP is a new faculty which man has only recently attained to as part of his evolution. On this theory ESP would be a human faculty only and absent from the rest of the animal kingdom. Others, including some distinguished zoologists, think that many animal species may have extrasensory perception and that its possession is advantageous to them. Indeed, there are many hints that domestic animals such as dogs and cats have a telepathic relationship with their owners, but this is difficult to prove on account of the normal sensitivity with which pets respond to their masters' attitudes (Secord, 1973). However, it is difficult to suppose that the capacity for "psi trailing" can be anything other than a form of extrasensory perception. Psi trailing is the name given to the extraordinary ability claimed from time to time for dogs and cats who find their way back to their "families" through totally unknown terrain, sometimes over hundreds of miles. Of course we do not know how many of these stories are actually true—some of these may be apocryphal like the tale of the ghostly pillion rider. Obviously all pets are not endowed with the psi-trailing ability or there would not be such enormous numbers of strays in the big cities. Those animals that can find their way home over great distances must be exceptional individuals like the great human psychics.

However, psychical research workers (or parapsychologists as they are sometimes called) particularly in the United States have carried out a number of laboratory experiments on ESP in animals. In Canada some experiments of this kind have been done by Dr. James G. Craig at the psychology department of the University of Waterloo with the participation of William G. Treurniet. In one such experiment rats born and raised within the laboratory were tested for activity in a standard situation. After testing, half of the rats were chosen by a random process which took no account of the amount of activity which they had shown. This group was painlessly put to death with chloroform a few hours after, while the other group was allowed to survive in comfort for another three weeks. It was found that rats of the first group, whose death was the more imminent, were to a significant degree more active than those fated to a delay of execution. It is as if some of the animals responded "precognitively" to their fate. It should be stressed that at the time that the experimenters were recording the activity of each individual rat they were completely ignorant of its fate, as the animal's destiny was decided by lot after the observations were made.

Dr. Craig's researches have not, of course, been confined to the psychic abilities of rats. Together with Dr. Gertrude Schmeidler of New York and Evelyn Garbatt of Waterloo he has studied the effect of mood on the manifestation of extrasensory perception in humans. Dr. Kenneth R. Keeling, also of the University of

Waterloo, did an interesting experiment to see if telepathy takes place in dreams induced by hypnosis. In the experiment a "sender" was hypnotized and given a card on which was written a description of a scene or episode. He was then instructed to have a dream incorporating this scene. In another room various percipients were also being hypnotized and told to dream about what the sender would dream. Later the sender and percipients were awakened and told to write down their dreams. A panel of "judges" then evaluated the dreams for resemblances between those dreams of the senders and those of the percipients. One group of percipients did well; their dreams showed a marked resemblance to those of the senders.

Dr. Keeling's work was inspired by a desire to exploit the well-known fact that the dream state is especially conducive to extrasensory perception, and to overcome the difficulty that in normal sleep we have many dreams which we forget. Hypnosis served as a means of limiting the spontaneous dream activity, helping to focus it on the senders. It should be stressed that this experiment was performed in a psychological laboratory and the hypnosis carried out by experts. Laymen should not attempt to imitate because inexpert hypnosis has real dangers.

Dr. Keeling's work is also in tune with the modern tendency to get away from the constrained artificiality of the card-guessing situation and to set up conditions more closely resembling those under which ESP occurs naturally in real life. That is why other Canadian psychical investigators have tried to replace the rather dull and uninspiring symbols of the Zener cards by more dramatic and exciting targets. Dr. Howard Eisenberg (now in Toronto) while qualifying for the M.D. degree at McGill University, Montreal, also did a piece of research for the M.Sc. degree in psychology. He chose a telepathy experiment but instead of getting his percipients to guess symbols on cards he used film sequences as targets. Twenty-four senders and twenty-four percipients participated on a voluntary basis. A sender located in a room at McGill would watch a randomly selected film sequence chosen for its emotional and dramatic impact. For example, one sequence was a scene from the movie *The*

Boston Strangler (Spraggett, 1973). The percipient in a room on another floor, and in the dark to minimize distraction, would try to tune in on the telepathic target.

Two methods were used to determine whether the percipient had received the sender's thoughts. Both percipient and sender wrote out an account of their thoughts and emotions during the attempted transmission. Also, the percipient was shown five photographs and asked to rank them in order according to how closely they corresponded to his predominant impressions. Unknown to him, one of these photos always was taken directly from the target film. If the percipient ranked that photo first, it was, of course, judged to be a bulls-eye hit. Careful statistical evaluation showed that over the twenty-four pairs of senders and receivers agreement was too close to be due to coincidence. The odds against the resemblances being due to chance were about 100,000 to one (Eisenberg, 1973).

Evelyn Garbatt of Waterloo, who was mentioned above, has devised an interesting approach to ESP experimentation via the ouija board. The board is not used to obtain messages from spirits. Instead, a group of percipients spell out their "guess" at a target picture or object. In a typical experiment a randomly drawn picture or object will be looked at by a sender in one room. In another room a group of people will be operating a ouija board. The idea is that instead of concentrating mentally to consciously receive the message they will be relaxed and leave it to their unconscious selves to guide the movements of the ouija board indicator. The method can equally well be used for clairvoyance.

The Toronto group have particularly interested themselves in long-distance experiments in ESP. This is because the relationship between ESP and distance is a particularly intriguing problem. Although telepathy has been called "mental radio," it seems to work differently from radio. As we know, the strength of a radio signal falls off sharply as the distance from the transmitter is increased. In empty space signal strength would obey the so-called inverse square law: at twice the distance the strength is one-quarter, at ten times the distance the strength is only one one-hundredth, and so on. Actually, with medium-length radio waves propagated between stations on the earth's surface, the falling off is not quite as sharp as this because the waves are reflected downward by the Heaviside layer of the atmosphere. However, there is still a very pronounced falling off. Extrasensory perception seems to be almost immune to distance. Spontaneous transmissions occur (as with the Wynyard apparition) over distances of thousands of miles. Similarly, card-guessing experiments with high-scoring subjects many miles, or even hundreds of miles, apart give results almost as good as those obtained with sender and receiver in the same room. There seems to be some slow falling off with increasing distance in the efficiency of ESP as manifested in card-guessing experiments showing weak ESP effects. Hence, it cannot be asserted that ESP is absolutely independent of distance. However, the falling off up to distances of 3,500 miles is far less abrupt than it would be for radio or any other form of radiation.

In a series of experiments conducted between sites in Toronto and between Toronto and Montreal we found that there was no effective difference in the power of ESP for distances of three miles, four miles, seven miles, and three hundred and fifty miles. In these experiments the actual scoring rate was very high; thus, the results at these big ranges were in every way just as good as could have been achieved between persons in the same room. We think that such high scores would not have been obtained with ordinary card guessing, and resulted from the way in which the experiments were set up. We were guided by the consideration that the group of senders should be both relaxed and interested in the images they would try to transmit. So we adopted the procedure of making telephone calls to the various percipients in Toronto and to Jan Merta in Montreal, saying that at a certain time we would be thinking about something or other, not yet decided, and that subsequently we would call again for them to tell us what impressions they had received. The group of senders would then have a free discussion as to the images they wished to send. Often we would have a picture drawn by Robert Neilly, a member of the group with a flair for graceful and humorous drawing. In the picture—or collage —we would incorporate whatever our fancy suggested—symbols, numbers, and sketches of scenes or objects. On one occasion the group forgot that they ought to be discussing what they would transmit and drifted innocently into an animated discussion of flying saucers and whether Ezekiel in the Bible had seen a UFO and extraterrestrial beings landing in the desert. When the time came this was made the subject for telepathic transmission with, as it turned out, excellent results (Owen, 1973).

The fact that up to distances of hundreds of miles telepathy (and probably other forms of ESP) is, so far as we can tell, independent of distance does not prove conclusively that it is not a form of radiation propagated like radio. For instance, the mind could be like an extremely sensitive radio receiver with a built-in automatic volume control. This possibility would be hard to deny. The only argument one could use against it would be to think it odd that nature should be so effective at concealing its mode of operation, like the White Knight in *Alice Through the Looking Glass* who "was thinking of a plan to dye one's whiskers green, but always use so large a fan that they could not be seen!" On the other hand, one could argue that the automatic volume control is a device to protect psychic sensitives from being shattered by titanic blasts of telepathy. Professor Michael Persinger of Laurentian University at Sudbury suggests that very low frequency electromagnetic waves may be involved in ESP. Unlike short-wave radiation, long waves are very penetrating and propagate to great distances. In a forthcoming book, *Patterns of the Paranormal,* he has assembled testimony concerning the times and seasons when ESP events seem most frequently to occur. Persinger believes there may be some relationships between the facility with which ESP happens and the state of the earth's magnetic field.

Clearly, Persinger is in sympathy with the school of thought that feels it would be wrong to assume that extrasensory perception does not have an explanation in terms of physical forces that we already know to exist, even though the mechanism may be a very obscure and subtle one. Another school of thought, however, is pessimistic of ever being able to explain ESP in terms of physical forces, whether forces that are already known, like electricity and magnetism, or forces yet to be discovered. According to this viewpoint telepathy, clairvoyance, and precognition are essentially nonphysical happenings; these events occur in another realm of being which interpenetrates the physical world but operates according to its own laws, which are not the same as those governing material things. For some people this is a repugnant idea as it is too reminiscent of the old notion that there is a material world and a spiritual or mental world—twin universes that intersect but are distinct from one another. The rise of modern science has tended to discredit the idea of two different realms of being. But this, of course, is not necessarily conclusive. During the last three centuries science has aimed deliberately at getting an accurate knowledge of how the material world works. Naturally, it has tended to find what it has been looking for. We have acquired a vast knowledge of the physical world but have learned little about mental and spiritual aspects of the universe. It is natural, therefore, to assume that a mental-spiritual realm is either nonexistent or a very subsidiary aspect of a basically physical universe. Whether or not this is true is an open question, which will have ultimately to be decided in the light of experience.

Various features of extrasensory perception suggest that it has a nonphysical basis. In precognition the percipient's mind is linked to events and objects that are not in fact physically existent. Only later do they come physically into being. It may be objected that the same is true of remembered events. Because the earth moves through space with a speed of many miles a second, when we remember an event that occurred a few months ago we are mentally putting ourselves in contact with a happening that took place millions of miles away. But this creates no intellectual problem because we are remembering by virtue of traces left in us which have traveled with us just like a letter carried by a postman. With precognition—"memory in reverse"—the situation (however we theorize about it) is quite different and we could claim that it operated by a physical process only if we revised our idea of what we mean by "physical" to such an extent that no physicist would recognize it.

Almost as mysterious is the ability of a telepathic message to go to its proper recipient like a homing pigeon flying to its nest. Psychic sensitives sometimes speak of themselves as "tuning in" on people they would like to have messages from. The comparison with tuning a radio set to the frequency of a broadcasting station is obvious. But are we to assume that the three billion or so persons on this planet are each broadcasting on a different frequency? Because ESP is comparatively insensitive to distance, some students of the subject prefer to liken telepathic contact to making a telephone call. This is called the "network theory" because it envisages that the minds of any two persons possessing ESP ability to send or receive are potentially capable of being linked by a channel of communication somewhat after the fashion in which two telephone subscribers can be linked by a series of telephone cables. If this is so, what and where are the telephone exchanges? Are they automatic ones or do they have operators? These questions may seem frivolous but are not really so; when we are trying to imagine how an unknown process could work we have to assist our thought by illustrations drawn from everyday life; this is the only approach available to us limited human beings. If the network theory is in any sense true the links in the network can hardly be physical.

As an alternative to the network theory we could postulate that contact between minds is mediated by a universal or cosmic mind such as we touched on when speaking of cosmic consciousness. The very concept of a universal mind tends to presuppose that if such an entity exists it cannot be a physical system. This is because no information can be transmitted by a physical system at a speed faster than light. The "cosmic mind," if physical, could not claim to have universal knowledge.

Because telepathy is, as we have seen, not necessarily a physical process we cannot assume that it is primarily an effect of the sender's brain on the brain of the percipient. We have to admit the possibility that each one of us, besides a brain, possesses something immaterial which for want of a better word can be called a mind. It is possible that in telepathy it is the mind and not the brain of the percipient that first receives the message. On this view it is only subsequent to the receipt of the message by the mind that related activity takes place in the nerve cells of the brain and nervous system of the percipient. In considering this possibility I do not, of course, wish to assert that telepathy does happen in this way. Indeed, there is no evidence yet available that is positively in favor of this theory. All that can be said is that it is by no means clear that telepathy takes place via a physical force or energy connecting brain to brain. This means that, even if some genius succeeded in performing the ideal experiment mentioned at the beginning of this chapter and showed that the electrical activity corresponding to a particular thought in the mind of a sender was paralleled by a similar burst of electrical activity in the brain of a telepathic receiver, we would have to be careful as to just what con-clusions we drew from the experiment. It would be easy to conclude that the electrical wave in one brain was the *direct* cause of the electrical response in the percipient's brain. As the electrical waves in both brains are certainly physical events it would be easy to suppose that the two events are connected by a chain of physical cause and effect. It would be true that the events are connected by a chain of cause and effect; what is not obvious is that the connecting link is a physical system. Also, as we have seen, it might be fallacious to suppose that one event is the direct cause of the other.

The ideal experiment which I outlined has not yet been per-formed. In fact, we do not yet have the technology to do it. How-ever, three years ago a group of Canadian physicians had a brilliant insight. They saw that the technology already existed by which one half of the ideal experiment could be carried out. This technology consists in a technique called *average evoked response,* which has been widely applied during the last few years though not previously used in psychical research. It is a branch of electroencephalography —the study of the electrical activity of the cortex of the brain.

The cerebral cortex is the layer of "gray matter" constituting the surface of the cerebral hemispheres of the brain and consists of a very great number of nerve fibers which themselves are made up of neurons—nerve cells. These neurons are always electrically active and at any time each point of the cortex produces a small electrical voltage. It is only a fraction of a volt. However, it is large enough to produce a small but measurable voltage on the scalp of the head. If an electrode is attached to a point on the scalp the voltage can be amplified and the resulting amplified voltage recorded on a chart recorder. The recorder works just like a recording barograph which registers changes in atmospheric pressure. In a barograph a pen is attached to a movable arm. The arm moves so that the height of the tip of the pen is proportional to the atmospheric pressure. Paper is moved on rollers at a steady rate. The tip of the pen thus traces out a graph in which atmospheric pressure is plotted against time. In this way all the variations of air pressure are recorded. In a precisely similar way the chart recorder supplies a record of the fluctuations of electrical voltage at the particular point of the cerebral cortex which is directly under the place on the scalp where the electrode is attached. The resulting graph is called an electroencephalogram, or EEG for short.

The electroencephalogram shows that the voltage which is developed at any one point of the cortex is not constant but varies markedly even within time intervals as short as one one-hundredth of a second. When one is awake and exposed to sensory input of all kinds—visual impressions, sounds, conversation, sensations in one's skin and muscles—and engaged in various physical or mental tasks —writing, doing arithmetic, haggling, conversing, walking, running, etc.—the EEG is a very irregular and wavering line. In other circumstances, however, it becomes much more regular. Thus, when one is in deep sleep the voltage at any point of the cortex rises and falls rhythmically at a frequency that is usually between one and four cycles per second. This is called the Delta rhythm. For instance, in a typical case the voltage on the scalp will reach a maximum value of one ten-thousandth of a volt twice in each second, and twice in each second will fall nearly to zero.

Most experiments on evoked response are done with a person in the so-called Alpha state. If one relaxes with one's eyes closed and abstains from thinking any elaborate thoughts and from carrying out tasks like mental arithmetic, the voltage at any point of the cortex tends usually to settle down into the Alpha rhythm. The peak value is then less than half that which occurs in the Delta state, but the frequency is considerably higher—between eight and thirteen cycles per second. Thus, in a typical case, the voltage will rise to a maximum about ten times a second and correspondingly fall to a low value ten times in each second.

We might note in passing that psychical research workers have attached great significance in recent years to the Alpha rhythm, or at least to the relaxed state in which it occurs, which is sometimes called the Alpha state. There is some evidence that people in this state score better in card-guessing experiments than when they are in the normal alert waking condition. There is also some support from spontaneous ESP occurrences which often do happen when the percipient is between sleeping and waking—a condition that somewhat resembles the Alpha state.

In a typical experiment on evoked response a person in a soundproof electrically shielded room and connected to an EEG amplifier is given a physical stimulus. The stimulus may be a pressure applied briefly to the surface of his arm or it can be a sound—a "bleep" lasting for about a fifth of a second. Whatever the stimulus is there will be an electrical response in the brain. This response consists of a rise in electrical voltage followed by a decline, then a smaller rise and another decline. After about half a second or so the response voltage dies away to zero. Now this response voltage does not replace the spontaneous Alpha rhythm voltage but is added to it, and the resulting graph of the cortical voltage does not show the response voltage in a clear-cut way; it is mixed up with the somewhat irregular Alpha rhythm voltage and it is hard to separate the two with any certainty.

However, there is a way around this difficulty. For simplicity, let us suppose that the stimulus is a bleep of sound lasting about a fifth of a second. What is done is to use an instrument called a tone generator to repeat the bleep every second, for about thirty seconds, i.e. half a minute. Each time this is done the evoked response voltage rises and falls, in almost identically the same way, so that its graph over each period of a second, if it could be drawn, would be of almost exactly the same shape. However, owing to the inherent fluctuation and irregularity of the Alpha rhythm or other spontaneous voltage produced by the brain cortex, the graph of this voltage will vary appreciably and be somewhat different in shape for each one-second interval. This gives a way of finding out the shape of the graph of the evoked response voltage. We can imagine that each second the chart recorder draws a graph of the mixed signal consisting of the evoked response and the spontaneous irregular Alpha rhythm added together. We can imagine also that a photograph is taken of the graph for each second and a negative developed so that sixty negatives result. The negatives are then superimposed so that a composite photograph results which represents, as it were, the average brain voltage. As the spontaneous voltage is irregular, it will be imperceptible in the composite photograph, but as the graph of the evoked response is fairly constant at each repetition it will stand out on the composite photograph as a bold line. In practice, the method of actually drawing separate graphs for each second and then photographing these is not done nowadays. The amplified EEG voltage is fed straight into a device known in the trade as a CAT, i.e., a "computer of average transients," which does the whole job automatically: the shape of the evoked response comes out the other end in any desired form— a column of figures, a graph drawn on paper, or a photograph.

A small group of Canadian physicians had the brilliant inspiration of replacing the repeated bleeping of the tone generator by repetitious projection of a thought at a percipient in a soundproof room. Before the experiment the receiver was told only that an attempt would be made to project a mental image to him, but he was not told what kind of image it would be or exactly when it would be projected. A sender outside the room and invisible to the receiver then repeatedly visualized a cup of coffee and willed the transmission of this image to the receiver. To get the correct timing the sender watched a synchronization light which flashed once a second and he tried to visualize the image briefly but very intensely once a second in phase with the light flashes. In the first experiment the percipient did not actually "perceive"—i.e. he got no impression of a cup of coffee or any other mental image—but the evoked response was traced out very clearly by the CAT. It resembled to some extent the response to the physical stimulus by sound, but the graph differed in some respects from that evoked by sound. The fact that the telepathic message did not register in the receiver's consciousness ties in well with numerous cases we have quoted of spontaneous ESP which is received unconsciously and makes itself known in a distinguished form.

Since the first experiment the procedure has been repeated many times with a similar result. Often the percipient has not been told that telepathy is being attempted, but nonetheless the brain shows an evoked response. Sometimes in the cases when he is told that it is a telepathic experiment the percipient has correctly guessed the particular image that the sender was attempting to transmit but most of the percipients have disclaimed receiving any psychic impression at all. Thus, usually, in these experiments the brain's reactions to the mental sending has not been reflected in the consciousness of the percipient. It should be stressed that when mental sending is not going on nor the tone generator being sounded the average signal delivered by the CAT is a flat straight line, at zero. This shows that the apparent response of the brain to a mental message is not merely apparent but real. Indeed, if it were otherwise we should have to suppose that the apparatus itself was defective and that the technique of average evoked response is faulty. This would be very serious as many important medical tests such as the determination of organically caused deafness would be erroneous, which of course they are not.

It should be mentioned that the persons chosen as percipients in the series of experiments that we are reporting (Lloyd, 1973) were all people who had a vague reputation for being psychic, but with the exception of one of them none had been tested for psychic ability in ESP experiments. The sender, however, was a person of marked psychic talent. Subsequent experiments will aim at discovering whether the evoked response is also obtained with nonpsychic receivers or senders. This may cast some light on the interesting question of whether or not it is true, as some people suppose, that all of us are constantly receiving psychic impressions which usually do not rise into our consciousness but which may have some effect upon the way we think and feel.

17

THE DEAD INDIANS SPEAK

When in the course of writing this book I had put the early chapters on paper I did not expect to refer again to the Indians of prehistoric Canada. But this was because I had not yet heard of the work of Professor Norman Emerson, a senior archaeologist at the University of Toronto. Professor Emerson is an authority on the mode of life followed in earlier centuries by the ancient peoples of Ontario—the Hurons, Iroquois, Ojibway, and others, of whom we have already spoken. Modern archaeology is a very laborious and painstaking discipline. The archaeologist has to piece together his knowledge of Indian life ways from the scattered fragments of material objects found on the sites of their ancient villages or in the fields which they cultivated. His first task is to find these sites and this itself is not always easy. Working with infinite care so as not to lose vital evidence, he has then to discover the ground plan of the houses and find the stumps of posts or locate the post holes that once supported timber and search over the original floor for debris of all kinds—bones, ashes, and the charred remains of food or of thatch and wattle. If he finds stone artifacts such as ceremonial tobacco pipes or human or animal effigies he counts himself lucky, for these will be in relatively good condition. Clay or pottery artifacts, however, are all too likely to be in the proverbial "thousand fragments" and have to be reconstructed by patient fitting together. The science of archaeology thus requires true dedication and a long apprenticeship.

Is there any "royal road" to knowledge, is there any quick and easy way? Emerson would say, "Not really," but in the light of some experience gained only within the last two years he would qualify this in one respect. As the result of working with a psychic Canadian, whom he refers to under the pseudonym "George," Emerson has come to believe that powerful psychics who happen to be emotionally attuned to archaeological material can be of real use in scientific archaeology.

Professor Emerson met George by chance. He had no reason to believe in George's abilities but, as an experiment, presented George with a fragment of pottery dug up on the Black Creek site in Toronto. George contemplated it, fondled it with his hands, and meditated upon it at length. He then correctly told Emerson that it was a pipe stem and gave the age of the site and its location. He described how the pipe was manufactured; he described the maker and provided details about the community and its living conditions. George then took pencil and paper and drew a picture of the pipe bowl which he stated had belonged to the broken pipe stem. Emerson was fascinated and impressed because he immediately recognized the picture as one of an Iroquois pipe of the kind that archaeologists call "conical ring bowl."

Emerson next gave George a fragment of the bowl of a pipe recovered from the shore of Bass Lake near Orillia. George again provided a wealth of information concerning this artifact—its age, location at finding, and how it was used by its original owners. He drew a picture of a modeled human effigy head which he stated had been broken off the edge of the pipe bowl. Emerson recognized the drawing as that of a pipe classified as "pinch-faced human effigy." Made by the Hurons, these pipes are found on late prehistoric and historic sites in Simcoe County, Ontario.

After a number of tests of this kind Emerson thought that a study of George's abilities would be eminently worthwhile. Two years of intermittent research in which George was tested with many many fragmentary artifacts led him to believe that the information George provided on prehistoric Indians was accurate about eighty percent of the time, i.e. about four times out of five.

Emerson also addressed himself to the problem of how George does it, and asked a number of important questions.

Has George gained his knowledge by study? No. A child of the Great Depression, he left school early to go to work and never became an avid reader. He has read little about Indians and appears to have only once visited the Royal Ontario Museum. In the field of Ontario prehistory George is uneducated and uninformed. Emerson is convinced that George's statements are intuitive; that is, they are in essence the product of intuition—immediate knowing without the conscious use of reasoning. By saying that George is uneducated in archaeology, Emerson (as he makes clear) means only that it is in this technical field that George is ignorant. He describes George as a warm, intelligent, and thoughtful human being, but just not cluttered up and overlaid with pedantic and restrictive book learning. George's archaeological insight is definitely not the result of scholarly study.

Does George read Professor Emerson's mind? George, says Emerson, does tell him things that coincide with his own knowledge and thus could be acquired from him by telepathy; but George also makes statements of new knowledge and statements which disagree with Emerson's knowledge and expectations. This suggests that the psychic is doing much more than just reading the professor's mind. For example, a woman sent Emerson an old coin she wished to know about. She mailed the coin from a place called Markstay. Emerson did not know the location of this place, nor did he mention the name to George. The coin was of George III vintage and could have come from anywhere in the world. George said immediately that it had been found in an area defined as "Sudbury, North Bay, Callender." Emerson checked the atlas; Markstay is twenty miles east of Sudbury and sixty miles west of North Bay and Callender—a very accurate identification in relation to the immense extent of the province of Ontario.

On another occasion George and the professor visited the prehistoric Iroquois Quackenbush village site, north of Peterborough. George said that these people did not cultivate corn, beans and squash. This was a surprise to Emerson, who found it hard to accept the idea that they did not have these traditional Iroquois crops. (Indeed, the "three sisters," as they are called, were grown by most Indian farmers in North America.) Also, the archaeologist working there said he had recovered abundant evidence of these plants on the site. So it looked as if George was wrong. However, it occurred to Emerson that these Iroquois might have obtained their vegetables by trade instead of cultivation; so he investigated the pollen grains in the soil. It turned out that the "three sisters" were totally unrepresented except for one solitary corn pollen grain, and that a rather problematical one. Whether a more extensive search for pollen will prove George right or wrong is immaterial: the point is that he could not have got the idea that the Quackenbush Iroquois did *not* cultivate corn, beans, and squash from Emerson.

Does George receive information by mental telepathy from persons other than Professor Emerson? This indeed cannot be ruled out. The "ESP channel" by which psychics receive information often seems to be obscure, meandering, and roundabout. Emerson says, "The strongest argument against mental telepathy of the more usual kind is the fact that the bulk of George's statements relate to a very dim and distant past. They relate to a period of anywhere from five or six centuries to five or six thousand years ago. It almost seems as if he is receiving telepathic information from people who were there at the time and who had specific information about those times. It is difficult to even begin to offer a comprehensive or even a comprehensible explanation of the above phenomena. They certainly involve more than traditional mental telepathy. I have explanatory thoughts of my own; but at this point in my studies it would seem most prudent to reserve judgment for the future."

The most usual response of the psychic research worker would be to classify George's skill as *psychometry*. This, of course, is only introducing a word for something we do not understand. How the psychic person can get knowledge of another human being just from physical contact with an object that has belonged to the other is a complete mystery. Perhaps the "ESP channel" runs back to a universal storehouse of knowledge. Perhaps the spirits of the makers of the artifacts convey their history to George. Has George had many, many incarnations as an Ontario Indian? It is I who am setting out this list of possibilities, not Emerson.

The form in which the knowledge comes to George is not mere thought or mental impressions. He sees visual images and hears sounds "in his mind's eye" when he is attuned to an artifact. George shows a remarkable sensitivity to the artifacts that he handles. He describes them as hot or cold, alive or dead. The older the artifact the colder it seems to George. Strange as it is, his age assessments by this means are quite accurate, so that this sensitivity is not illusory.

According to Emerson, like many psychics, George is a specialist. Old objects do not bring out his talent unless they are Indian. He is interested in Indians as it is in this area that his pronouncements prove out most accurately and the area in which he exhibits the most interest and enthusiasm.

George's psychic ability where ancient Indians are concerned is not restricted to the psychometry of artifacts. He is also sensitive to archaeological sites. "Upon a site, he almost quivers and comes alive like a sensitive bird dog scenting the prey," says Emerson. Knowing where to dig is one of the archaeologist's chief problems, and a person like George can save him weeks of fruitless effort. The psychic person is, of course, no substitute for the basic and approved methods of archaeology. But he can be a useful auxiliary provided he has been proved reliable. The proving out of George and the uses of "Intuitive Archaeology" will be the themes of a forthcoming book by Norman Emerson.

18

TORONTO BREAKTHROUGH: PSYCHOKINESIS FOR ORDINARY PEOPLE

In this book I have not tried to discuss either Spiritualism in general or Canadian Spiritualism in particular. My reason for this is not on account of any hostility to Spiritualism—indeed I think many of the criticisms of Spiritualism and of spiritualistic churches are not justified. I abstain from treating this important subject for the best of reasons; I have neither the personal experience nor sufficient historical knowledge of Spiritualism in Canada to do justice to it. An inadequate treatment would, I feel, be likely to mislead and is therefore best not attempted.

There is, however, an area in which PK phenomena and Spiritualism overlap—the physical phenomena in the séance room. Over the last hundred years or so there have been many groups of people who meet regularly to sit in what are called mediumistic circles. This is done in the hope of receiving messages from the spirits of deceased friends and relatives. In a typical sitting or séance the participants are seated with their hands on top of a table, sometimes with their fingers touching, sometimes not. It is said that the spirit who is supposed to be present often causes a variety of strange physical effects to occur: the table may rock or even be lifted up from the floor; rapping noises may come from the table or elsewhere in the room. Other objects in the room may move, even ones as substantial as chairs and other heavy furniture.

In the old days there was serious doubt as to whether these phenomena were genuine. This was because it was believed that for them to occur a specially endowed person known as a spirit medium was required. It was also easy to cheat because it was believed that the sittings or séances had to be in darkness or in subdued light. However, not all mediums appear to have been fraudulent or to have worked in darkness. Research by Sir William Crookes, who worked with the famous medium D. D. Home in a good light, and by Harry Price and other famous investigators who studied Stella Cranshaw in 1923, proved that some of these physical phenomena were genuine and not the result of trickery.

In 1973 a group consisting of eight members of the Society for Psychical Research in Toronto decided to find out more about these mysterious effects. They wanted to find out, first, whether they could be produced in full light; second, whether a spirit medium was necessary or if, instead, they could be generated by ordinary people; and third, if the force involved was produced by a disembodied spirit or instead was generated by the living participants in the circle. The group was an ordinary cross-section of the population: an accountant, an engineer, an industrial designer, a scientific research assistant, and four housewives. None of them claims to be a medium. Psychical research is just one of their many diverse interests.

Their work had started as early as the fall of 1972. For a year they met weekly for a couple of hours, in a sustained attempt to summon up an apparition or ghost. Perhaps when it came it might be merely a collective hallucination, but for all they knew to the contrary, it might come as a materialized figure of ectoplasm, or of astral material of pure mental energy, if such things do exist. The point is that though by nature they were all skeptical and scientific, they were also truly open-minded. One could say that the group's point of view was that one cannot absolutely deny the existence of phenomena that one has not taken the trouble to look for. So that their effort would not be aimless and uncoordinated they did not sit around in the casual hope that any passing spirit (if such there be) would choose to drop in on them. Instead, they decided to concentrate their thoughts as a group on a single character, "Philip."

Philip's story in brief is as follows. Philip was an aristocratic

Englishman living in the middle 1600s at the time of Oliver Cromwell. He had been a supporter of the king and was a Catholic. He was married to a beautiful but cold and frigid wife, Dorothea, the daughter of a neighboring nobleman. One day when out riding on the boundaries of his estates Philip came across a gypsy encampment and saw there a beautiful dark-eyed raven-haired gypsy girl, Margo, and fell instantly in love with her. He brought her back secretly to live in the gatehouse near the stables of Diddington Manor—his family home. For some time he kept his love nest secret, but eventually Dorothea, realizing he was keeping someone there, found Margo and accused her of witchcraft and stealing her husband. Philip was too scared of losing his reputation and his possessions to protest at the trial of Margo, and she was convicted of witchcraft and burned at the stake. Philip was subsequently stricken with remorse that he had not tried to defend Margo and used to pace the battlements of Diddington in despair. Finally one morning his body was found at the foot of the battlements where he had cast himself in a fit of agony and remorse.

The story continues that Philip has been reincarnated several times since then, but once every century or so his ghost is seen on the battlements at Diddington. The group decided that the present time is a period between incarnations and that his ghost should again be evident. The theory was that if he could be materialized and reassured that Margo had forgiven him, and is indeed "on the other side," then he would be at rest.

The group spent some time fixing in their minds a picture of Philip which tallied with his legend and with all their individual ideas of him as a person. In fact, a "portrait" of Philip was drawn by an artist member of the group. The group members agreed that this picture was consistent with the ways in which, individually, they visualized him. They could not trace a Diddington Manor but deemed the legend to relate to Diddington Hall, a small mansion in Warwickshire, England, built of red brick in Tudor or Jacobean times and which one of the group had visited some years before. Subsequently two other members of the group visited it while in

England and brought back pictures of the house, the stables, and surrounding countryside.

The séances started with the group sitting in a circle around a table and meditating in silence, initially for periods of ten minutes, later increasing the time of meditation, and the place would not necessarily be constant, the group meeting in various homes. After the period of meditation the group would discuss their experiences and feelings during meditation and also discuss the story and personality of Philip.

At this stage, also, an observer was stationed outside the group to witness any unusual phenomena that might occur. This observer, who is an "aura viewer," frequently described auras around the participants, and also energy fields, passing from one member to another, and around different persons. On occasion all members were aware of a certain mistiness in the room or around the center of the table, although the atmosphere was quite clear. Smoking was not allowed until after the period of meditation.

The group continued to meet in this way weekly for a whole year, and during this period the members had come to relate to each other extremely well; they were completely relaxed in each other's company and a strong bond of affection and friendship was becoming evident.

In the summer of 1973 work which had been done in England during the previous ten years came to the attention of the group. This work had been started in 1964 and continued with intermissions until 1972 (Batcheldor, 1966; Brookes-Smith and Hunt, 1970; Brookes-Smith, 1973). However, those members who had read of it previously had not realized its relevance to their current experiment. Batcheldor and, later, Brookes-Smith and his associates were specifically interested in producing physical effects such as table levitation and raps, but our Toronto group wondered if a similar approach might also work in the creation of Philip. In any case it was felt at that time that a different approach was needed, as the effects produced so far had been minimal.

Batcheldor and Brookes-Smith and Hunt recommended an approach to physical phenomena more closely approximating the old type of séances as performed during the Victorian era. Instead of quiet, concentrated meditation, an atmosphere of jollity and relaxation should be created, together with the singing of songs, telling of jokes, and exhortations to the table to obey the sitters' commands. In their papers they gave a completely reasoned philosophy as to why this method worked. Our Toronto group decided that, as we had worked for a whole year on the other method without many obvious results, we would try this recommended method. Consequently, at a meeting in late August 1973 at the home of one of the members the group tried this new method. They found it a little difficult at first to dispense with the meditation method they had become accustomed to and were a little inhibited in producing an atmosphere of singing and jokes. Apart from a feeling of "vibration" in the table at times nothing happened in this session.

But at the following session, and on subsequent evenings, using this method, very extraordinary things happened indeed. The first experience was the "feeling" of raps in the table. "Feeling" is the right word because these raps were definitely felt rather than heard at this initial stage, and also because the group was making a degree of noise at the time and would not necessarily have been able to hear the raps if they were audible. It should be stated that these sessions were conducted in a fair degree of light. During the first two or three there was a lamp in the corner of the room and sometimes also a lighted candle on the table. Later the group worked in a general rosy light which made it perfectly possible to observe clearly everything happening. At no time did the Toronto group work in the dark.

The year's building up of rapport now paid off. After the initial hesitation the group found no difficulty in relaxing, singing jolly or sentimental songs, telling jokes, and generally creating the kind of atmosphere recommended by Batcheldor and Brookes-Smith. When the group sang particular songs, especially songs associated with the period that Philip lived in, the table began to respond by producing raps, which became louder and more obvious as time went on.

The group adopted the procedure of addressing the table as "Philip." Philip himself adopted the procedure of one rap for yes and two for no with slight, hesitant knocks when the answer was doubtful or the question apparently not understood. He would also give a loud series of raps for a song of which he approved and very soon adopted the habit of actually beating time to favored songs. At the beginning of each session the members of the group would address him in turn, saying, "Hello, Philip," and under each hand in turn there would be heard a loud and definite rap. Again, at the end of the session the group would individually say "Good night" and get individual responses. Questions were asked regarding Philip himself, his likes and dislikes, his habits and customs, and the Philip of the table responded exactly in the manner one would expect. In other words, the table recreated the personality of Philip. However, on occasion, the table would rap out an answer inconsistent with the story, which intrigued the group—for instance, he twice denied quite vigorously that he had loved Margo—the keystone of the story! This the group found most interesting and unexpected.

It should be stated that the initial sessions were held in the home of one of the members. An ordinary plastic-topped metal-legged card table was used. After two or three sessions the group moved to the home of another member where a room was set aside for the sessions. A similar card table was used—in actual fact several tables were experimented with, all with a similar result. The floor was thickly carpeted, and in ordinary circumstances it was very difficult to move the table by pushing it on this floor. Needless to say, the raps could not have been produced by someone's feet tapping the floor. The raps became louder and were clearly audible during quiet moments during the sessions. They moved about the table, often appearing to come from within or underneath the table. They were equally audible and prolific if the group were all standing up around the table, with all hands in view, fingertips lightly resting on top of the table. Later it was found that it did not matter if everyone was not resting hands on the table, and various combinations of members of the group were able to produce the phenomena alone—the last occasion being when only four members of the group were able to be present, and another member of the Society who had not been aware of this work had come in, and the phenomena occurred with just the four group members and the complete stranger.

After some four weeks of sittings when raps were produced, one night suddenly the table started to move and it moved around the room in random fashion. The sitters were forced to vacate their chairs and follow it. It would move right into corners, forcing most of the sitters to relinquish their contact, and then shoot across the room at great speed, so that at times it was difficult to keep up with it. When it came to rest, the sitters, standing around the table, would continue their questions, and the raps would come forcibly and apparently intelligently, as before, thus demonstrating again that no one was tapping from underneath.

The table developed quite a personality, and the sitters were enjoying the whole thing immensely; at times the situation became hilarious. Philip was showing preferences—likes and dislikes, and also apparent preferences for members of the group—together with an aptitude for mischievous pranks—he was apt to chase a particular person; on one occasion a member had left the room, having said good night, and then had to come back for her jacket. Philip made a very definite and obvious attempt to prevent her getting the jacket and finally whooshed across the room in chase! At times he showed a tendency to sulk at something he did not like, while becoming completely noisy and appreciative of songs or jokes he approved of. He particularly liked drinking songs, as befitted a Cavalier!

On one occasion, on a hot evening, the table had been particularly vigorous, and the group had been trying to persuade Philip to lift the table, as in the Brookes-Smith experiments. This had been unsuccessful, and to date there has been no real and obvious levitation. One of the members said, "Well, Philip, if you are not hot and tired, we are; we would like a rest. Why don't you just flip right over, and then we'll all have a glass of lemonade and a rest." Whereupon the table immediately tilted and, with all hands on top of it, gave a curious little "flip" and landed completely upside down with all four legs in the air. (It should be stated that the group were all standing up at the time, and so there was no question of a push with the knees—there was nothing underneath the table.)

During this period of rest, with the table still upside down, another member of the Society came into the room, a member who had not been associated with this experiment in any way and who was quite skeptical of all the phenomena. The group righted the table and introduced the visitor, R. The table responded with a slight tap. "That's not loud enough," said one of the group. "You can do better than that." Whereupon a very loud rap was heard from the center of the table. R. was allowed to join the group and on his speaking to Philip very loud raps were heard immediately under his hand in reply. At that stage the group invited me into the room. Previously all visitors had been excluded in case they disturbed Philip.

That was the beginning of Philip's social coming out. That same evening the group let five more people come into the room, and two of them were allowed to take places at the table with their fingers resting on top. Philip continued to perform; the raps could be heard clearly and distinctly from several feet away. Prior to hearing the raps and seeing the table movements the visitors were highly skeptical but went away satisfied that these happenings were produced paranormally and not by the group members tapping with their hands, feet, or knees. On subsequent evenings Philip became even more sociable and has "conversed" for long periods with a number of guest sitters. It was found that if it was desired to converse with Philip only by raps a good deal of the boisterousness could be omitted. Philip would reply immediately without an elaborate build-up.

Shortly after this there was a period when various members of the group were obliged on occasion to be absent from the sittings, either on account of minor illnesses or having business out of town. As a result it was found that Philip will still converse in raps even when as few as four group members are present. Also, it was found that no particular member of the group is essential for the phenomena to occur. Each member of the group has at some time been absent, yet raps and table movements have taken place. This is very interesting as it shows that the phenomena are not regulated by a single mediumistic individual. If it is the case that the physical force which makes the raps and table movements is generated by the group members themselves, then it is a case of collective psychokinesis or, as one might say, PK by committee. As with other committees, only a quorum need be present for business to be transacted. It will be recalled that the members of the group were not selected because they had PK ability, indeed none of them had experienced poltergeist activity or spontaneous physical phenomena. Our result suggests, therefore, that most people have some latent or potential PK ability that is too feeble and unchanneled to produce phenomena; however, when a group is working together, the PK powers are combined and, in aggregate, are large enough to be effective.

Is the spirit of Philip really present at these sittings? Or are the phenomena merely the result of the group members directing their thoughts to the same end because they share the same idea of Philip? To decide this question would require a much fuller discussion of the sittings and the background to them. All this will be given in a forthcoming book by Iris Owen and Margaret Sparrow, which deals with all these problems. Irrespective of how these questions are decided, however, the Philip research has been valuable because it shows that group psychical phenomena can be produced in full light and without darkness and without a spirit medium. The Philip research does not necessarily validate the full spiritualist assumption that the presence of a disembodied spirit is necessary for physical phenomena to occur in the séance room. This is because, in this instance at least, the operative factor is not the actual spirit of Philip but, instead, the *idea* of Philip in the minds of the group members. On this line of reasoning, although Great Turtle of the Ojibways was a purely imaginary being, if the shaman had the idea of Great Turtle fixed sufficiently in his mind, then genuine paranormal phenomena might result, perhaps even the "direct voice." However, the Philip research does show that, regardless of their interpretation, the physical phenomena of Spiritualism cannot be dismissed out of hand as being, in all cases, the results of fraud or poor observation. Instead, it would seem that the physical phenomena in some séances are genuine paranormal phenomena—examples of PK.

Since October 1973 many many visitors have sat at the table with the Philip group, and conversed with Philip, receiving yes and no answers to their questions, often delivered by raps under their own hands. The raps do not sound the same as blows on the upper or lower surface of the tabletop would. They seem to come out of the woodwork itself, as if the molecules of the wood had been set in vibration by an internal force. Philip's visitors, however friendly and well disposed, usually start off with a skeptical attitude, but after an hour or so at the table leave as complete converts to the reality of the phenomena. In January 1974 we made a film called *Philip: The Imaginary Spirit*, showing the group at work and recording Philip's raps in response to questions. This movie, which may be rented or purchased from George Ritter Films, Ltd., 2264 Lakeshore Boulevard West, Toronto, Ontario, Canada M8V-1A9, is a landmark in physical research.

19

AN AFTERNOON WITH URI GELLER

Philip's outstanding performances under bright lights and in the presence of strangers seemed a fitting climax to our 1973-74 research session. We were well pleased and did not think that within a few days we would be witnessing other strange physical phenomena in Toronto. However, it proved to be a case of one thing leading to another, and most interestingly too. Joan Schafer, CITY-TV's producer, told us that Uri Geller had agreed to record an interview for Channel 79 some time during his visit to Toronto, which was scheduled for the next week. She invited the TSPR to form the main part of the studio audience and to advise on the way in which the interview should be carried out. We were happy to agree to this because we had long been interested in Uri's remarkable phenomena.

I should explain that Geller was born in Tel Aviv in Israel in 1946, the only child of an army officer. His mother is a distant relative of Sigmund Freud, the founder of psychoanalysis. When he was eleven years old his family moved to Cyprus, where Uri gained an excellent command of the English language. Somewhat earlier he had become aware that psychokinetic events happened in his presence. The hands of his watch would behave in a peculiar and erratic manner and the wristband broke inexplicably. These were the first instances of Uri's effects on metals which have since become so much a subject for discussion. In 1965 at the age of eighteen Uri returned to Israel and served for three years as a paratrooper in the Israeli army. He was wounded in the Six-

Day War and sent to a rehabilitation center. In 1968 he was sent on leave from the army to work as an instructor in a children's summer camp. Another young man at the camp took a special interest in Uri's phenomena. Uri says that in the presence of this friend his powers of mental telepathy manifested very strongly. The young man taught at a school in Tel Aviv and one day persuaded Uri to give a demonstration there of both his mental phenomena and his ESP powers. The teachers were impressed and the students fascinated. He was invited to demonstrate at other schools. Soon he was in great demand for lecture-demonstrations before large audiences.

Uri came to the attention of Dr. Henry Puharich, a physician in the United States well known for his work in medical research and related subjects, as well as for contributions to psychical research. Dr. Puharich visited Israel in 1971 and observed Uri's phenomena over a period of some weeks. Convinced by his own observations that Uri's phenomena were entirely genuine and very remarkable, Dr. Puharich persuaded Uri to come to the United States in 1972. He demonstrated his phenomena on many university campuses and to groups of prominent people, including many scientists. Very little in the way of formal reports on these demonstrations has been published, but word has it that the select and high-level audiences were often genuinely astonished and sincerely impressed. Some distinguished persons have gone on public record as convinced of the paranormality of those of Uri's phenomena that they have seen. These include Dr. Edgar D. Mitchell, the scientist and astronaut. Soon after his arrival in the United States, Uri spent five weeks at the Stanford Research Institute at Menlo Park, California. This is a private corporation which carries out research in various branches of science, working under contract to various organizations, industries, or government agencies. Though not part of Stanford University, it has a distinguished staff and high reputation.

The findings of the research done there by Dr. Harold Puthoff and Russell Targ have just been published. The institute has just also issued a film in which Uri performs the feat of finding which of ten identical metal cans contains a ball bearing. He does this by passing his hands over the cans at a height of a few inches. In the film he correctly picked out the can containing the bearing. In fact, he succeeded in ten independent repetitions of the experiment. The odds against doing this purely by chance are ten billion to one, which shows that in appropriate circumstances Uri manifests a remarkable ESP ability. The film also shows Uri exerting, by mental concentration from a distance, a PK force on a delicate electric balance. (This instrument is operated electrically but measures mechanical not electric force.) The force was not large, about one and a half grams, i.e. a force about equal to that which would have been exerted if a weight of about a twentieth of an ounce had been laid on the platform of the balance. This is indeed not a large force, being of about the same order as that which Jan Merta exerts in moving his feather, but the sensitivity of the electric balance is such that I, for one, have no doubt that it was correctly measured and that Uri did produce this force by mental concentration.

Otherwise, at the time of Uri's visit to Toronto we knew that objects were said to be sometimes teleported away in his presence, or to arrive as apports. In this respect he is somewhat like the poltergeist person in that he does not have full control over these appearances and disappearances and can regulate them voluntarily only to a limited degree. It was this fact that inclined me to believe that Uri was sincere and his phenomena paranormal, because the element of capriciousness is very characteristic of real PK as opposed to magicians' tricks—which never never fail. As regards his mental phenomena I had met witnesses who testified that their own keys, spoons, or forks, held in their own hands, had bent while they watched. Sometimes Uri was gently stroking the object in question, but sometimes he was a few feet away. However, there had been talk that he was a "showman." Various magicians around the world had declared that Uri was a magician and that his phenomena were magician's tricks. I did not give much weight to this because I have heard magicians say this kind of thing before about other parapsychological phenomena. I have never been particularly impressed, because these vociferous conjurors seem to be better at talking than doing, and rarely, if ever, reproduce the phenomena in exactly the same form and exactly the same circumstances as PK happenings actually occur. To make his case good, it seemed to me, a magician-critic of Uri must be capable of bending a metal object provided by an experimenter, and preferably held by the experimenter, and retained by the experimenter afterwards so that there is no possibility of substitution or sleight of hand.

Correspondingly, if Uri could do this with my own objects in my presence I would be quite convinced of his paranormal abilities and would not hesitate to announce this fact publicly. As it happened, this is exactly what occurred. While in Toronto Uri was interviewed on the morning of 7 March by Pat Murray on the *Toronto Today* program. Only the morning before, Murray had interviewed my wife Iris and Margaret Sparrow in connection with the work of the Philip group. In his interview with Uri, Murray mentioned the Philip phenomenon and asked Uri's opinion. Uri said that in the light of his own experience it was most believable that other people could produce psychical phenomena and he would like to meet the Philip group and see them in action. This expression of interest was indeed sincere because Uri told Joan Schafer that he would be willing to record an interview at CITY-TV provided the only audience (apart from a few friends of his own and some studio personnel) were the Philip group and their close associates in the TSPR.

I saw Uri in a TV interview with Pat Murray. I have listened to many fast talkers during my life and was able to recognize immediately that Uri was *not* of that ilk. Instead, he seemed an honest person, who spoke with sincerity and without affectation. In a discussion with Joan Schafer and Patricia Murphy (who was to conduct the CITY-TV interview) I said that I thought Uri was a sincere person and therefore that his phenomena were probably genuine. We decided that the interview should be directed primarily at letting Uri talk about his phenomena and how they seemed to him both in their mode of occurrence and in their possible significance. This alone would be thoroughly worthwhile. However, we also thought it likely that in a genuinely friendly atmosphere Uri might successfully demonstrate some of his phenomena. It was agreed that members of the audience should bring their own metal objects and that during the interview these should lie on a low table in front of Uri and Patricia Murphy and always in full view of the audience.

About 3 P.M. on Friday, 8 March, my wife and I and five members of the Philip group with other members of the TSPR convened at CITY-TV studio. The audience was otherwise made up of some friends of Uri and some friends of Joan Schafer. On arrival I met Uri in the corridor and introduced myself briefly to him. He asked me to collect together plenty of "stuff" for him to work on and to ask the audience to be actively "willing" for things to happen so that good phenomena would result. I looked through my own pockets and found some extra keys, while Uri went down to the makeup room. He passed through the basement café where the audience was congregated and briefly said hello to them, and asked them to actively "will" him to succeed.

The objects I had collected previously had been handed to Valerie Elia of CITY-TV, who had put them with the other material brought by the audience on a bronze tray which was resting on a low glass-topped table on the dais in front of the two chairs in which Uri and Patricia Murphy would be seated during the interview. I deposited the extra keys on it; there were already about twenty metal articles and a few watches. The metal objects included some nails and large screws, spoons and knives, forks, car keys, and door keys. I verified that all the objects I had brought (which will be specified later) were there. Also, I spent a few moments handling every object and verified that so far as could be disclosed by visual inspection and application of moderate manual pressure, each object was a normal one of its type and not made of especially soft metal. It seemed clear to me that none of them had been prepared by cutting and rejoining with soft metal, glue, or pliable material.

Though I was not continuously in the studio thereafter I did in fact visit it several times while it was being got ready and the lights and cameras positioned. Needless to say, during this period technical crews were in the studio all the time and the focus of attention was the dais—so it would have been impossible for any-one to do anything to the objects on the tray without being ob-served. Each time I came in I went to the tray and verified by a *coup d'oeil* that the objects were the same as when I had last seen them. Finally, about two minutes before Uri and Patricia Murphy took their places on the dais, I made a last inspection, confirming that the objects were the same ones I had looked at originally. Meanwhile Andrienne Henwood had talked to Uri, who asked her to get still more material. She went to the basement and com-mandeered an additional batch of house and car keys from the Philip group. Returning to the studio, she dropped this material on the tray and took her place in the studio audience only seconds before recording started. Uri and Pat had taken their places on the platform only a short time before. The tray on its table was at all times in the full view of the audience (and also of the TV cameras when they were on wide angle). After my final inspection I had kept the tray under continuous observation and saw that none of the objects had subsequently been handled by Uri or Pat or anyone else.

Until the first commercial break the interview was concerned with mental phenomena (telepathy, clairvoyance, etc.). It included an illustration of Uri's ESP ability which Uri stressed was only an illustration not a rigorous experiment.

During the first commercial, matters began to take a different turn. My wife, who was sitting with Mrs. Sparrow and Bernice Mandryk on the top row of the set of wooden bleachers, or terraces, provided for the accommodation of the audience, opened her purse and inspected her bunch of six keys of various kinds. Previ-ously they had all been inspected by herself, Mrs. Henwood, Mrs. Sparrow, and Bernice Mandryk, and declared normal; this was in the basement after Uri had gone up to the studio. Though my wife and Uri might have passed one another in the studio while he and the audience were getting to their respective stations, there was no further conversation or physical contact between them. She did not open her purse until the first break. To her surprise one of the six keys was noticeably bent at a point about a quarter-inch from the shaft. This key was a Yale-type and stamped REILLY'S LOCK CORP. LTD. TORONTO. The angle of bending appeared to me to be about 25 degrees of arc. The key was kept on the key ring but inspected by myself and Iris, Mrs. Sparrow, and Bernice. We called out to Uri, who asked that it be brought down to him. He looked at it, held it in front of the cameras, then tossed the whole bunch of keys to a point on the carpeted floor about four feet away from him, and said, "Let's look at it again later." It should be reiterated that this was the only occasion that he had touched or even seen this key.

When the interview was resumed Uri discussed his ability to rehabilitate broken watches. He picked out from the objects on the tray two "fob" or "turnip" watches (which Pat confirmed were not working), placed them on the tabletop, and made two or three passes of his hands over them. Pat testified to the fact that they immediately started ticking. I mention this for interest only as the matter was not investigated in depth.

Uri next talked about his metal-bending ability. He casually picked up and replaced several of the spoons and forks on the tray. Finally he selected a fork about seven inches in length. He asked Pat to hold it in such a way that the whole of the stem would be visible to the audience and cameras. This was achieved by Pat holding the blade, or tined part, of the fork between her thumb and forefinger. The fork was oriented broadside to the audience. Uri, using the tips of the thumb and forefinger of his right hand, then gently "massaged" a section of the stem of the fork, the traverse of his fingertips being about three-quarters of an inch. The portion of the stem which he stroked was situated just below the blade. It was the part narrowest in width. However (as we ascertained later) the *thickness* was the same as that of the rest of the stem, which in this respect was uniform throughout its length. Uri first said that he thought nothing was going to happen. Then he smiled and nodded and said, "It's going" (or words to that effect). With the thumb and finger of his right hand he held the bottom of the stem and gently waggled it. The stem moved relative to the blade (which Pat kept immobile), thus showing the audience that the section he was stroking had lost its rigidity. So that this could be seen more clearly Uri asked Pat to present the profile of the fork to the audience. Then, holding the narrow portion of the stem in the thumb and first finger of his right hand and the end of the stem with his left thumb and first finger, with what appeared to be minimal effort he waggled the stem to and fro, the blade being kept immobile. The total angle traversed between extreme positions appeared to me to exceed 40 degrees. After five or six wagglings he released the bottom of the stem and pushed it lightly with a fingertip. The stem suddenly parted at a point in the portion that Uri had stroked and fell to the floor of the dais. Uri picked it up and handed the two parts to Pat Murphy. When the applause had subsided she read the inscription on the stem, which said, KOBA, STAINLESS, JAPAN. It was at this stage that I realized the fork was one that I had brought from home.

The day previous to the interview I had taken this fork, together with two others (of dull gray metal not matching the first one and stamped 1847 ROGERS BROS. I.S.), and two old spoons from the kitchen cutlery. I supplemented this collection of expendable material with a couple of long steel screws and some derelict watches. I had not noticed that among the forks of various vintages we had a second Koba fork, the exact mate of the one that Uri had divided. I discovered this on returning home with my material, which I recovered from the tray the moment that the recording ceased. I was pleased that the divided fork had a mate because it affords a good comparison of the before and after states of the object. I need hardly point out that the Koba forks are somewhat out of date and so are relatively individual objects. Even if, for the sake of argument, it were supposed that despite the considerable evidence to the contrary Uri had substituted a prepared Koba fork for the one on the tray, the odds against his selecting one by chance for this purpose are astronomically large. A severe critic might argue that conceivably Uri knew by extrasensory perception that a Koba fork would be there and obtained one by teleportation; but this would be a rather self-defeating criticism.

After his success with the fork Uri noticed two keys on the tray. These I immediately recognized because they were not on a key ring but tied by string to a buff-colored cardboard label. These keys were in fact unique. They were both of the long variety stamped YALE, THE YALE AND TOWNE MFG. CO. MADE IN ENGLAND. One of them was stamped RKC 25A 13. It was in fact a Fellow's key of Trinity College, Cambridge, issued to me many years before. The number 13 was its own individual number and it is registered as issued to me personally. It gave us therefore a uniquely identified object. The other key opened a door in the Department of Genetics, Cambridge, and bore the individual number 6 as well as a type number 8150. The label bore an annotation in my hand-writing done in (now rather faded) blue ink, T.C.C. GEN. CAM-BRIDGE U.K. Remarking that these seemed an interesting pair of keys, Uri picked them up by the label without touching the keys themselves. It was then noticed that the Genetics Department key was in process of bending. This was actually seen by the audience and by the TV cameras in close-up. Uri supported this key with a finger of his other hand. It continued to bend and finally stopped at about 15 degrees of arc.

By now we had reached the second commercial break. Uri sug-gested that the bunch of keys, including the bent Reilly key, be put together with other material that the audience still had in their pockets, in a pile at the back of the audience. This was done; the pile was made on the back seat between myself and Mrs. Sparrow. Uri then answered three questions put by members of the audience. He then suggested that the pile be looked at. It was discovered that only the top half of the Reilly key was still attached to the bunch. The blade had separated from it, the metal being divided at a point close to the original bend, an operation that normally would require either a hacksaw or a cold chisel and mallet. The blade was found among the other keys in the pile.

When the fork and the Reilly key were examined it was noted that they were divided at their narrowest points, which suggests that the paranormal forces responsible tend to be applied in conformity with a principle of least effort.

The selection of our own fork can doubtless be put down to chance. The pair of Cambridge keys were eye-catching and it may well be that Uri picked them out just because they looked interesting. It is just conceivable that Uri chose these objects intuitively. I was certainly concerned that the interview should constitute what, for me, would be a good experiment.

After the recording Uri talked to various members of the audience. He said to Iris that it was she who had (paranormally) bent and broken the Reilly key. This is indeed possible, though mysterious, because similar events have been reported from England, which suggest that Uri can temporarily endow other people with the metal-bending ability. Among the material on the tray was an old-fashioned teaspoon contributed by Mrs. Sparrow. It was of a very standard design and previously had nested in perfect congruity with a spoon of twin design. When Mrs. Sparrow retrieved it, it appeared normal, but back at home, after a period of an hour or so, it was visibly bent. When inspected later it was still more curved. When the process terminated there was a gap of half an inch between the middle of this spoon and its mate when they were placed together for comparison.

Such were the results of our afternoon with Uri Geller—an hour or two well spent. We had received totally adequate proof of the existence of yet another mysterious force subject to some degree of mental control, and, whatever its origin, a physical force in the sense that it produces physical effects. For myself, I felt that the afternoon with Uri Geller represented the end of one stage in a long pilgrimage which had occupied some fifteen years of my life. Since 1959 I had, so far as time and opportunity permitted, been on the track of physically expressed forces of seemingly psychic or mental origin. In the intervening time I had come on verification of the poltergeist force, Jan Merta's force, and the table-rapping force of the Philip phenomenon. I had also had reason to believe in the thoughtography force that affects the emulsion of photographic plates, and the healer's force that can modify enzymes. Now I had seen for myself the operation of Uri Geller's metal-bending and dividing force. Perhaps I should add to this list the force (if it can legitimately be described in these terms) that registers the evoked response in the brain when a telepathic message is received. It would be tempting to regard all these forces as different varieties of one underlying psi or PK force, even perhaps the missing link in psychology—the force that mediates between the mind and the brain. But this is to be too speculative. I did feel, however, and still do, that 8 March indicated the beginning of an epoch in the development of parapsychology. With all its rough edges and unanswered questions, psychical research has, nonetheless, in one department at least, come of age. It can now present for the consideration of physicists and chemists a galaxy of physical forces, whose explanation is a task worthy of the mighty disciplines they represent.

20

LOOKING AHEAD:
NEW HORIZONS IN SCIENCE

Which way does progress lie? This is a question never easy to answer, even in sciences less knotty than parapsychology. I think it was the Greek philosopher Plato who said that it was impossible to do research by purely rational means. He argued that to solve a problem one had to know the right step to take, but how could one know this unless one already essentially knew the problem's solution? Plato's own answer to this conundrum was that every great innovator does have the requisite knowledge in his own soul; he brings it with him from a higher state of existence preceding his reincarnation in a living body. This is a fascinating assumption but not very useful as a guide to action as it would imply that the only course is to wait passively in faith or fatalism until the appropriately inspired geniuses come along.

It would be equally fatalistic to expect that in due time selected men and women will receive key insights from higher beings—the spirits of the dead or higher civilizations in the stars. It is true that many great discoveries and inventions have been made through sudden inspirations that seem to come abruptly out of the blue rather than as a consequence of logical thinking. But usually the advent of the new and brilliant idea is preceded by its recipient having long immersed himself in the problem and all its associated technology. Inspiration would therefore seem to be in part the reward of perspiration. It would be unwise to ascribe it entirely to ESP; to do otherwise would be to make us lazy. This is not to deny that ESP may play a role in human creativity. But to assume that every sudden insight comes by extrasensory perception would be rash indeed. I have, it is true, cited many instances that suggest that ESP messages prior to rising into consciousness are first received in that part of the psyche which we vaguely term the unconscious or subconscious. But to suppose that every brilliant idea that leaps abruptly into consciousness is the result of extrasensory perception would be to go much too far and neglect the normal creativeness of the unconscious.

As I have implied above, great insights fail to come to the idle. It would seem that we cannot lie back and wait for the unconscious to deliver the goods. It does so only when it has been stirred up and goaded into activity by the conscious mind after the latter has long wrestled with a problem that it longed to solve. Furthermore, mind, whether conscious or unconscious, cannot sparkle in a vacuum. Some kinds of progress can be made only if the required technology exists. The genius of whoever it may have been in the Canadian medical group who first realized that the evoked EEG response technique might be applicable to ESP reception consisted in the ability to make a bold intellectual leap. He saw a possibility un- noticed by others. This is very typical of certain forms of scientific advance, but these advances are possible only when the appropriate technique already exists. There are other kinds of advance which result mainly from the rare faculty of logical persistence. The en- zyme breakthrough resulted from the consistency of Dr. Grad's reasoning. He argued that if healer's hands do good to both humans and horses, then perhaps they may sometimes be actual conductors for a physical force that produces real and detectable physical effects on biological material. With equal consistency of logic Dr. Justa Smith followed through with her theory that some healers actually modify the chemistry of the enzymes in our bodies.

The enzyme work and the EEG research have in common the feature that they aim at getting objective results. In the past it has been the bane of work on ESP that it deals only in the transmission of information, and information is not a tangible commodity. Even when the odds against two people thinking simultaneously of the same thing by chance are astronomically large, it is difficult not to regard such a happening as merely a statistical fact and not a real fact. This is not entirely a rational attitude but it reflects a psychological truth: we like what we can *see*, whether it is the deflection of the needle of a voltmeter, the trace on an oscilloscope, the digestion of beef broth by tripsin, the levitation of a table, the softening of a steel fork, or the flight of a spoon. This is a good instinct; those sciences that have advanced most are those which either deal with material things or, as occurs in physics, study fields or influences that can be described in terms of physical effects that they produce.

This was my line of thinking some fifteen years ago when I concentrated my attention on the poltergeist force at a time when many parapsychologists were unenthusiastic about it. A prolonged and detailed study convinced me of the reality of the PK force in poltergeist situations, and I did not hesitate to make my conclusions known. This was because I believed, as I still do, that parapsychology as a scientific discipline has sometimes been hindered in its development by an excessive timidity on the part of psychical research workers who have often failed to publish important findings, which had they been known would have guided the thought of other investigators, as well as putting them in good heart. "If the trumpet give an uncertain note, who then shall prepare himself for battle?"

The Toronto group have not neglected the study of "pure" ESP unaccompanied by physical effects or the recording of EEG evoked responses. However, if there has been a guiding philosophy underlying their work, it is the belief that strange physical effects and forces do exist and are potentially more accessible than is usually supposed. We believe that the study of these "fields" or influences which manifest themselves physically provides the best hope for progress in understanding psychic phenomena in general. We also see them as having a general scientific importance going far beyond the traditional concerns of parapsychology. In this respect (like precognition in the sphere of mental phenomena) the now proven existence of the galaxy of PK and other forces which I listed at the close of the last chapter is awesome in its testimony to the power of mind in the realm of physical matter and energy.

In their work, however, the Toronto investigators have been mindful not so much of Plato as of his famous pupil Aristotle, a man of more practical outlook, who, if he lived today, would be an eminent science professor. Aristotle remarked that if one wished to study a phenomenon, then one should first verify its existence before devising a plan for further researching it. The Toronto group, whenever they could, have looked into various alleged phenomena such as the influence of pyramids or the physical reality of the rim aura. These are necessary episodes in the general process of "cleaning up" the subject. If we had a motto it would doubtless be "We Speak as We Find." What we find out, we declare; but also, if after a reasonably complete investigation we discover that an alleged phenomenon is actually a nonphenomenon, then we are not afraid to say so. It is wrong for mistaken beliefs to stand uncorrected; they distract attention from discoveries that are both true and profoundly interesting; their effect is like that of Gresham's Law in the field of public finance where "bad coin drives out good." As every good investigator knows, whether he is a police detective, a physician, a laboratory scientist, or a historian, negative research is just as important as making positive discoveries. Indeed, it is an essential part of all successful exploration that unless we clear the ground we cannot see the wood for the trees!

But enough of proverb mongering and riding of metaphors! The Canadian experience of parapsychology, as summarized in this book, besides opening magic casements leading on to new profundities in human life, also suggests a number of lines of research of real practical and humanitarian value. They are also forms of research for which the necessary scientific technology or expertise already exists. The enzyme discovery is highly amenable to objective study by biochemists and enzymologists in particular. Furthermore, like dowsing ability, the capacity to heal (or relieve) chronic ailments by proximity of the hands seems to be more widespread in the general population than are the manifestations of high-grade

ESP or other psychic talents. Indeed, though attention has been drawn to the subject by scientists with an understanding of psychic research, the enzyme phenomenon may not be psychic at all, but possibly depends on physical fields so subtle in their origin and action that they can be detected only by the particles which make up living matter. To see that this is a possibility to be seriously considered we need only note that typical protein molecules such as those of insulin or hemaglobin (which are among the simplest of biological materials) are made up of thousands of atoms. It would take a bold man to deny absolutely that biological substances have no unexpected properties.

Work of the kind indicated fulfills the conditions required of a good scientific venture; it is fundamental research calculated to advance our knowledge of basic features of living matter; it is also good applied science. The chronic diseases or discomforts are precisely the ones most resistant to medical treatment, but also, as several leading doctors have recently pointed out, are coming increasingly to represent a major responsibility of modern medicine. The scientific community in the relevant disciplines could, it seems to me, embark on this research with a very clear scientific conscience, because it is very likely to yield dividends adequate to justify the relatively minor diversion of scientific resources it would entail. If research in this field took the course which is almost normal in medicine, one can envisage the mechanism of the healer's action becoming understood. At that stage, medical research would, doubtless, direct itself to finding an alternative method of treatment and, on past showing, would have a good chance of succeeding.

Our experience with ESP also suggests work which could be seriously undertaken as both "pure" and "applied" science of humanitarian relevance. Here I draw on an address I gave recently to medical and social work staff at a large mental health center in Toronto. The capacity for ESP, like all other human talents, varies extremely between people. At one end of the scale are people with no ESP talent at all; like myself, they are "psychic morons." At the other extreme there may be persons who are completely inundated with psychic impressions; they continually receive ESP signals from their environment. This does seem actually to be the case. Though a pronounced degree of psychic talent is uncommon, it is not excessively rare. From time to time we encounter people who seem truly to be inundated with psychic impressions. Some of these, of course, successfully cope with the problem that this presents and incorporate it in their lives without its being too distressful. This group includes many professional psychic sensitives but also people who follow other vocations.

Coping with psychic inundation of course depends on recognizing it for what it is. But suppose a person was picking up random messages from his environment and, unlike the people in the many examples of ESP which I have given in this book, could not correlate them with any external cause. He might well think his mind was giving way! This is sometimes the reaction of people who have never heard of PK when, for the first time, they witness psychokinesis. I know of several cases where the persons concerned, though differing greatly in their level of general education, have used exactly the same words, "I thought I was seeing things. I thought I was going mad." This serves as a parable; it warns us not to dismiss out of hand what we may be told by people who may in fact be subject to psychic inundation. Indeed, such people, unless they are showing clear signs of real mental illness, deserve sympathetic investigation.

Often the psychically inundated persons find themselves in a real predicament. They fear the onset of insanity, they fear the reactions of their friends and relatives; it is a difficult thing to talk about. In some cases I have known of they eventually confide in their family doctor, who may refer them to a medical psychologist. Thereafter it depends on how aware the psychologist is of ESP as a real possibility. Sometimes the anxiety of these unwilling psychics is completely relieved by talking it over with an experienced parapsychologist. In other cases they achieve tranquility by working for some months with a group of people who are capable of discussing psychic experiences in a temperate and informed way. On occasion, however, they admit themselves as voluntary patients in mental health centers, until finally they can be reassured that there is nothing basically wrong with them. But this is perhaps a distressing and socially expensive way of dealing with what, if originally looked at in the correct perspective, would be a minor personal problem. Research aimed at methods for reliable early diagnosis of psychic inundation would be quite worthwhile both as pure or applied psychology, and of real social value. There is a piece of research also waiting to be done which is parallel with this and which to some extent overlaps it. This would be a survey of the content of the "mental messages," visions, auditory hallucinations, etc., experienced by normal people as psychic impressions in order to compare them with those received by patients suffering various degrees of definite mental ill health.

The potentialities of the evoked response technique for isolating the brain's response to its owner's reception of a mental message are so diverse that we cannot hope to mention them all, even in outline. But if it proves not to be merely a local phenomenon, in its further development this technique may provide an objective method of measuring a person's ESP sensitivity. Clearly this would aid in the diagnosis of psychic inundation. But it would have a wider application. From time to time I have drawn attention to the possibility that ESP is often received at the subconscious level. For all we know to the contrary this happens in many people who are not overtly psychic. We could guess that some persons receive ESP messages frequently but they do not emerge into consciousness. Sometimes the effects of the ESP signal express themselves in a borderline way—the sudden onset of a state of feeling that cannot be accounted for. People who also get conscious ESP messages tell me that on occasion they are plunged into oppressive despair or anxiety, or feel frightened or desolate, or "out of focus, hushed and jarred," or "out of focus and cold," or experience a "great sense of dissociation from self." Their testimony is valuable precisely because these feelings, in their cases, actually precede conscious ESP impressions that come later. However, if he or she never got

conscious psychic impressions we could not tell whether these
feelings were neurotic or physical symptoms or whether instead
they were caused by subconscious ESP. The brain wave technique
might however disclose these people's unconscious receptivity to
ESP messages.

The foregoing paragraphs have brought us into contact with a
new scientific discipline, which I have christened "parapsychological psychology." No textbooks on it have yet been written; I would
like to hope that the first one will be written in Canada. Be that
as it may, someone, somewhere, sometime, will certainly write it.
Not surprisingly, PK will be represented in that manual. Tension
plays a part in generating poltergeist outbreaks. As I have always
tried to be logical it occurred to me that psychokinetic phenomena
of poltergeist type would occur occasionally in association with
patients undergoing treatment by psychiatrists and medical psychologists. Indeed it seemed to me to be almost a logical necessity.
But the first intimation that this was so did not come to light
until 1964, when a leading analytical psychologist in London,
England, published a paper in the *International Journal of Parapsychology*, on which I was invited to comment. This consultant
reported the occurrence of rappings and movements of objects
while a certain patient was in her office. Quite recently I have
learned through private conversations with Canadian medical
psychologists that this kind of happening is not altogether uncommon. Clearly the phenomena are related in some way to the
patient's emotional conflicts. If the precise relationship can be
ascertained, these happenings will certainly be useful and possibly
important in determining the causes of the emotional disturbance,
and so be an aid in deciding on the type of remedial treatment that
is indicated.

Here there is a point of contact with some aspects of the "Philip"
phenomenon. The Philip research has many implications which
need to be followed up. They are too numerous to be dealt with
here, and for an adequate treatment must await the publication of
the Philip group's own book. However, it is permissible to dwell on

one or two of the issues it raises. Looked at from one point of view, the Philip rappings are like poltergeist phenomena; indeed, they sound strikingly similar to poltergeist noises that, from time to time, have been recorded on audiotape. But they are produced collectively by normal people simultaneously directing their thoughts to the same idea. Though the Philip situation with our Toronto group is not, so far as we are aware, a therapeutic one, nevertheless it does suggest the possibility of a new form of group therapy. On the plane of ordinary psychology it reminds us how little we understand of the nature and purpose of drama and humor in human life. It is very hard to explain convincingly why human beings need to participate in drama or comedy even merely as spectators. It was Aristotle who first raised this question when, in his *Poetics*, he speculated as to the precise reasons why audiences gained benefit from watching a tragedy in the theater. He thought it did them good because it enabled them to undergo a *catharsis*—i.e. a purging or working off of "pity and terror." Aristotle died in 322 b.c. It is a curious reflection on the way in which gaps can persist in man's knowledge of his own nature to note that Aristotle was the last thinker to make any serious contribution to the psychology of drama in relation to the spectator.

As regards humor, the only serious attempt to understand its why and wherefore was by Sigmund Freud, who died thirty-five years ago and wrote *Wit and the Unconscious* in 1916. Here, in what I regard as one of his most brilliant works, he sought to interpret humor in terms of release of unconscious or semi-conscious tensions. His analysis is no doubt incomplete and imperfect but remains the best one we have. It may be love that makes the world go round but the wag who extended the proverb by saying that it's money that greases the wheels was not entirely correct. It is humor that takes so much of the friction out of human relationships. Research of the Philip type that seems to depend so much on humor may cast some light into an obscure but important region of social psychology.

As the reader will see I have sketched out new areas of scientific research. This may seem daring but I think they are all logically indicated by the results of parapsychological research, especially the recent Canadian work. Each type of investigation has the merit of being practicably feasible because ESP talent, though not superabundant, is available if one knows where to look for it, and the Philip research has shown that PK can be generated by ordinary people. Each of these fields of research has the further merit of contributing to fundamental knowledge, while also having a practical and humanitarian end in view. The work requires expertise; amateurs can play a part, but the work will fall mainly on professional scientists in hospitals, universities, and other research centers. While it may attract some private donors to aid in its financing, like a great deal of research in medicine and the social sciences, though ultimately it results in social benefit to the community at large, this kind of work offers no immediate prospect of buttering anyone's parsnips. Doubtless, therefore, it will draw its financial support from disinterestedly philanthropic donations, or governments, research councils, and large foundations. I hope that some of it will be undertaken in Canada before too long.

An area that does offer some promise of early financial gain to the community or to investors is that of dowsing. As I have said, it is possible that there is something in this art. Also, there are indications that in a somewhat clandestine way it is usefully employed by hard-headed concerns such as oil companies. It is hard to form a definitive judgment because of the small number of proper experiments that have been done. The pilot experiment carried out on campus by the University of Toronto professors does indicate that if sufficiently rigorous and numerous experiments were carried out, then the subject might be validated. From a practical point of view it would be important if dowsing is to become an applied science, not only to check whether dowsing sometimes does work but to assess its reliability. This is the crucial point with all practical uses of ESP or similar talents. People should certainly ascertain the success rate of their fortune-tellers before basing any important actions on what they are told! Similarly, "psychic diagnosis" of medical complaints should be treated with the utmost discretion. That is why the best sensitives always tell clients with health problems to see their doctors. There is much said nowadays about diagnosis from the "aura," but the matter should be approached with great caution.

I have indicated various lines of research the ideas for which have grown out of our own parapsychological experience in Canada. There are others I could have spoken about. However, I have emphasized those which first came to mind as being enterprises that are scientifically responsible and which respectable scientists could undertake with a good conscience. In the past few years the Canadian contribution to psychical research has been a distinguished one, and the relatively small number of people concerned in it can take pride in what has been achieved. I have suggested ways in which this progress can be maintained in a more systematic fashion. I do not suggest that there will be no place for the competent amateur—the kind of person who in earlier centuries actually founded what are now professional sciences: physics, astronomy, chemistry, biology, and psychology. (The era of the professional scientist is a comparatively recent one.) There will also be a role for those private donors or foundations who might wish to aid financially. Research funds for parapsychology are practically nonexistent in Canada. In comparison with the vast amounts dispersed on all kinds of scientific research, the sums required for useful work of a genuinely scientific character in parapsychology are not large.

Let me conclude by considering the deepest problem that parapsychology in its present stage of development can offer for the serious consideration of scientists. This is undoubtedly the nature and mode of functioning of the PK force, or forces. Thus far, physics recognizes four distinct kinds of force operating between elementary particles. Elementary particles are the basic building units of matter; the best known are the proton, electron, and neutron, but there are many others. The four forces are gravitation, electromagnetism, the "strong" nuclear interaction, and the "weak" nuclear interaction. The last two were discovered only in the present century. Like the speculative parapsychologist with *his* forces, speculative physicists wonder if the four known physical forces are really only different manifestations of a single underlying field. In fact, Einstein spent forty years trying to "unify" gravitation and electromagnetism, but without success. (This should serve as a warning against trying to oversimplify parapsychology.) Recently, however, some progress has been made in unifying the weak interaction and the electromagnetic field, so that the goal of unification may perhaps be achieved at some future date.

Psychical research has now brought into prominence a galaxy of mysterious forces. This is an important physical discovery because these forces are physical (within the meaning of the act) because they express themselves physically. What is to be done with these strange forces? Are they *too* strange for the professional physicist to tangle with? Perhaps we can answer this with a parable taken from the history of physics itself and turning on this very word "strange." It arises from the work of high-energy physicists. High-energy physicists are those who shoot streams of elementary particles at very high speeds so that they are highly energized. This is done by very high-cost machines (the price of any one of them would finance parapsychology on a very handsome scale for a century). About two decades ago high-energy physicists found that certain new elementary particles were generated in atomic collisions. The behavior of these new particles was so odd that they were dubbed "strange particles." Furthermore, they were found to differ in their degree of strangeness. In addition, the strange particles could be grouped into different species. Each species was labeled with a number called its "strangeness." However, in physics what is strange today becomes commonplace tomorrow, and students in physics departments think no more of writing down the "strangeness number" of a particle than they do of listing its magnetic moment, spin, or isotopic spin, each of which specifications was in its time a discovery and a nine days' wonder.

Modern physics has a certain ideological resemblance to parapsychology. This goes back to a maxim of Galileo: "When the senses fail us, reason must step in." Consequently, whenever the facts require it, physicists have accepted the existence of the appropriate force fields, even though the force or field, as opposed to its effects, is invisible and intangible. They have also, when the facts demanded it, postulated the existence of completely unknown particles. This was done by Fermi when he postulated the existence of the neutrino. Only very recently has a method been devised for detecting it. For at least twenty years its existence had been accepted and used by physicists in their calculations though no direct proof that there was such a particle had been given.

If first-class physicists would be willing to study the family of PK forces, bringing to the problem not only their technological expertise and the resources of their laboratories, but also their own special form of mathematical and physical insight, then it is possible that the greatest of scientific breakthroughs will result. It may be that the time is not yet ripe; perhaps there is a fundamental barrier to progress which will be overcome only some decades or even centuries from now. But, nothing ventured, nothing gained. Nature will certainly stay deaf to questions that we do not trouble to ask Her. It would be foolish to leave the problem to remote posterity and abandon it as inherently insoluble, without making at least one good try. We would still be living in caves if no one had ever tried to solve problems. If the nature of the PK force or the metal-dividing force can be elucidated, even in part, it will expand enormously our view of the universe.

What of practical results? This question hardly needs to be answered; it has long been accepted that fundamental physical research has a guaranteed practical outcome, which is partly why it has little difficulty in getting itself financed. It was not always so. We all know the story of the young woman who asked Michael Faraday what was the use of electromagnetic induction. "What is the use of a baby?" he replied. Faraday's baby certainly grew up— all the dynamos and electric power stations the world over sprang from his demonstration of what must have seemed a mere academic toy.

Talking of babies, Canadian parapsychology is at present a very young but vigorous infant, robust enough to have made a significant contribution to research in this field. What happens now? Canada, population-wise, is one of the smaller nations of the world. That has not, in the past, prevented Canadians from making outstanding contributions to world science. However, it would be unwise to suppose that Canada can assume and maintain a leading role in the international science of parapsychology. I would like this to happen, but failing that, I would hope that Canada will continue to occupy an honorable place in this international adventure. Whether it does or not depends largely on the enthusiasm of those who read this book, whether scientists or laymen, whether private persons or in the public service. I hope that what I have written will show that psychic research is a humane and productive study, worthy of a place in the national life, and that some at least of my readers will be inspired to seek to aid the work either as direct participants, or through financial aid, or by using their good offices to secure the adoption of sound schemes of parapsychological investigation in research institutes and places of higher learning.

BIBLIOGRAPHICAL REFERENCES
TO CHAPTERS

CHAPTER 1: *The First Canadians*

Dewdney, Selwyn, and Kidd, Kenneth E. *Indian Rock Painting of the Great Lakes*, 2d ed. Toronto: University of Toronto Press, 1967.

Landes, Ruth. *Ojibway Religion and the Midewiwin*. Madison: University of Wisconsin Press, 1968.

Taylor, William E., Jr., and Swinton, George. *The Silent Echoes. Prehistoric Canadian Eskimo Art*. Ottawa: National Museum of Canada, n.d.

CHAPTER 2: *Canada's First Psychical Investigators*

Barton, Winifred G., ed. *Canada's Psi-Century*. Bartonian Metaphysical Society, P.O. Box 4022, Station E, Ottawa, n.d.

Lambert, R. S. *Exploring the Supernatural*, 2d ed. Toronto: McClelland and Stewart, 1966.

CHAPTER 3: *Canadian Poltergeistery*

Branden, Vicki. "The Age of the Bubble-Gum Witch." *Saturday Night* Vol. 88, No. 3538, April 21-24, 1973.

Lambert, R. S. *Exploring the Supernatural*. Toronto: McClelland and Stewart, 1966.

McInnis, Frank, and Owen, Iris M. "A Psychokinetic Event of Poltergeist Type." *New Horizons* Vol. 1, No. 1 (Summer 1972) p. 24.

Owen, A. R. G. *Can We Explain the Poltergeist?* New York: Taplinger, 1964; "Poltergeists." *Man, Myth and Magic*, No. 79 (1971) pp. 2223-2228.

CHAPTER 4: *Extrasensory Perception*

Barton, Winifred G., ed. *Canada's Psi-Century.* Bartonian Metaphysical
    Society, P.O. Box 4022, Station E, Ottawa, n.d.
Creighton, Helen. *Bluenose Ghosts.* Toronto: Ryerson Press, 1957.
Lambert, R. S. *Exploring the Supernatural.* Toronto: McClelland and
    Stewart, 1966.

CHAPTER 5: *Crisis Communications*

Barton, Winifred G., ed. *Canada's Psi-Century.* Bartonian Metaphysical
    Society. P.O. Box 4022, Station E, Ottawa, n.d.
Creighton, Helen. *Bluenose Ghosts.* Toronto: Ryerson Press, 1957.
Hervey, Sheila. *Some Canadian Ghosts.* Richmond Hill, Ontario:
    Pocket Books, 1973.
Lambert, R. S. *Exploring the Supernatural.* Toronto: McClelland and
    Stewart, 1966.

CHAPTER 6: *Ghosts and Haunted Houses*

Barton, Winifred G., ed. *Canada's Psi-Century.* Bartonian Metaphysical
    Society, P.O. Box 4022, Station E, Ottawa, n.d.
Creighton, Helen. *Bluenose Ghosts.* Toronto: Ryerson Press, 1957.
Hervey, Sheila. *Some Canadian Ghosts.* Richmond Hill, Ontario:
    Pocket Books, 1973.
Ingus, Thomas, et al. "Auditory and Visual Phenomena in an Allegedly
    Haunted House." *New Horizons* Vol. 1, No. 1 (1972) pp. 35-39.
Lambert, R. S. *Exploring the Supernatural.* Toronto: McClelland and
    Stewart, 1966.
MacGregor, Roy. "The Great Canoe Lake Mystery." *Maclean's*, Sep-
    tember 30, 1973.
Owen, George, and Sims, Victor. *Science and the Spook.* New York:
    Taplinger, 1971.
Sonin, Eileen. *Especially Ghosts.* Toronto: Clarke, Irwin & Co., 1970.

CHAPTER 7: *Cosmic Consciousness*

Bucke, Richard Maurice, M.D., *Cosmic Consciousness.* New York:
    Dutton, 1969.
Greenland, Cyril. "Richard Maurice Bucke, M.D." *Canadian Psychi-
    atric Association Journal* Vol. 2 (April 1966) pp. 146-154.

MacDonald, Flora. "Horace Traubel." *The Sunset of Bon Echo,* Vol. 1., 6. April, May, 1920, 4-11.

Prince, Raymond, ed. *Personality Change and Religious Experience,* n.d.; *Trance and Possession States,* 1968; *Do Psychedelics Have Religious Implications?* n.d.; R. M. Bucke Memorial Society, 1266 Pine Ave. West, Montreal, P.Q.

Renardin, Paul. *Une grande mystique français au XVIIe siècle. Marie de l'Incarnation.* Paris, 1938.

Zaehner, R. C. *Mysticism, Sacred and Profane.* Oxford: Clarendon Press, 1957.

CHAPTER 8: *Reincarnation*

Stearn, Jess. *The Search for the Girl with the Blue Eyes.* New York: Doubleday, 1968.

Stevenson, Ian. *Twenty Cases Suggestive of Reincarnation.* 2nd ed. rev. Charlottesville: University Press of Virginia, 1974.

CHAPTER 9: *Healing: Enzyme Breakthrough*

Grad, Bernard; Cadoret, René; and Paul, G. I. "An Unorthodox Method of Treatment of Wound Healing in Mice." *International Journal of Parapsychology* Vol. 3, 2 (Spring 1961) pp. 5-24.

Grad, Bernard. "A Telekinetic Effect on Plant Growth." *International Journal of Parapsychology* Vol. 5, 2 (Spring 1963) pp. 117-133.

Lambert, R. S. *Exploring the Supernatural.* Toronto: McClelland and Stewart, 1966.

Mann, W. Edward. *Orgone, Reich and Eros.* New York: Simon and Schuster, 1973.

Owen, A. R. G. *Hysteria, Hypnosis and Healing.* New York: Taplinger, 1971.

Rindge, Jeanne P. "Are There Healing Hands?" *Response* (Rosary Hill College, Buffalo, N.Y.) Vol. 2, 2 (Spring 1968) pp. 18-21.

Spraggett, Allen. *The Unexplained.* Toronto: New American Library of Canada, 1967; *Probing the Unexplained.* Toronto: Nelson, Foster Scott, 1971.

CHAPTER 10: *Pyramids, Orgone, and Cosmic Forces*

Alter, Allan. "The Pyramid and Food Dehydration." *New Horizons* Vol. 1, No. 2 (1973) pp. 92-94.

Mann, W. Edward. *Orgone, Reich and Eros.* New York: Simon and Schuster, 1973.
Owen, A. R. G. "The Shapes of Egyptian Pyramids." *New Horizons* Vol. 1, No. 2 (1973) pp. 102-108.
Ostrander, Sheila, and Schroeder, Lynn. *Psychic Discoveries Behind the Iron Curtain.* Englewood Cliffs, N.J.: Prentice-Hall, 1970.
Simmons, Dale. "Experiments on the Alleged Sharpening of Razor Blades and the Preservation of Flowers by Pyramids." *New Horizons* Vol. 1, No. 2 (1973) pp. 95-101.

CHAPTER 11: *Water Divining, Dowsing, and Radiesthesia*

Hopkins, Rae. "Man versus Machine." *Ontario Hydro News* Vol. 58. No. 6 (June 1971) pp. 17-21.

CHAPTER 12: *Auras and Force Fields*

Kilner, W. J. *The Human Atmosphere.* London: 1911.
Mann, W. Edward. *Orgone, Reich and Eros.* New York: Simon and Schuster, 1973.
Owen, A. R. G. "Generation of an 'Aura' a New Parapsychological Phenomenon." *New Horizons* Vol. 1, No. 1 (1972) pp. 9-23.
Owen, A. R. G. "The 'Rim' Aura; an Optical Illusion a Genuine but Non-psychic Perception." *New Horizons* Vol. 1, No. 3 (January 1974) pp. 19-31.

CHAPTER 13: *Astral Projection and Psychic Photography*

Cook, William. "Photography of Psychic Imagery; An Hypothesis." *New Horizons* Vol. 1, No. 1 (Summer 1972) pp. 33-34.
Lambert, R. S. *Exploring the Supernatural.* Toronto: McClelland and Stewart, 1966.
Rindge, J. P.; Cook, W.; and Owen, A. R. G. "An Investigation of Psychic Photography with the Veilleux Family." *New Horizons* Vol. 1, No. 1 (Summer 1972) pp. 28-32.
Spraggett, Allen. *The Unexplained.* Toronto: New American Library of Canada, 1967.

CHAPTER 14: *Mind over Matter: Jan Merta's Breakthrough*

Gaddis, Vincent H. *Mysterious Lights and Fires.* New York: David McKay, 1967.

Ostrander, Sheila, and Schroeder, Lynn. *Psychic Discoveries Behind the Iron Curtain.* Englewood Cliffs, N.J.: Prentice-Hall, 1970.
Owen, A. R. G. "A Demonstration of Voluntary Psychokinesis. Report of a Seminar." *New Horizons* Vol. 1, No. 1 (Summer 1972) pp. 25-27.

CHAPTER 15: *Psychic Canadians*

Katz, Sidney. "Extrasensory Perception." *Maclean's,* 29 July 1961.
Owen, A. R. G., and Owen, I. M. "An Experiment with Mr. James Wilkie involving Handwriting Samples." *New Horizons* Vol. 1, No. 2 (1973) pp. 88-91.
Spraggett, Allen. *The Unexplained.* Toronto: New American Library of Canada, 1967.
Watson, A. D., and Lawrence, M. *Mediums and Mystics.* Toronto: Ryerson Press, 1923.
Wilkie, James H. P. *The Gift Within,* introduction by Allen Spraggett. New York: New American Library, 1971.
Zmenak, Emil. "An Odd Experience Involving a Prediction." *New Horizons* Vol. 1, No. 1 (Summer 1972) pp. 61-62.

CHAPTER 16: *Canadian Breakthrough: Telepathic Waves in the Brain*

Blewett, Duncan. "Psychedelic Drugs in Parapsychological Research." *International Journal of Parapsychology* Vol. 5, No. 1 (Winter 1963) pp. 43-70.
Craig, James G. "The Effect of Contingency on Precognition in the Rat," in *Research in Parapsychology 1972.* Metuchen, N.J.: Scarecrow Press, 1973.
Eisenberg, Howard. "Telepathic Information Transfer of Emotional Data," in *Research in Parapsychology 1972.* Metuchen, N.J.: Scarecrow Press, 1973.
Keeling, Kenneth R. "Telepathy Transmission in Hypnotic Dreams: An Exploratory Study." *Proceedings of the Parapsychological Association* No. 8 (1971) pp. 55-58.
Lloyd, D. H. "Objective Events in the Brain Correlating with Psychic Phenomena." *New Horizons* Vol. 1, No. 2 (Summer 1973) pp. 69-75.
Owen, A. R. G. "Experiments on ESP in Relation to (a) Distance and (b) Mood and Subject Matter." *New Horizons* Vol. 1, No. 2 (Summer 1973) pp. 76-87.

Persinger, Michael A. "Patterns of the Paranormal." Unpublished.
Secord, Alan. "Of Pets and People." Lecture to the Royal Canadian Institute. Unpublished, 1973.
Spraggett, Allen. "Telepathy." *The Sunday Sun.* 30 September 1973, M12.

CHAPTER 17: *The Dead Indians Speak*

Emerson, J. N. "Intuitive Archaeology: A Psychic Approach." *New Horizons,* Vol. 1, No. 3 (1974) pp. 14-18.

CHAPTER 18: *Toronto Breakthrough: Psychokinesis for Ordinary People*

Batcheldor, K. J. 1966 Report on a case of table levitation and associated phenomena. *Journal S. P. R.* Vol. 43, No. 729, Sept. 339-356.
Brookes-Smith, C. and Hunt, D. W. "Some experiments in psychokinesis." *Journal S. P. R.* Vol. 45, No. 744 (1970) pp. 265-281.
Brookes-Smith, C. "Data-tape Recorded Experimental P.K. Phenomena." *Journal S. P. R.* Vol. 47, No. 756 (June 1973) pp. 69-89.
Owen, Iris M., and Sparrow, Margaret H. "Generation of Paranormal Physical Phenomena." *New Horizons* Vol. 1, No. 3 (1974) pp. 6-13.

CHAPTER 19: *An Afternoon with Uri Geller*

Owen, A. R. G. "Uri Geller's Metal Phenomena; An Eye-Witness Account." *New Horizons* Vol. 1, No. 4 (1974).
Targ, Russell, and Puthoff, Harold. "Information Transmission Under Conditions of Sensory Shielding." *Nature,* Vol. 251 (Oct. 18, 1974) pp. 602-7.

INDEX